# THE STATE OF
# BLACK AMERICA 1988

Published by **National Urban League, Inc.**
January 1988

# THE STATE OF BLACK AMERICA 1988

## Editor

*Janet Dewart*

Copyright © National Urban League, Inc., 1988.
Library of Congress Catalog Number 77-647469
ISBN 0-914758-08-X

Price $18.00

*The cover art is "The Family" by James Denmark. "The Family" inaugurates the "Great Artists" series of limited edition lithographs on black Americans created for the National Urban League through a donation from the House of Seagram.*

# National Urban League, Inc.

The Equal Opportunity Building ▪ 500 East 62nd Street ▪ New York, New York 10021

Founded in 1910, the National Urban League is the the premier social service and civil rights organization in America. The League is a nonprofit, community-based agency headquartered in New York City, with 112 affiliates in 34 states and the District of Columbia. Its principal objective is to secure equal opportunity for blacks and other minorities.

# TABLE OF CONTENTS

# About The Authors

### DR. LEE P. BROWN
*Chief of Police*
*Houston, Texas*

Dr. Lee P. Brown is a distinguished criminologist and outstanding career law enforcement official. The Chief of Police in Houston since 1982, Dr. Brown has served as Public Safety Commissioner in Atlanta and as Sheriff and later Director of Justice Services in Multnomah County, Oregon.

At Howard University he was Associate Director of the Institute of Urban Affairs and Research, Professor of Public Administration, and Director of Criminal Justice Programs. Prior to joining Howard University, he chaired the Department of Administration of Justice at Portland State University.

He began his career as a police official in the San Jose, California Police Department in 1960.

He earned a doctorate and a master's in criminology at the University of California at Berkeley. He also earned a master's in sociology at San Jose State University and a bachelor's in criminology at Fresno State University.

His professional activities include Vice President of the International Association of Chiefs of Police and National Correspondent to the United Nations Program for the Prevention of Crime and Treatment of Offenders. He is also associated with the National Advisory Commission on Higher Education for the Police and the National Organization of Black Law Enforcement Officials.

Dr. Brown is the author of numerous articles and *The Police and Society: An Environment for Collaboration and Confrontation.*

### DR. PRICE M. COBBS
*President*
*Pacific Management Systems*

Dr. Price M. Cobbs is the President of Pacific Management Systems and the Chief Executive Officer of Cobbs, Inc. He co-authored with William Grier two books, *Black Rage* and *The Jesus Bag.* Both books are considered classics in understanding the inner drives of black Americans. He has written and lectured extensively on the dynamics and effects of racism and has developed a clinical model to change attitudes and assumptions that arise from racial, ethnic, and value differences.

For the past 20 years he has been an internationally recognized management consultant to Fortune 500 companies, government agencies, and community projects. Most recently, he has conducted seminars at the United Nations headquarters in New York and for the city government of Oakland, California. In 1986 he was a speaker at the annual National Urban League Conference and was an invited Eminent Scholar at Norfolk State University, Norfolk, Virginia.

Dr. Cobbs is a Fellow of the American Psychiatric Association, a member of the Institute of Medicine of the National Academy of Sciences, Certified Consultants International, and a Life Member of the N.A.A.C.P.

He received a B.A. from the University of California, Berkeley and his M.D. from Meharry Medical College in Nashville, Tennessee. He is presently an Assistant Clinical Professor of Psychiatry, University of California, San Francisco.

## DR. BRUCE R. HARE
*Associate Professor of Sociology*
*State University of New York at Stony Brook*

Dr. Bruce Robert Hare is an Associate Professor of Sociology at the State University of New York at Stony Brook, Long Island, New York. He is also a nationally respected author of articles and papers that have appeared in scholarly journals.

His publications include "Stability and Change Among Black Adolescents: A Longitudinal Study of Self-Perception and Achievement" for the *Journal of Black Psychology,* the Task Force Report on Black Americans for the President's Commission on Mental Health (1978), and *The Rites of Passage,* a youth development monograph for the National Urban League.

Dr. Hare is a graduate of the University of Chicago, where he received his M.A. in Sociology of Education and his Ph.D. in Social Psychology, and of the City College of the City University of New York where he received both his B.A. in Sociology and his M.S. in Elementary Education. He has taught at a number of institutions including the Manhattanville Child Development Center, the University of Massachusetts at Boston, and the University of Illinois; he has done post-doctoral study at the Johns Hopkins University Center for Social Organization of Schools in Baltimore and Stanford University in California.

He is the recipient of the Rockefeller and Social Science Award fellowships and is a frequent lecturer at national meetings and conferences dealing with child and adolescent development, social psychology, and education.

## DR. DIANNE M. PINDERHUGHES
*Associate Professor, Department of Political Science*
*University of Illinois at Urbana-Champaign*

Dr. Dianne M. Pinderhughes is a noted political scientist, a prolific writer, and a much-sought-after lecturer on the political history of blacks and women. Her most recent book is *Race and Ethnicity in Chicago Politics, A Reexamination of Pluralist Theory.*

Since 1984, she has been on the faculty of the University of Illinois at

Urbana-Champaign; an Associate Professor, she directs the Afro-American Studies and Research Program.

Among her academic achievements are a term as Adjunct Fellow at the Joint Center for Political Studies (Washington, D.C.); a guest scholar at the Brookings Institution (Washington, D.C.); Assistant Professor of Government at Dartmouth College; and Postdoctoral Fellow at the University of California at Los Angeles.

She is active in a number of professional organizations; she is President Elect of the National Conference of Black Political Scientists and serves on the editorial boards of the *Urban Affairs Quarterly* and the *National Political Science Review.*

Dr. Pinderhughes earned her academic degrees in political science: her Ph.D. and M.A. from the University of Chicago, and her B.A. from Albert Magnus College in New Haven.

### DR. ALVIN J. SCHEXNIDER
*Associate Vice President for Academic Affairs*
*Virginia Commonwealth University*

Prior to his appointment as Associate Vice President for Academic Affairs at Virginia Commonwealth University in Richmond, Virginia, Dr. Alvin J. Schexnider held previous faculty and academic administrative positions at the University of North Carolina at Greensboro, the Federal Executive Institute, Syracuse University, and Southern University.

Dr. Schexnider completed undergraduate study at Grambling State University. He received the M.A. and Ph.D. in Political Science at Northwestern University, where he was a Woodrow Wilson Fellow.

Dr. Schexnider is a past president of the Virginia Chapter of the American Society for Public Administration. He was appointed by Governor Charles Robb to the Governor's Commission on Virginia's Future and by Governor Gerald Baliles to the Board of Visitors of Virginia State University.

He is co-author of *Blacks and the Military,* published by the Brookings Institution and is a previous contributor to *The State of Black America.*

### DR. NIARA SUDARKASA
*President*
*Lincoln University of Pennsylvania*

Dr. Niara Sudarkasa is the first woman to head the formerly all-male Lincoln University of Pennsylvania.

Dr. Sudarkasa came to Lincoln from the position of Associate Vice President for academic affairs at the University of Michigan in Ann Arbor, where she was the first black woman to receive tenure and the first to be promoted to full professor in the arts and sciences. At Michigan, she also served as Director of the Center for Afro-American and African Studies and Research Scientist in the Center for Research on Economic Development. Before joining the faculty at Michigan, she taught at New York University and was a visiting faculty member at Columbia University.

She received her undergraduate education as a Ford Foundation Early Entrance Scholar at Fisk University and Oberlin College. She graduated from Oberlin in 1957 at the age of 18, ranking in the top ten percent of her class. Her master's and Ph.D. degrees in anthropology were awarded by Columbia University in 1959 and 1964, respectively.

An internationally known anthropologist with a book and over thirty published articles to her credit, she has conducted extensive research in Nigeria, Ghana, and the Republic of Benin. Her articles on higher education have appeared in the *Chronicle of Higher Education* and the *Bulletin of the American Association for Higher Education*.

A former Senior Fulbright Research Fellow, Dr. Sudarkasa has received numerous fellowships, grants, and awards. She has served on a number of national boards, including the executive board of the American Anthropological Association. Her current assignments include the board of directors of a national study of new immigrants, sponsored by the Ford Foundation, and the board of the Pennsylvania Economic Development Partnership, to which she was appointed by Governor Robert P. Casey.

### DR. DAVID H. SWINTON
*Dean, School of Business*
*Jackson State University*

Dr. David H. Swinton is recognized as one of the country's leading economists. The former Director of the Southern Center for Studies in Public Policy at Clark College, he has written for national publications, including National Urban League publications.

Dr. Swinton has held positions as Assistant Director for Research, Black Economic Research Center; and as Senior Research Associate and Director of Minorities and Social Policy Programs at the Urban Institute.

Dr. Swinton received his undergraduate degree from New York University and his M.A. and Ph.D. degrees from Harvard University. He has served as a Teaching Fellow at Harvard and a lecturer at City College of New York.

### DR. BERNARD C. WATSON
*President and Chief Executive Officer*
*William Penn Foundation*

Dr. Bernard C. Watson has been President and Chief Executive Officer of the William Penn Foundation since 1981. During an 11-year tenure at Temple University, he was Professor of Urban Education and of Urban Studies. For five years he served as Academic Vice President.

Prior to his university experience, Dr. Watson had served as a teacher, counselor, and department chairman in the public schools of Indiana and as Deputy Superintendent of the public schools of Philadelphia, Pa.

Author of a book, *In Spite of the System,* he has authored 13 monographs, chapters in 14 books, and numerous articles in professional journals. His most recent publication is a monograph: *Plain Talk About Education: Conversations With Myself.*

Dr. Watson earned his baccalaureate degree from Indiana University, a Master's degree from the University of Illinois, and his Ph.D. from the University of Chicago. He has done post-doctoral work at Harvard University.

The recipient of numerous awards and honors, including seven honorary degrees, he was appointed by President Lyndon Baines Johnson to the National Advisory Council on Education Professions Development and by President Jimmy Carter to the National Council on Educational Research.

\*\*\*

An honors graduate in Economics from LaSalle University, Mrs. FASAHA TRAYLOR earned her M.A. in Urban Studies at Temple University. She is currently a doctoral candidate in Sociology at Temple University where she is studying under a National Science Foundation Fellowship. Mrs. Traylor has been a teacher and administrator and is currently serving as a part-time Research Intern at the William Penn Foundation.

## DR. CHARLES V. WILLIE
*Professor of Education and Urban Studies*
*Graduate School of Education*
*Harvard University*

Dr. Charles V. Willie, a sociologist, is Professor of Education and Urban Studies at the Graduate School of Education, Harvard University. Before his Harvard appointment in 1974, Professor Willie was affiliated with Syracuse University 25 years as a graduate student, professor, chair of the Department of Sociology, and vice president.

A baccalaureate degree was received from Morehouse College in 1948 where he and Martin Luther King, Jr. were classmates. He earned a master's degree at Atlanta University and was awarded the Ph.D. degree in sociology by Syracuse University in 1957.

Contributing to the development of sociology as an applied discipline, Professor Willie has served as president of the Eastern Sociological Society, member of the American Sociological Association's Council, and on the Board of Directors of the Social Science Research Council. He is also a member of the Association of Black Sociologists and Sociologists for Women in Society. His research interests are education, health, race relations, and the urban community.

Professor Willie was appointed by President Jimmy Carter to the President's Commission on Mental Health. Among other public service activities is his participation as expert witness in several school desegregation cases. He served as court-appointed master during the controversial Boston school desegregation case.

Professor Willie's scholarship has been recognized by his alma mater, Morehouse College, and by the Berkeley Divinity School at Yale University that awarded him honorary doctoral degrees. He was designated distinguished alumnus by the Maxwell School of Syracuse University. He is author or editor of eighteen books and approximately 100 articles and chapters in books. His most recent books are *Metropolitan School Desegregation* (1986) (with Michael Grady), *Five Black Scholars* (1986), *Black and White Families* (1985), *School Desegregation Plans That Work* (1984), and *Race, Ethnicity and Socioeconomic Status* (1983).

# Black America, 1987:
# An Overview

John E. Jacob
President
National Urban League, Inc.

Black Americans, like their fellow-citizens, closed 1987 beset by economic uncertainties that were not dispelled by the superficial glow of an arms control treaty or the hoopla of a presidential election campaign moving into high gear.

When the stock market crashed in October, it raised the specter of economic turmoil and greater fiscal austerity, along with growing fears of worldwide economic depression and accelerated racially-based disadvantage.

In the wake of the market's crash, it became popular to say that the long bull market prosperity and economic recovery era of the 1980s was ended — "the party's over."

But when parties end, bills become due. And the nation's "party" of deficit-driven prosperity will have to be paid for. The big question is: who will pay?

The pundits foresee an extended period of belt-tightening, spending cuts, and "sacrifices" to pay for the binge of the 1980s. Such statements are usually accompanied by token promises to screen the poor from the effects of the necessary fiscal adjustments.

But we heard that before—when President Reagan came to office with his plans for a party of tax cuts and increased military spending while preserving the safety net for the "truly needy."

We all know what happened: the party roared on, but the safety net for the poor was shredded. So assurances that the poor will be protected carry little weight today. The poor were shut out of the party, and now that the bills are due, those who had the most fun should pick up the check.

The poor and moderate-income families were the most obvious victims of recent policies. The numbers of the poor increased by four million in the 1980s. The real income of the lowest fifth of the population, adjusted for inflation, *declined* between 1979 and 1986 by $663 per family. Meanwhile, the top fifth of the population *gained* $12,218 in real income during those years.

Black people, too, were not at the party. The 1980s were a time of increasing black hardship, with inner-city communities decimated by crack and crime, and national policies of withdrawal from efforts to increase opportunities for blacks.

Programs that benefited the black poor the most were cut the most. Between 1981 and 1987 the federal government slashed subsidized housing programs by 79 percent, training and employment programs by 70 percent, the Work

Incentive Program by 71 percent, compensatory education programs for poor children by 12 percent, and community development block grants and community services block grants by well over a third.

Black youth weren't at the party either. Even as their high school graduation rates increased, black college attendance rates plummeted throughout the 1980s, helped in part by a shift in federal college aid programs from direct assistance to loans.

Black youth unemployment remained high, and the economic deterioration experienced by young black males is directly responsible for the tragic weakening of the black family. As the Children's Defense Fund pointed out in a 1987 study, the majority of young black males in 1973 earned enough to keep a three-person family out of poverty. Now, less than half do. Young men aged 20 to 24 who earn enough to stay above the poverty line marry at rates three to four times higher than young men with below-poverty line earnings. Constricted opportunities for young men have cut their marriage rates in half over the past 15 years and have led to the alarming rise in single female-headed households.

Many of the elderly weren't at the party, either, but some want them to pay the tab through a Social Security cost-of-living-adjustment (COLA) freeze. But over 20 percent of the elderly live on incomes below 125 percent of the poverty line — a higher percentage than all Americans do — and the majority of the elderly rely on Social Security for over 70 percent of their incomes. Restricting COLA payments would mean increased hardship for the non-affluent elderly and for most black older citizens.

Children weren't at the party, but the coming austerity targets include domestic programs such as education, training, nutrition and other essential social services that benefit youth.

A fifth of all children grow up poor and a majority of black children are in poverty. The Reagan administration's spending binge did not include efforts to draw those youngsters into the mainstream, to help their families, or to create opportunities for them.

The unemployed and the homeless weren't at the party, either. Black unemployment has improved slowly to the point where it now stands at recession-levels of about 12 percent. But counting discouraged workers, and part-timers who want full-time work, the true black unemployment rate hovers around the 20-percent mark — after five years of economic recovery.

In fact, the Reagan boom was a false prosperity era, a period in which gains were concentrated on a relatively small portion of the population while large segments of the citizenry saw a real deterioration in their living standards. It was a period marked by growing homelessness, and the homeless population included a far higher portion of families and children than ever before.

The major task for 1988 will be to reverse that ugly trend, and to assure that those who were brutally excluded from the prosperity party of the 1980s will not be forced to pay its bills.

Whether sound economic policy dictates higher taxes or lower spending or both, the nation must make investments in its people necessary to create the infrastructure of human capital without which future prosperity will be impossible.

Education is one such investment. The demographics suggest that a third of America's work force will be minority, but most will come from poverty backgrounds. They have high dropout rates and few of the skills needed in a high-tech society. It is in the national interest to invest in educating at-risk children, as numerous studies and private sector groups have urged. In 1987, the prestigious business group, the Committee for Economic Development, published a report "Children in Need" that documented the urgency of such investments.

With less than one of five eligible children in Head Start and less than half of the eligible children in compensatory education programs, and with nutrition, medical, and other programs reaching too few of the children in poverty, it is essential that such programs be funded at levels sufficient to reach all eligible children and families.

The emerging consensus on a welfare reform program that encourages work, education, and training should be implemented through legislation that retains strict federal controls, establishes inflation-adjusted benefit levels above the poverty line, provides universal coverage of all the poor, and assures child care, transportation, counseling, and other services that enable people to get training and to work.

The refusal to invest in the nation's physical infrastructure also acts as a brake on future growth while constricting job opportunities. Long-overdue investments in affordable housing, roads, and bridges must be made. In the process, jobs can be created and skills learned.

Such investments lay the groundwork for future prosperity that is shared by all, generate tax revenues, and actually save federal resources. A dollar invested in immunization or in nutrition programs pays for itself many times over through lower medical costs. Similarly, a dollar spent on education or on training is repaid with rich dividends through future tax payments and reduced social welfare benefit costs. Even in times of fiscal austerity, we have to take a long view of social investments that increase society's fairness and enable it to become more competitive and productive.

And as America totters near the brink of recession, we must understand that the thin line separating us from economic hardship is the purchasing power of masses of people who spend their paychecks, their Social Security checks, and their transfer payments on goods and services that keep the economy afloat. An austerity that punishes those who were excluded from the party will result in a decline in consumer spending and a fast slide into recession, while raising taxes for the affluent will merely impinge on sales of luxury items.

The view that social programs are actually investments in human capabilities that pay off in the future is confirmed by the rise of the black middle class. A series of articles in *The Washington Post* in late November highlighted blacks' entrance into the mainstream, but a less-noted follow-up article by the author of the series made a point neglected in the articles themselves: that in an extraordinary number of instances, the members of that emerging middle class were enabled to escape from poverty through the intervention of federal social programs — whether Title One compensatory education, a federal training program, or a minority contractor program.

The writer, Joel Garreau, identifies himself as "a true believer in the forces of the market place," but he also realizes the value of some Great Society programs: "Despite the views of those who would rewrite history for ideological reasons, not all that money went down the drain."

Indeed, those programs proved far more efficient and cost-effective than the Pentagon expenditures and federal subsidy programs to the affluent. They unleashed the energies of people who were enabled by government's helping hand to contribute to our society. Their success proves that fairness and compassion must be an integral part of the nation's policies as we move into the difficult period ahead.

The focus in 1988 will be on government's role because our fate will be decided by national economic policies and because it is a presidential election year.

But that does not mean private sector responsibilities should be ignored. In fact, the private sector which had most of the fun at the Reagan-era party, failed to pay its entrance fee in full. The president slashed social welfare programs partly on the premise that voluntarism and the private sector would fill the gaps left by government. In fact, despite increased voluntarism and a higher level of interest by corporate America, those gaps were not filled. And in recent years the wave of mergers and a new spirit of austerity among many companies threaten to leave widening gaps.

In 1988, the private sector needs to reassess its role in helping to solve national problems, and I am hopeful that reassessment will lead to expanded participation in the solutions to those problems. The most enlightened companies understand that their future work force needs and their need for social stability will be threatened unless new opportunities can be created, and unless people have opportunities to escape from the bitterness of deep poverty.

Within the black community, 1987 was a year of expanded efforts to do what can be done to overcome our disadvantages. Prime among these efforts was the Urban League's Education Initiative.

After a year of planning, community mobilization, and coalition-building, most Urban League affiliates are moving their local education initiatives into the operational phase, with several already making significant contributions to black student achievement. In Harrisburg, Pennsylvania, for example, students participating in the League's academic support program have raised their scholastic aptitude test scores in math, science, and language skills by 70 to 100 points.

Other national and local black community-based organizations are also deeply involved in programs to make our schools work for our kids. The black community is making a long-term commitment to do what is necessary to ensure that our children's educational achievement levels equal and *exceed* those of others.

Black underachievement is intolerable and unacceptable. Ending that underachievement requires systemic changes that help our kids to fulfill their potential.

Too often, discussions of urban school problems center on the kids, with claims that their home environment, their supposed cultural failings, and similar stereotypical excuses are to blame for the schools' failure to educate students.

But minority youngsters aren't the problem — the problem is the inferior education they're getting.

We can no longer allow our kids to be processed for failure — we have to start training them for success, and an active, concerned black community can make it happen.

In 1988, the black community will also have to direct its energies to assuring that its needs are addressed by the presidential candidates and their parties. We must recognize that blacks come to the political table, not as supplicants, but as sharers of power. Today, minority political clout has to be widened, for the presidential election of 1988 will be a major turning point.

There can be no more urgent task in the coming months than to register as many black voters as possible. Every black community organization must do its part in national voter registration efforts. We need black and minority citizens in both parties and in *every* candidate's camp. We've seen what happens when blacks are frozen out and we can't let that happen again. Exercising black voting power can influence policies that bring opportunities to poor people.

A 1987 Census Bureau report found that for the first time in history, young blacks registered and voted at rates higher than those for young whites.

This trend to increased political participation is especially important for black people—who don't have economic power. The black population has a far higher percentage of young adults than the general population. Using that potential political clout can pay off in more responsive government policies that help the poor and open doors of opportunity.

For both parties, the road to the White House leads through Houston's Third Ward, through Watts, through Harlem, through Chicago's South Side. The major parties are in peril if they ignore that fact.

They certainly should have understood that it was the power of the black vote that defeated Judge Robert Bork's Supreme Court nomination.

The White House thought it could win a Senate showdown by keeping the Republican minority in line and adding enough southern Democrats to put Judge Bork on the Supreme Court. But when those southern senators looked at his record, they found enough to make them leery of routinely backing the president's candidate. The decisive factor, however, was their reliance on black votes. That hard political reality determined the outcome of the Bork nomination.

Exercising our constitutional right to vote is the surest means of preserving black rights. And it is the appropriate means of paying tribute to the generations of blacks who sacrificed to secure those rights despite blatant oppression.

We were reminded of that in 1987 by Supreme Court Justice Thurgood Marshall, who brought badly needed perspective to the mindless hype surrounding the celebrations of the 200th anniversary of the framing of the Constitution.

Justice Marshall eloquently pointed out that the famous first three words of the Constitution, "We The People," did not include women, who were denied the right to vote, or blacks, who were enslaved. They also excluded poor whites, who could not meet the property test qualifications for voting. He also pointed out that the document itself was seriously flawed — caught in the contradiction between guaranteeing liberty and justice to all and denying both to blacks. It took a century of struggle before slavery was ended and before the Constitution was amended to guarantee rights to all and to assure the equal protection of the laws.

Justice Marshall's message needed to be said — and it needed to be said now, when the Attorney General and a group of newly-appointed federal judges seem to think that constitutional issues can best be resolved by going back to determine the intent of the framers.

By calling the nation's attention to the fact that intent of the framers included preserving slavery for blacks and second-class status for women, Justice Marshall helped us see that the "original intent" school of argument is not to be taken seriously.

The Founders created a flawed structure, a structure that became democratic through the pain of civil war and reconstruction, and in the fitful, periodic drives to reform and renew our society.

We may be nearing another one of those cycles of renewal, a period in which Americans will once again recover the spirit that fights the racism and poverty that stain our democracy.

In 1988, we must work to lay the foundations for a Great Awakening that brings our society to a higher stage of fulfillment of the potential of all our people.

: : :

Within the following pages, *The State of Black America* presents papers from outstanding scholars. Their independent evaluations are intended to inform and to stimulate but their views do not necessarily reflect the official position or policies of the National Urban League. Our own summation and recommendations appear at the end of this report.

This *State of Black America,* like past ones, serves to increase the nation's awareness of the reality of life within Black America and to influence the decision-making process in 1988. We express our gratitude to the authors.

# Black Enrollment In Higher Education: The Unfulfilled Promise Of Equality

Niara Sudarkasa, Ph.D.

"Twenty-five years after James Meredith became the first black to enroll at the University of Mississippi, the outlook for minorities in higher education is bleak." (*The Chronicle of Higher Education,* September 2, 1987)[1]

"In recent months, racial incidents have been reported at colleges across the country . . . Though no one keeps statistics on such incidents, officials at the colleges and experts in race relations say they seem part of a growing pattern of bigotry and animosity toward minority students on campus." (*The New York Times,* March 9, 1987)[2]

## INTRODUCTION

Nineteen eighty-seven was barely a month old when two flagrant racial insults to blacks at the University of Michigan in Ann Arbor triggered an outpouring of protests which, in turn, led State Representative Morris Hood to convene a formal legislative hearing on racism at that university. Ultimately, Reverend Jesse Jackson was called in to mediate negotiations between the university administration and the students around the latter's "non-negotiable proposals" for change.[3] The nation was reminded that such incidents had become all too common on our college campuses.

Three of the most widely publicized racial incidents of 1986 occurred at Dartmouth College in New Hampshire, at The Citadel Academy in Charleston, South Carolina, and at the University of Massachusetts in Amherst. At Dartmouth, white students destroyed the "shanties" that had been erected by black students in protest over the college's failure to divest from companies doing business in South Africa. At The Citadel, a group of white students dressed in white sheets and hoods threatened a black cadet with racial obscenities and a burnt paper cross.[4]

At the University of Massachusetts, a black student was beaten unconscious and several others injured when a crowd of white students attacked several blacks after the New York Mets won the World Series from the Boston Red Sox. It required a black professor's investigation and report on the incident to force some campus security officials to admit that this was a racially motivated attack rather than mere "hooliganism."[5]

A number of racial incidents were reported at other Massachusetts institutions that pride themselves on their liberalism. At Smith College, Mount Holyoke College, and Tufts University, there were reports of harrassment of black students and other incidents linked to racism. In February 1987, a member of the board of trustees at Wellesley College resigned when the campus reacted with outrage to her comment, made during a classroom lecture, that blacks preferred pushing drugs to working in a factory.[6]

In March 1987, eight black students at Columbia University in New York City were beaten by white students in a brawl described as being racially motivated.[7] Before that, white students at Northern Illinois University had reportedly shouted racial epithets at blacks gathering for a speech by Reverend Jesse Jackson.[8] As the quote from *The New York Times* suggests, these are only examples of a more widespread pattern of racial animosity toward blacks at predominantly white colleges and universities.

Along with the news of these hostilities against blacks came equally disturbing reports of a continuing decline in black enrollment in higher education. The decade-long pattern of decline, which had begun in 1976, showed no signs of reversal. For the most part, that decline reflects the precipitous drop in black enrollment at the predominantly white colleges and universities.

A decade ago, in 1976, black undergraduate enrollment reached a high point of 10.5 percent of the national total, up from six percent in 1968. By 1980, it had declined to 10.1 percent, and by 1984, the last year included in the American Council on Education's *1986 Report on Minorities in Higher Education,* it was down to 9.5 percent. Between 1980 and 1984, the decline in numbers was from 932,254 to 897,185, representing a net loss of 3.8 percent. Blacks were the only major racial or ethnic group whose undergraduate enrollments declined between 1980 and 1984; other minorities and whites experienced an increase.[9]

Black enrollment in graduate school also declined substantially over the decade. Only black enrollment in professional schools increased, but not enough to offset the overall loss in enrollment beyond the bachelor's level.[10]

In 1987, two years after the College Board published *Equality and Excellence: The Educational Status of Black Americans,* warning of the seriousness of the downward trend in black higher education, the nation still has not moved with a sense of urgency to remedy this situation.[11] The article on minorities in higher education in the back-to-school issue of *The Chronicle of Higher Education,* cited at the beginning of this essay, is typical of those that have appeared in the wake of the College Board report.

These articles remind us of the complexity of the problem of declining black enrollment, and conclude that little can or will be done to reverse the trend. Yet, many sound proposals for increasing the numbers of blacks in higher education have been put forth by various conferences, committees, and commissions, as well as by individual faculty members and administrators.[12]

The bottom line in all these plans and proposals calls for increases in spending and a major commitment of other resources. To date, neither the federal government, the states, nor the individual colleges and universities have been willing to commit the necessary resources on a *long term and sustained basis* to reverse this decline. Had such a commitment been made in the mid-seventies to safeguard the gains from the sixties, the black enrollment picture would look very different today.

The downward trend in black enrollment in higher education and the growing hostility toward blacks in predominantly white colleges and universities have served to underscore the vital role of the historically black colleges and universities (HBCUs) in American higher education. As this author has noted elsewhere, black colleges have borne, and still bear, the brunt of *America's* responsibility for providing equitable educational opportunities for black students.[13]

Predictably, in 1987, historically black colleges only made headlines when they were facing financial or academic difficulties. Nevertheless, as most of these institutions struggle to thrive academically and survive financially, their continued existence is crucial in the face of the retreat by predominantly white institutions from their promise of equal educational opportunities for black students.

A recent study by the sociologist Walter Allen (1986), comparing black students at predominantly black colleges with those at predominantly white colleges, provides yet another piece of evidence that black colleges do a better job than their predominantly white counterparts of educating black undergraduates.[14] Allen shows, as Jacqueline Fleming had earlier (1984), that black colleges offer a more nurturing academic and social environment, and graduate proportionally larger numbers of black students. They also provide students with the skills and self-confidence necessary to compete effectively in graduate and professional schools, as well as in the world of work.[15]

What does it all add up to—this picture of declining black enrollments in higher education; of increased hostility towards blacks on majority campuses; of struggling black colleges that still produce the lion's share of the blacks who earn graduate and professional degrees? In the pages that follow, an attempt is made to provide a more detailed picture of the trends, to understand their causes, and to assess their implications.

The conclusion makes the point that equity in higher education still eludes blacks as a group. When the statistics on minorities are disaggregated, they show clearly that blacks are the only ones who are consistently losing ground in the quest for educational equality.[16] This finding alone should be sufficient to make black higher education a priority on the nation's educational agenda.

## WHAT IS BEHIND THE ENROLLMENT DECLINE?

Total black enrollment in higher education declined from 9.4 percent in 1976 to 8.8 percent in 1984. As stated earlier, black *undergraduate* enrollment declined over the same period from 10.5 percent to 9.5 percent.[17] Since 1976, the proportion of black high school graduates who go on to college has declined from 33.5 percent to 26.1 percent. In terms of absolute numbers, there were 15,000 fewer black high school graduates entering college in 1985 than there were in 1976.[18] According to Alexander Astin's estimate, only 42 percent of the black students who enter college continue through graduation.[19]

This downward trend in college enrollment by blacks is particularly disturbing because it has been occurring at a time when black high school graduation rates have been going up. The proportion of blacks graduating from high school rose from 67.5 percent in 1976 to 75.6 percent in 1985.[20] The result of these two opposite trends has been to negate much of the ground blacks gained in higher education in the late sixties and early seventies.

Samuel Myers, president of the National Association for Equal Opportunity in Higher Education (NAFEO), the umbrella organization for the 117 historically and predominantly black colleges and universities, recently wrote that the expansion of black enrollment in higher education that occurred between the decade of the mid-1960s and mid-1970s was the most dramatic in history.[21]

The spurt in black enrollment to which Myers referred was the direct result of federal legislation adopted during the Johnson administration in response to the momentum of the Civil Rights Movement. The Economic Opportunity Act of 1964 authorized funding of the college work-study program to assist academically and financially disadvantaged students. The Civil Rights Act of 1964 prohibited federal funding for institutions that discriminated on the basis of race, thereby virtually mandating that colleges and universities open their doors to minority students.

Under The Higher Education Act of 1965, work-study programs were expanded, a program of need-based student grants established, federal assistance to struggling colleges provided, and a broad set of egalitarian educational objectives outlined. In 1968, the TRIO outreach and academic support programs (Upward Bound, Talent Search, and Special Services for Disadvantaged Students) were created. The 1972 amendments to the Higher Education Act provided additional financial assistance to needy students through the Basic Educational Opportunity Grants, later known as Pell Grants.[22]

Just as federal assistance for financial aid and academic support programs spurred the increase in black enrollment between 1966 and 1976, so the shifting emphasis in some of these aid programs and the cutbacks in others have been mainly responsible for the decline in black college enrollment since 1976. Although the total dollars spent on financial aid have increased somewhat, that increase has not kept pace with inflation. And financial aid allocations have certainly not expanded sufficiently to meet the needs of the growing number of students who require assistance.

In the late sixties and early seventies, most federal financial aid went to lower income whites and blacks. As the numbers of other minorities in higher education increased, and as middle class whites demanded financial aid assistance, there was a commensurate need for additional financial aid dollars. The response to this increased demand was to cut the financial aid pie into thinner and thinner slices.

The government also sought to meet these increasing demands by shifting the emphasis of its financial aid programs from grants to loans. This reduction in gift aid occurred during the period of back-to-back recessions in the late seventies, when black parents could least afford to make up the difference between the financial aid available and the rising costs of a college education. Moreover, the precarious financial situation of many black parents made them unable or unwilling to take on the burden of student loans.[23]

A recent issue of *The Chronicle of Higher Education* summarized the changes that have occurred in financial aid funding and packaging between 1980 and 1987. In terms of "constant 1982 dollars", the total amount of federally funded gift aid rose a mere five percent, from 3.288 billion in 1980 to 3.455 billion in 1987. The total amount of federal student loan dollars increased by 13.4 percent, from 7.754 billion to 8.794 billion. Funding for college work-study programs, on which many black students depend for supplementary income, *declined* by 22 percent over the seven-year period.[24]

Other statistics in the *Chronicle* article confirm that as the demands on financial aid funds grew, the monies were divided into smaller and smaller lots. Between 1980 and 1987, Supplemental Educational Opportunity Grant aid per recipient declined by 16.6 percent; aid in the form of loans per person declined by an average of 14.5 percent; college work-study aid per recipient declined by 15 percent. Only aid in the form of Pell Grants increased by 17.5 percent per person.[25]

What emerges from these data is a strong case for the proposition that economic factors have been the main cause of declining black enrollment in higher education over the past decade. The key elements in this decline have been the reduction and redirection of financial aid dollars; cutbacks in federal funding for pre-college outreach and academic support programs; the rising costs of a college education; and the erosion of the earning power and income of black families as a result of back-to-back recessions.

The attempt by the Department of Education to refute the importance of financial aid in determining the levels of black college attendance simply does not stand up. In a study released earlier this year, the Department noted similar college-going rates among blacks and whites with similar income levels and achievement backgrounds. This was cited as proof that it is not a shortage of federal financial aid that discourages black college enrollment.[26]

What the study *does not* point out, but what is shown in *Equality and Excellence,* is the disproportionately large number of blacks who fall in the lower income group, which is heavily dependent on financial aid:

The importance of financial aid for black students is apparent when one considers that in 1981, nearly half (48 percent) of black college-bound seniors came from families with incomes under $12,000, as compared to only 10 percent of their white counterparts.[27]

In other words, nearly five times as many college-bound blacks as college-bound whites have family incomes under $12,000. Thus, even though the rate of college enrollment may be the same for blacks and whites with family incomes under $12,000, that income group includes proportionally five times as many black students as white students.

The Department of Education's study simply confirms something we already know, namely that lower income students are less likely to attend college than those in middle income groups. The Department should have also pointed out that lower income students are precisely those who depend on financial aid to enroll in college and to remain in college. It happens that the overwhelming majority of black students fall in the lower income groups.

Of course, no one maintains that financial aid and other economic factors have been the only ones contributing to the decline in black enrollment in higher education over the past decade. Other factors such as changing college admissions requirements and growing opposition to affirmative action helped to curtail recruitment activities on many campuses.

Another factor contributing to the decline has been the poor quality of the elementary and high school education which many blacks receive in our public schools. The inferior quality of this education, especially that provided by many inner-city public schools, has left many black students unprepared for, and uninterested in, continuing on to college.

Moreover, the high cost of college has helped to enhance the attractiveness of the military as a stepping-stone to a higher education or as a career option in its own right. Economic and other considerations have also led a number of black high school graduates to turn to private "proprietary" institutions for courses and credentials that hold out the often unrealistic promise of quick entry into well-paying jobs.

## BLACK STUDENTS ON BLACK AND WHITE CAMPUSES

Historically, America looked to the black colleges to fulfill its responsibility to provide educational opportunities for black students. Although the resources available to these institutions—public and private alike—could not compare with those available to the better endowed predominantly white institutions, black colleges proved remarkably successful in graduating men and women who formed the core of the black professional class and the black leadership.

As recently as the 1960s, black colleges still enrolled over 50 percent of all the blacks in higher education. In the southern states where most of the historically black colleges are located, in 1965, 75 percent of the black students enrolled in college were attending black institutions.[28]

Contrary to popular belief, overall enrollment in historically black colleges did not decline as a result of the desegregation of predominantly white institutions. The black institutions also benefitted from the spurt in black enrollment that occurred in the sixties and early seventies. Many of the public black colleges also gained substantially in white enrollment as a result of the integration of public higher education ordered by the Federal Court in the *Adams v. Califano* decision of 1972.[29]

As a group, black colleges experienced their largest enrollment increases in the period between 1954 and 1976. Between 1976 and 1980, while black enrollment dropped steadily at predominantly white institutions, it remained relatively stable at the historically black colleges and universities.[30]

These trends notwithstanding, the 1970s were the years when the preponderance of black enrollment shifted from historically black institutions to predominantly white colleges and universities. Since 1970, nationwide, the proportion of blacks enrolled in black colleges has declined to 27 percent. The proportion is about 37 percent in the 19 states and the District of Columbia (the "*Adams* states") where the traditionally black institutions are located.[31]

The opening up of mainstream academia to black students held out the promise of equal opportunities for advancement for large numbers of these young people. Yet, after nearly two decades of substantially increased numbers of black students on white campuses, glaring inequalities remain between the opportunities they offer black students as compared to those available to white students.

The differential treatment and experience of black students at predominantly white institutions is reflected in their limited participation in extracurricular activities other than sports; the dearth of leadership roles they have available to them; the limited range of academic concentrations they are encouraged and helped to pursue; the relative absence of mentoring by the faculty, other than black or minority faculty; and their limited overall success as judged by their academic performance and rates of graduation.

Of course, there are a number of black students who excel at predominantly white colleges and universities, and their experiences and accomplishments must be taken into account in assessing the effectiveness of these institutions. In far too many cases, however, predominantly white institutions have only provided revolving doors through which black students enter and exit with little more for their efforts than outstanding loans and a shaken confidence in their own abilities.

Because of the high attrition rates and correspondingly low graduation rates of blacks in many predominantly white institutions, few universities release these statistics to the public. The available data indicate that the drop-out rate is significantly higher for blacks enrolled at predominantly white colleges than for those in historically black institutions.[32] A 1986 research report prepared for the Educational Testing Service (ETS) notes that:

. . . from 10–40 percent of all students who enter college will drop out before degree completion, but for minorities the proportion is substan-

13

tially higher, particularly in predominantly white schools.[33]

My own researches indicate that a four-year graduation rate of 35 percent and lower is not uncommon for blacks in predominantly white institutions. *Six-year* graduation rates of approximately 51 percent and 59 percent, respectively, were reported for black students by Michigan State University and the University of Michigan at Ann Arbor, two of the few institutions that regularly release such data.[34]

Although it might be presumed that most blacks drop out of predominantly white institutions for academic reasons, existing studies show that most of those who leave do so because of financial and other non-academic reasons. The availability of financial aid not only plays a key role in the recruitment of blacks to college, it is a major factor in their retention.[35]

Many black students at some of the more expensive predominantly white universities enroll from term to term, frequently uncertain as to whether the aid they will receive will be sufficient to allow them to remain in school. When these financial insecurities are added to what for many black students are already high pressured academic environments, it is not surprising that many students drop out or opt out. Indications are that some opt for lower cost four-year institutions or community colleges.[36]

Financial aid problems are not unique to black students at predominantly white institutions. However, a number of factors make the problems there somewhat different from those at historically black institutions. On the one hand, because of the low parental incomes of students at historically black colleges (the median income was $8800 in 1980), most of those students qualify for a combination of grants and loans to cover all their tuition and fees.[37] On the other hand, since most predominantly black colleges and universities are less expensive than their predominantly white counterparts, parents whose incomes require that they contribute to the costs are more likely to be able to afford them.

Ironically, because predominantly white institutions enroll a larger share of black students who are technically part of the middle class, they have a larger proportion of black students who need assistance but do not qualify for certain types or amounts of federal (or state) aid. Often, however, the family responsibilities of middle class black parents do not permit them to make the contributions to their children's education which government regulations require. When their children cannot secure the financial aid they need, they often transfer to historically black colleges or other less expensive institutions.

A related point is the fact that many high-achieving black students are recruited to predominantly white institutions with generous but non-renewable one-year scholarship offers. Such students often find themselves in financial difficulties when the scholarships run out and they have no other source of comparable gift aid. Without support from their parents, they often have no option but to take out a loan or transfer to another institution.

Next to financial aid problems usually comes dissatisfaction with the academic and social environment as a reason why black students drop out of predominantly white institutions. In fact, if there is one common thread that runs through the studies of black students on predominantly white campuses, it is their sense of isolation and alienation from activities that form the core of the white students' college experience.[38]

In Allen's comparative study of blacks on historically black and predominantly white campuses, nearly two-thirds of the students on majority campuses (62 percent) felt that activities *were not* representative of their interests. By contrast, two-thirds of the students on black campuses felt that the activities *were* in line with their interests.[39]

Most of the difficulties which black students perceive in the environment on white campuses are attributed to racial discrimination and/or negative racial attitudes exhibited by faculty, students, or staff in the environment. Blatant manifestations of hostility toward blacks, such as those cited at the beginning of this essay, represent but the tip of the iceberg, according to reports of students at many predominantly white institutions.

It is not only the social climate that is perceived as racist on white campuses, it is the academic climate as well. Students complain of insensitivity of faculty to their presence in class, and in some instances accuse faculty of deliberately seeking to humiliate them by means of negative references to black people and/or black culture.

The racial tension that is prevalent on predominantly white campuses seems to be ameliorated in the black campus environment. Whites usually comprise upwards of 30 percent of the faculty in these institutions. The student bodies at most of these institutions are five percent to 25 percent interracial and international. (Now, a few of the public *historically black colleges* are predominantly white.) In Allen's study, a substantially larger percentage of black students at black colleges (than those at white colleges) reported having good to excellent relationships with white faculty and staff.[40]

Even though non-academic factors such as financial aid and campus climate head the list of reasons why black students drop out of predominantly white colleges, it is obvious that many of them leave for academic reasons as well. Both their own academic performances and their perceptions of the academic climate are factors in individual students' decisions to drop out or transfer out of these institutions.

A recurring and particularly disturbing finding concerning black students on predominantly white campuses is that many very good students do not thrive academically in these environments. Various researchers have pointed out, as Allen does, that "the high school academic superiority of black students attending white universities is incontestable."[41]

Yet, despite these superior academic backgrounds, black students on white campuses tend to lose more ground academically in the transition from high school to college than do their counterparts in black institutions. Allen describes the decline in academic performance of blacks at predominantly white institutions as "nothing short of spectacular."[42] (See Table 1.)

## Table 1
### Black Students' Academic Performance At Predominantly Black and Predominantly White Colleges

| College Grade Point Average (GPA) | College Campus Predominantly | | H.S. GPA* of Black Students College Campus— Predominantly | |
|---|---|---|---|---|
| | Black | White | Black | White |
| Below 2.5 | 28.0% | 36.4% | 15.1% | 4.1% |
| 2.6 to 2.99 | 38.1 | 39.2 | 27.8 | 15.9 |
| 3.0 to 3.49 | 26.1 | 20.7 | 39.2 | 31.5 |
| Above 3.5 | 7.8 | 3.7 | 17.9 | 48.5 |
| | 100.0 | 100.0 | 100.0 | 100.0 |
| N = | (884) | (653) | (747) | (629) |

* H.S. GPA = High School Grade Point Average

After Allen, Walter, *Gender and Campus Race Differences* (1986), Tables 1 and 9, pp. 33 and 48.

Table 1 shows that in Allen's study, almost half (48.5 percent) of the black students on predominantly white campuses entered with high school grade point averages higher than 3.5 (B+/A-). Yet, over one-third of them (36.4 percent) reported college GPAs of less than 2.5 (C+). Whereas 80 percent of them entered with averages of B or better (3.0 and above), only 24 percent of them maintained a college average of B or better.

By contrast, Table 1 shows a decidedly less pronounced shift in the distribution of grades from high school through college at the historically black institutions. There, 57 percent of the students entered with grade point averages of B or better (3.0), and 34 percent of them maintained a B average in college.

Some of the slippage in academic performance by blacks in predominantly white institutions can be attributed to the actual or perceived high level of competitiveness in the environment. But most students say, and scholars agree, that much of the decline in achievement has to do with other factors in the predominantly white college environment.

After all, many of these students had been high achievers at competitive high schools, with various degrees of integration. What most of them do not get in college, and which they had in high school, is a supportive environment in which faculty take the lead in rewarding them, reassuring them, and helping them with difficulties when they arise. Such support is particularly important for the majority of black students who do not have family members or others to whom they can turn for the type of advice and assistance that helps students from academic and professional backgrounds learn to "negotiate the system." In a very perceptive paper entitled "Nonformal Education and Strategies for Black Retention," Beauvais and Gould make the point this way:

> . . . heavily recruited Black students, the best and the brightest, are failing at major universities in alarming numbers. The major problem is not academic preparation, or intelligence, or motivation. Substantial numbers of Black students fail or surrender, because of incomplete nonformal, rather than formal, education . . . Successful mentoring relationships and networking [results] in Black students feeling as though they can impact and control their environment . . . Study skills, time management, academic information, note taking, and decision-making are areas [where] the Black students' pre-university nonformal education has rendered them less competitive than their white colleagues . . . Students should not be assisted in remediation efforts by individuals who believe they will fail. This mentality is always destructive and, unfortunately, fairly typical of most university attempts with special tutorial programs for Black students. What Black students need is an ongoing support group which not only provides skill-building and networking opportunities, but affirms and validates the importance of these activities . . .[43]

At historically black colleges, it is recognized that students need these support mechanisms and considerable attention is given to providing them. Jacqueline Fleming, Walter Allen, and others have noted that the nurturing atmosphere and the presence of active mentors and role models enable students in black colleges to out-perform their better prepared peers in predominantly white institutions. The proof of the effectiveness of this support is that black students in black institutions graduate in larger numbers in shorter periods of time.[44]

The accomplishments of historically black colleges in educating black students are all the more noteworthy since most of these institutions lag behind their white counterparts in terms of the credentials of their faculties and the caliber of their facilities.

The academic credentials and scholarly output of faculty members at black colleges are seldom comparable to those of faculty at the predominantly white institutions which the black schools regard as their peer institutions. The point is usually made that as primarily teaching institutions, effectiveness in the classroom is given more weight than scholarly research in recruiting and evaluating faculty.

Nevertheless, the relative absence of incentives for faculty to engage in scholarly research and keep abreast of general developments in their fields in some institutions and/or departments definitely impairs their effectiveness in attracting and keeping the brightest students.

The absence of a sufficiently stimulating academic environment is a common reason given by those very good students who choose to transfer out of predominantly black institutions. They usually opt for what they expect will be a more challenging environment at a predominantly white institution. Of course, once they are there, they also find challenges of a different sort.

Another point on the down side of the black college success story is the apparent lack of success in training professional teachers. In some southern states where teacher competency examinations have been introduced, on the whole, reportedly, graduates of black colleges have not performed as well as blacks or whites from other institutions.

Some of the difference between the success of black college graduates in the arts and sciences and those in education may be due to the different academic backgrounds and performance records of students who opt for one or the other course of study. Certainly there is a nationwide concern with the quality of students being attracted to teaching. A national effort is underway to attract better students into the field. In any case, more research is needed before we can identify the factors affecting the competency and performance levels of teachers who graduate from historically black colleges.

That black colleges *can* improve their records in this regard is indicated by the turnaround in the success rate of Grambling State University's graduates on the National Teachers Examination required for certification in the state of Louisiana. When the test was introduced, as few as 20 percent of Grambling's graduates passed. For the last several years, however, as a result of innovative changes in the education curriculum, the pass rate of Grambling's graduates is 95 percent or more. The university was honored by the American Association of State Colleges and Universities (AASCU) for its accomplishments in the teacher training field.[45]

For those who would question the overall quality of the education students receive at historically black colleges, suffice it to say that the public record of the accomplishments of black college alumni speaks for itself. Their performance in graduate and professional schools as well as in the world of work attests to the quality of the preparation, and the effectiveness of the motivation, they received as undergraduates.[46]

Black colleges award 34 percent of the undergraduate degrees earned by blacks nationwide, and 59 percent of those earned in the South. By comparison, they enroll 27 percent of all black students and 37 percent of those in the South. They graduate over 50 percent of the students earning bachelor's degrees in mathematics, and approximately 40 percent of those with majors in business, computer science, engineering, and the biological and physical sciences.[47]

The American Council on Education's *1985 Report on Minorities in Higher Education,* issued by the Office of Minority Affairs, points out that 55 percent of the 6320 blacks who received doctorates between 1975 and 1985 received their undergraduate training at only 87 historically black colleges. The remaining 45 percent of those who earned doctorates in that period received their bachelor's degrees from a total of 633 predominantly white institutions.[48]

There is no question but that black colleges are still carrying more than their share of the weight of preparing black students for academic and professional careers. As is evident from the statistics quoted above, without black colleges, the number of blacks entering the pipeline to careers in science, engineering, and related fields would be reduced by nearly half.

In some critical fields, the loss would be even greater. In 1987, for example, according to the American Institute of Physics, nationwide 51 blacks earned baccalaureate degrees in physics; 12 of those graduated from Lincoln University in Pennsylvania. No doubt, most of the others also graduated from historically black colleges.

When the records of historically black and predominantly white colleges are compared with respect to their success in educating black students, it is clear that the edge goes to the black institutions. As the present author noted in a recent address:

> Black colleges . . . instill in black students what eludes them at many predominantly white institutions . . . [namely] the boldness to dare to compete at the cutting edge, and the confidence and the skills to succeed once they are there.[49]

Yet, given the demographic realities of the 1990s and beyond, it is clear that the majority of black students will continue to enroll in predominantly white institutions. There are too few black colleges, and these are too small, to meet the enrollment needs of black students in this country. Moreover, the day has long since passed when it could be expected that all blacks should, or would choose to, study in predominantly black colleges. These students have a right to expect and receive the support necessary to ensure their success in, as well as access to, predominantly white and historically black institutions.[50]

It is clear that in the decades ahead, the two types of institutions should strengthen their collaborative efforts to provide a quality education for blacks (and other minorities) in both settings. Predominantly white institutions can make available to black colleges some of their resources and facilities to enable black colleges to do an even better job at what they do well. At the same time, black colleges need to share the techniques and approaches that will enable predominantly white institutions to provide blacks with a genuinely equal opportunity for success on those campuses. Everyone stands to gain by pooling strengths on behalf of students in both environments.[51]

## CONCLUSION: FULFILLING THE PROMISE OF EQUALITY

To answer the question of where we are in 1987 with respect to equal opportunities for blacks in higher education, we must look backward to measure the distance we have covered. The mid-1960s constitute an important benchmark because federal legislative initiatives during that period led to an unprecedented opening up of predominantly white colleges and universities to black students. When we look back over the two decades, we must affirm that progress has been made.

We note, however, that the direction of change is now reversed. Between 1966 and 1976, the number of black undergraduates doubled, and the proportion of blacks at all levels of higher education reached nearly 10 percent. Over the decade since 1976, however, those gains have been steadily eroding, so that the overall black enrollment in higher education is about 8.8 percent. Today, there are fewer black high school graduates entering college than there were in 1976. The progress made in the sixties and early seventies is in danger of being obliterated.

Between 1980 and 1984, blacks were the only racial or ethnic group whose undergraduate enrollments went down. Those of whites, Hispanics, Native Americans, and Asians all went up. The decade-long decline in black enrollment in higher education is rightfully a cause for alarm. There is a clear and immediate imperative to call the nation to action to remedy this situation.

It is not only the issue of access to higher education that is a cause for concern. As Alexander Astin and others have noted, there is also the question of what choices or options are available to blacks seeking a higher education. Although community college enrollment was not dealt with in this paper, the data show that over 40 percent of the black enrollment in higher education is in community colleges. This enrollment is not by choice. In fact, it reflects an absence of choice.

Many blacks are forced to attend community colleges or no college at all. There are already signs that some of these institutions are being allowed to degenerate into second-class educational palliatives for second-class citizens. The glaring overrepresentation of blacks and other minorities in the community college sector of higher education must be eliminated in as much as it is both the result of discrimination and discriminatory in its effect.

As to recommendations that might be made to rebuild the overall black enrollment in higher education, whatever can be said there has been said before. There was no mystery as to the cause of the increase in black enrollment that began in the sixties. It resulted from a massive infusion of resources in the form of financial aid to students and to academic institutions. Similarly, there is no need to mystify the present situation and what is necessary to change it.

The data show clearly that black enrollment declined when the resources sustaining it were reduced and redirected. To make a difference now, there must be a sustained commitment of additional resources at federal, state, and local levels. After 20 years, in various institutions around the country, there are many successful programs for recruiting and retaining blacks in college. These can be duplicated or modified to meet the needs of other institutions. What is required is money, personnel, and facilities to mount the programs.

One of the things that should be learned from the efforts of the late sixties and early seventies is that we must not be too quick to pronounce our efforts a failure. One excuse that was used to justify cutting back support for programs for enhancing minority recruitment and retention was that "they didn't work."

Some did and some did not; but it is clear that this was not an undertaking for which a definitive evaluation could be rendered after a few years.

We were just beginning to see the fruits of the investments of the sixties and seventies when these investments were seriously curtailed. Any undertaking to achieve a lasting increase in black enrollments in higher education must involve a commitment of decades, not years.

Education is "All One System," as noted educator Harold Hodgkinson so succinctly put it. Positive intervention at any level has the potential of reverberating throughout the system. The higher education community must overcome its own inertia in the face of declining black enrollments, and stop insisting that it can do little until the K-12 system changes. Whatever is done at the level of the colleges and universities will have an impact on the K-12 level and vice versa.

What is urgently needed is for the nation's colleges and universities to take the initiative to step up their collaboration with the K-12 system in order to enhance the preparedness of blacks and other underrepresented minorities for full participation in higher education. As pointed out earlier, there also needs to be collaboration across the higher education spectrum to link predominantly black and predominantly white institutions to improve the chances of black student success in both environments.

The issue of student enrollment in higher education is not the only one that must be addressed. The continuing underrepresentation of blacks among the ranks of faculty and senior administrators in higher education is as acute a problem as that of declining enrollments. Obviously the two issues are linked, but we cannot be content with the argument that there can be no recruitment of black faculty until we get substantially greater numbers "coming through the pipeline."

There are issues of black faculty recruitment and retention that deserve immediate attention, particularly on majority campuses. Recent essays by Reginald Wilson and by the present author outline the ways to reverse the trend of the "dwindling black presence" among the faculty ranks.[52] The formation this year of the National Congress of Black Faculty, under the leadership of Ronald Walters at Howard University, signals the urgency with which black faculty around the country regard the need to address the problems they face.

The rationale for having black and other minority faculty on our nation's campuses should not be simply one of meeting affirmative action goals. An ethnically and racially diverse faculty is important because the perspectives which these faculty bring to scholarship help to define what *is* good scholarship in the modern world.

We live in a world where it is no longer intellectually defensible to presume to discuss human history or human affairs from the perspective of any one cultural or racial group, no matter how important its contributions to the world as we know it. Modern scholarship in the sciences as well as in the humanities is already infused with the racial, ethnic, and cultural diversity that characterizes this country and the world.[53]

As we move into the 21st century, our universities should acknowledge and affirm the value of that diversity. It should be reflected in our curricula and in our faculties. Exposure to the views and works of black scholars and of others who are minorities in this country, but majority peoples elsewhere, should be regarded as a necessary element in the education of students who must understand and function in the world of today and tomorrow.

# Tomorrow's Teachers:
# Who Will They Be,
# What Will They Know?

Bernard C. Watson, Ph.D.
with
Fasaha M. Traylor, M.A.

## INTRODUCTION

In this decade of "educational reform," known primarily for the many reports issued by national organizations, it is interesting to note that most of the action has taken place at the state or local level. Recommendations which purportedly would lead to improvement in the quality of education for all of America's children have included almost every area of schooling: curriculum, textbooks, length of school day and year, organization of schools, standards of performance for staff and students, relationships between the private sector and public schools, and the nature and quality of pre-service and in-service education and training for teachers. It is probably fair to suggest that most people would agree that:

- Public education provides a significant percentage of its students with an education which enables them to pursue higher education or to enter the primary labor market. Yet, for a smaller and growing percentage of students, the education they receive fails to prepare them for either the job market or higher education.

- Although there are many teachers who are superbly prepared and who do a commendable, even outstanding, job with their students, the quality of the teaching staff in this country needs to be upgraded, particularly among those entering the field as beginners.

- There are many good, even excellent, schools in this country that are doing an excellent job educating the children and youth who are enrolled. Yet, there are too many schools which do an inadequate job of educating their students.

- The best education is probably offered to students who attend schools in more advantaged communities and the poorest education is probably offered to students in the more disadvantaged and poorer communities.

- Schools located in big cities, in poor neighborhoods, with large or majority minority-student populations, especially black and/or Hispanic minorities, usually do the poorest job of educating their students.

- There is widespread inequality of educational opportunity in the public schools of the United States.

- As with all generalizations, there are exceptions, many of which can be and have been identified and analyzed to one degree or another.

- However one feels about the public schools of this country, there is a need for immediate and significant improvement across the board if students now attending those schools are to be prepared to cope effectively with the society in which they will live their adult lives. It is equally obvious that, if this country is to remain competitive with other countries, the quality of its work force must be improved.

Perhaps the one thing with which almost everyone would agree is that the teaching cadre is the crucial element in the improvement of education. All of the other changes recommended will have little, if any, effect if those who teach young people are not equipped to do a far better job than they are doing today. It is, therefore, no surprise that the recommendations for improving or "professionalizing" the teaching force have attracted so much attention during the past few years. But it is precisely because there is *so little disagreement* about the need to improve or to "professionalize" teaching that the various proposals and recommendations must be examined carefully.

Many of the recommendations for "professionalizing" the teaching force have begun to find their way into collective-bargaining agreements, and into deliberations over the future direction and requirements of college and university teacher-training programs. Some have even become national or state-level legislative proposals. It appears that many people are prepared to take seriously the claims made by this latest wave of educational reform: that professionalization of teachers is the key ingredient to improving the quality of education for American children. We take issue here with that proposition, because "professionalization" will not necessarily result in an educational system that is accessible, responsive, and responsible to all American children. In fact, there is every reason to believe that changes in the structure of the teaching profession such as those recommended by the Carnegie Forum Task Force on Teaching as a Profession, The Holmes Group, and others might just as easily lead to increased inequality of educational opportunity—particularly for black, poor, and minority children concentrated in our nation's urban centers. The same could be said for rural children of all descriptions. Avoiding this outcome requires a realistic appraisal of this country's future teachers, and institutional resources. Even more important will be our willingness and determination to direct immediately both effort and resources to those parts of the teacher preparation system—conceptual, programmatic, and institutional—that now are very weak. If these "weak links" are strengthened, America's children can benefit. If they are not strengthened, then future reformers may well look to 1988 as the year America began the *construction of its second dual educational system.*

## A Brief History

As the quality of teaching moved to the top of the agenda of educational

24

reform in the mid-1980s, proposals designed to improve teacher performance spread to virtually every state. Using the rationale that teachers could not teach what they did not know, reformers at every level set out:

- to ensure that teachers knew more;
- to develop policies, procedures, and evaluations that would make it obvious to teachers that more was being expected;
- to see that teachers who met new and higher standards were more adequately compensated for their work.

The efforts of state lawmakers to mandate accountability and foster higher standards of performance have included proposals to mandate or encourage post-baccalaureate degrees or training in education, competency testing of new teachers and recertification of veteran teachers, salary increases, merit pay, career ladders, and both loans and loan-forgiveness programs for prospective teachers.[1]

Although states have been leaders in the reform movement, they have not been the only source of proposals to change American teachers. In 1983, *A Nation at Risk,* the report commissioned by former Education Secretary Terrel Bell, proposed changing teacher education requirements to reduce the number of required "educational methods" courses so that prospective teachers could take more undergraduate courses in "substantive" areas such as mathematics, English, history, economics, or the sciences. Citing a "survey of 1,350 teacher-training institutions," the commission complained that "41 percent of the time of elementary school teacher candidates is spent in education courses."[2]

With so much attention directed at the quality of preparation of the teaching force, deans and professors at many of the country's premier teacher-training institutions convened to assess the need for changes in the undergraduate education of American teachers. Published in April 1986 as the Report of The Holmes Group, *Tomorrow's Teachers* was the first of two reports to focus on teachers as a professional group, quite apart from their roles and responsibilities as employees of school districts. *A Nation Prepared,* the report issued one month later by the Carnegie Forum Task Force on Teaching as a Profession, built upon and extended the recommendations of The Holmes Group. These two reports are worth reviewing in some detail because their recommendations are at the core of current efforts to restructure teaching.

## THE HOLMES GROUP AND CARNEGIE FORUM TASK FORCE: TOMORROW'S TEACHERS/A NATION PREPARED

No one, it seems, feels that the current preparation of teachers is adequate. The first of The Holmes Group goals was therefore to "make the education of teachers intellectually more solid," by which they meant that teachers should have "greater command of academic subjects" (an objective shared by numerous states) and which would require the abolition of the undergraduate education major.[3] Unlike many others, however, The Holmes Group insisted that knowledge of subject matter does not a teacher make; it upheld the importance of teaching teachers how to teach. In a pointed rebuttal to *A Nation at Risk* and other reports, The Holmes Group maintained that the real problem is not that education methods courses are unnecessary or undemanding, but that *only elementary school teachers* take such courses. The result is abysmally poor teaching in both high schools and liberal arts courses in most colleges and universities.[4]

As a second goal, The Holmes Group suggested that in place of the states' emphasis on merit pay proposals, there should be changes in what is required (and, by implication, compensated) at different stages of a teaching career. This would involve "distinguish[ing] between novices, competent members of the profession, and high-level professional leaders."[5] The Holmes Group would replace the uncertainty involved in determining what qualifies for "merit pay" with a formal system of preparation that links increased pay to the assumption of clearly defined, professional responsibilities.[6]

The third goal of The Holmes Group, also related to the issue of teacher competency, is to "create standards of entry to the profession—examinations and educational requirements—that are professionally relevant and intellectually defensible."[7] Again taking issue with state-level reforms that were geared to measuring only the most minimal of skills needed by the "good teacher," The Holmes Group advocated a system where "students [are required] to demonstrate mastery of important knowledge and skill through multiple evaluations across multiple domains of competence."[8]

The fourth goal of The Holmes Group was to establish a connection between teacher-training and research institutions and the actual sites of teacher work. Universities must "make better use of expert teachers," and schools must become places where practitioners and researchers can feel equally at home.[9] To this end, *Tomorrow's Teachers* recommended the establishment of "Professional Development Schools, analogues to teaching hospitals in the medical profession" that would serve as the institutional site of collaboration between teacher-educators/researchers and teaching practitioners.[10] Finally, they argued, schools must be made "better places for teachers to work, and to learn. This will require less bureaucracy, more professional autonomy, and more leadership for teachers."[11]

The Holmes Group also took issue with many other assumptions of education reformers, including the "bright person model" of teaching, in which it is assumed that somehow a brilliant student automatically becomes an inspired teacher.[12] But it was primarily the five goals listed above that in substance formed the core of the Carnegie proposal. Moreover, the admonition that schools "require less bureaucracy, more professional autonomy and more leadership for teachers" was actually the organizing theme of the report published by the Carnegie Forum Task Force on Education and the Economy in May 1986. By then, autonomy had become the official pathway to excellence.

The similarity between *Tomorrow's Teachers* and *A Nation Prepared: Teachers for the 21st Century* is more than a coincidence. The two proposals had in common a few key people, funding sources (the Carnegie Corporation helped to fund The Holmes Group deliberations), and a knowledge base. Where The Holmes Group focused almost exclusively on teacher preparation, the Carnegie Forum Task Force defined as its goal "a system in which school districts can offer the pay, autonomy and career opportunities necessary to attract to teaching highly qualified people who would otherwise take up other professional careers."[13]

The Carnegie Forum Task Force recommended a series of steps that are meant to be implemented together: "None will succeed," the report states, "unless all are implemented."[14] In many ways, *A Nation Prepared* drew upon the elements of The Holmes Group report. It recommends:

- the restructuring of "schools to provide a professional environment for teachers";
- introducing "a new category of Lead Teachers with the proven ability to provide active leadership in the redesign of the schools";
- requiring "a bachelor's degree in the arts and sciences as a prerequisite for the professional study of teaching"; and
- developing a "new professional curriculum in graduate schools of education leading to a Master in Teaching degree."

Where the Carnegie Forum Task Force departed from The Holmes Group proposals was in its recommendation of a salary scale for a restructured teaching profession that would significantly increase the salaries of each of the teacher grades, from entry-level to Career Professional/Lead Teacher.[15] It also called for, and subsequently created, a national Board for Professional Teaching Standards, which was to "establish high standards for what teachers need to know and be able to do, and to certify teachers who meet that standard."[16]

## THE NATIONAL BOARD

The National Board for Professional Teaching Standards is an organizational innovation that is expected to supplant eventually (by making irrelevant) existing licensing requirements. The Task Force itself lists several functions for the Board, including the granting of teachers' certificates and advanced teachers' certificates; the determination of "what teachers need to know and be able to do"; giving assistance to teacher education institutions in "preparing candidates for certification"; and the creation of "state or regional organizations of certified teachers . . . to oversee Board functions at the regional and state level."[17]

The Task Force emphasizes that the certification requirements of the Board are to be "Initially . . . voluntary, [but should in time] be incorporated in the structure of state standards."[18] Teachers will be motivated to seek the certificate because it will be "an unambiguous statement that its holder is a highly qualified teacher." The value of the certificate can be expected to be incorporated into compensation systems because "intense competition" will develop for Board-certified teachers.[19]

It is not insignificant that the shift from competency to professionalization also entailed a shift from shoring up the existing teaching force to attracting a different kind of teacher. Yet, few observers have commented upon the transitional effect of having a two-tiered teaching force, one of which is presumably "more qualified" than the other. What is most important—the revolutionary kernel of these proposals—is that they unveil a set of policies and programs that shift the responsibility for upgrading the teaching force and eventually supervising its more highly qualified members *from* the state and local districts that have traditionally been responsible for the delivery of public education *to* a wholly different set of procedures and institutions.

What is surprising about this conceptualization of the National Board is that it is a *national* board, chartered to develop national standards, without any real attention to how the centralization of teaching standards can be expected to affect diverse educational districts. Teaching standards will be centralized not only through the issuance of certificates by the National Board, but also—and this was never made quite explicit in the report—through its power to decide "what teachers need to know and be able to do." This power will be magnified and expressed through the connection of the National Board to university-based teacher-education programs and, once in place, would seem to be far beyond the reach of any particular locale to alter or oppose it.

Whether this was its intended effect is not easy to say. There is, however, not much evidence that the implications of this for local districts or even states have been well thought out. The National Board for Professional Teaching Standards is, among other things, an organization that will centralize and standardize the production of the teaching force, quite apart from the particular needs or problems of any local school district. The role of the local district vis-a-vis the new professional teacher is not exactly clear, but certainly its best understood role will be to raise the money to hire them at higher salary levels. While this arrangement may not be entirely analogous to "spinning off" the teaching profession into the private sector, it may be as close as any public employees could expect to get.

The pursuit of professional autonomy through organizational innovation has both strengths and weaknesses. Locating the source of professional authority outside local school districts—in teacher education programs and the National Standards Board—obviously bypasses entrenched bureaucratic resistance in school systems, states, the public, and labor organizations.

It also empowers representatives of the emerging profession to control closely both the "knowledge base" of teaching and its new entrants through what must soon become a reciprocal relationship between professional education programs and the standards board. Eventually, the standards board, or some yet-to-be-devised, closely related entity, will have to be charged with accrediting teacher training programs, because it would be impossible for the standards board to "certify" that individuals meet certain professional standards without it also having some level of formal control over the nature of the preparation of future members of the profession.[20] It is only through these "two overlapping systems"—issuance of the certificate of professional competence to individuals, and the development of new accreditation standards and systems to implement them—that the profession can expect to control effectively both the production of teachers and what they are to know.

Determining what teachers "should know and be able to do" cannot be separated from the characteristics of the upcoming generation of American students. It is also intimately related to one of the fundamental values of American public education: the principle of local control. How will teachers prepared in this new way cope with the diversity of the public school systems of America? How will changes in the roles of teachers impact on how schools and school systems serve local needs? We will return later to these questions, but for now we want to turn from teachers to the question of students. As Harold Hodgkinson has already pointed out, "changes in the composition of the group moving through the educational system will change it faster than anything else except nuclear war."[21]

## DEMOGRAPHIC CHANGES

Both *A Nation Prepared* and *Tomorrow's Teachers* commented on anticipated demographic changes in America's student population over the next twenty years. The Carnegie Forum Task Force on Teaching as a Profession decried "a future in which both white and minority children are confronted with almost exclusively white authority figures in the schools."[22] The Holmes Group warned that "we may soon have a teacher force composed overwhelmingly of people from majority backgrounds teaching students who are primarily from low-income and minority backgrounds."[23] Despite these warnings, however, the substance of professionalization proposals glides too smoothly over what is likely to be an almost cataclysmic demographic change. Consider:

- One of the most forthright measures of who will be students is the rate at which different population groups are having children. In 1984, the fertility rate (number of children per woman of childbearing age) was 1.3 among Cubans, 1.7 among whites, 2.1 among Puerto Ricans, 2.4 among blacks, and 2.9 among Mexicans.[24]

- Regional differences in population growth are primarily a reflection of ethnic differences in fertility rates.

- Varying birth rates also create average age differences between populations that are likely to have troubling implications both for who the next generation of parents are likely to be as well as for which groups will have vested interests in the support of the public educational system. In 1980, the average age of whites was 31 years; of blacks was 25 years; and of Hispanics was 22 years.[25]

- These demographic realities have already changed the character of American public school systems and may soon change the way we think about the terms "majority" and "minority": The majority of students in California elementary schools is a member of a minority group; 46 percent of students in Texas schools is minority; the public school population of half of the states is more than 25 percent nonwhite. All of the 25 largest school systems serve a majority of minority students; blacks are concentrated in urban and big-city school systems.[26]

- America's Asian population is also making its presence felt in the schools: Asians represent 44 percent of all immigrants currently admitted into the U.S. A large majority of America's Asian population (66 percent) is foreign-born, and though the average Japanese-American speaks English as a native language, the influx of Indochinese will continue to pose language problems for schools, since almost none of them speaks English.[27]

- That so many new Asian immigrants do not speak English should not be allowed to obscure the unusually high level of education of this population. Almost 30 percent of Asian immigrants arrive here with four complete years of college; almost 39 percent of Asian adults in America are college graduates. Scores on the verbal portion of the SAT are far below whites; scores on the math portion are equally far above whites.[28]

- A disproportionate number of minority students in elite colleges and universities are Asian because of their proficiency in math and sciences.[29]

In addition to these ethnic changes in the composition of the American student population, there will be social changes as well. Births of premature infants to teen mothers reached 750,000 in an annual cohort of 3.3 million; many of these premature infants will become victims of education disabilities or are destined to become otherwise "difficult to teach." Of 100 children born today:

- 12 will be out of wedlock
- 40 will be to parents who will divorce before the child is 18
- 5 to parents who will be separated
- 2 to parents of whom one will die before the child is 18
- 41 will live in a "normal family"[30]

What teachers need to "know and be able to do" has changed drastically and irrevocably since 1950, 1960, or even 1970. And yet, the importance of reaching these new student populations has never been greater. In 1950, there were 17 workers to pay for the retirement benefits of each retiree; in 1992, there will be only three, and one of these will be a member of a minority group.[31]

## IMPACT OF CHANGES IN SUPPLY AND DEMAND FOR MINORITY TEACHERS

The two-part warning issued by The Holmes Group and the Carnegie Forum Task Force concerned not only the composition of the student population, but also, and perhaps primarily, the composition of the teaching force. Although who the students are is beyond our ability to direct or control, the teaching force can be molded by the effective targeting of policies and programs. Advocates of professionalization must realize that naming a problem is not solving it: minority candidates will not be wished or hoped into teaching.

It is well known that black teacher candidates have been failing various tests for entry into teaching at much higher rates than have others. What is less well known is that effective programs have been implemented to do something about these failure rates. Coppin State in Maryland, the University of Arkansas at Pine Bluff, Tuskegee, Xavier, Grambling, and Jackson State have all instituted programs that have raised the pass rates of black teacher candidates. However, as Joan Baratz has remarked, the "program" that will most increase the number and quality of black teachers will be the improvement of elementary and secondary education, because only an increase in the pool of black college students can significantly increase the number of potential teachers.[32]

There are two separate but equally important paths to preparing teachers to deal effectively with the changed student population. Elaine Witty, of Norfolk State, has called upon major white universities to take seriously their responsibility to teach white teachers how to teach minority students. One mutually beneficial way to meet this obligation is through establishing relationships between historically black colleges and research universities. Establishing collaborative relationships is also important from another standpoint: as Norman Francis makes clear, "what happens at the HBCs will have the greatest impact because, although they constitute only 5 percent of the higher education universe, they produce 66 percent of the nation's black teachers."[33] Black teachers constitute no more than 10 percent of the teaching force, and even that small proportion is declining. Moreover, the percentage of black teachers has never approached the percentage of black students in the schools, not even where systems have been led by blacks.

To reiterate: naming this problem does not solve it. The clear and present danger inherent in the reform proposals is the explicit and implicit elitist nature of the "voluntary" system. At the time The Holmes Group issued its report, for example, it included no representatives of historically black colleges or universities; the 63-member National Board for Professional Teaching Standards did finally reach out to include representatives of Xavier University and Tuskegee Institute.[34] What neither group included was any specific measure designed to ensure that black teachers would be among the elite, nationally-certified cohort. This is especially important since it seems to be expected that the schools preparing the teachers will be the elite or "superior" colleges and universities, and not the HBCs which provide over two-thirds of black teachers.

The demographics of the student population coupled with the likely composition of the future teaching force compel us to move the recruitment and preparation of minority teachers from the periphery to the center of efforts at teacher professionalization. Most highly qualified black students pursuing college degrees now have options—as they should. But because the number of black students in the college pipeline is declining, and because the decline is even steeper at the graduate and professional-school level, where teacher preparation is likely to be concentrated within a short period of time, the recruitment and preparation of minority teachers is doubly urgent. We must avoid further diminution of the number and percentage of black teachers, especially those "new breed" teachers who are projected to assume more and more responsibility and power in the new "one best system."

Although Myron Atkin and The Holmes Group tried to make the point that pedagogy was important to improving education, it bears repeating that too little attention has been focused on one of the most potentially damaging consequences of the renewed push for "teacher competence"; there is precious little evidence that teachers who are expert in their subject matter or who are well and/or liberally educated are able to foster higher performance and achievement from young people. This is especially true in view of the large and growing mismatch between the composition of the teaching force and those whom they teach.

The most recent *Handbook of Research on Teaching,* which reviews the paradigms, methodologies, and designs of major research on teaching and learning, offers little to guide teachers, teacher-educators, or education officials about what works. There remain many questions and uncertainties, even about the relationship between teacher attributes—characteristics, degrees, experience, methods—and student outcomes (learning, achievement, behavior). What this suggests is that we do not know as much about teaching and learning as we need to; we must certainly use caution, therefore, in setting standards about "what teachers need to know and be able to do." In this context, standardization could easily become the enemy of excellence.

Finally, it is worth remembering that annual Gallup polls on education have clearly established that adults—whether they have children in the schools or not—have consistently rated nurturing qualities above both cognitive and intellectual qualities in their opinions about "good teachers." These clear statements, from average Americans, should remind professional educators that it certainly takes more than *just* subject-matter knowledge to motivate children and youth to take advantage of a higher quality of education. The idea of teacher professionalization as the pathway to educational improvement for America's students—particularly its minority and poor students—is a dangerously naive notion that blithely incorporates most of what everyone thinks is good about "the professions" and ignores the depressing evidence of what is bad. To borrow from Langston Hughes, professionalization in America "ain't been no crystal stair."

## LESSONS FROM THE MEDICAL PROFESSION

The Holmes Group, the Carnegie Forum Task Force, and others refer approvingly to the evaluation of medical education conducted in the early 1900s by Abraham Flexner, an educator hired by Carnegie to assess and recommend measures to improve the medical profession in the United States. At the time, the medical profession was plagued by many of the same problems, and some which were worse than those now plaguing teachers: low and unpredictable salaries; widespread disagreement about what constituted the core of medical training; a perception by the public that "doctoring" was not any special form of expertise. In essence, doctors had not been effective in persuading the public—in part because they could not persuade themselves—of the nature and extent of their "superior competence."[35] In any case, although scholars of the professions disagree about many of the direct effects of Flexner's report, there is no disagreement about two: first, a series of institutional reforms that ended in higher costs for medical education and more uniform and stringent requirements drove women, blacks, many Jews, and other immigrants out of the profession.[36] This result was induced only partially by *direct discrimination against applicants to the remaining medical schools;* more fundamentally, it resulted from the demise of many of the schools which had been educating and training women, blacks, and other people of more working class origins for the profession. One scholar succinctly describes the problem: "before the Flexner report, there had been seven medical schools for blacks in the United States; only Howard and Meharry survived."[37] And although there is some question about whether the decline in female physicians was the cause or effect of fewer medical colleges for women, the restriction of entry into coeducational medical schools unquestionably led to a rationing of the places available, and to "outright discrimination" against women.[38]

Another scholar argues persuasively:

"The 'qualitative' argument of the reform leaders—get better doctors—fused, therefore, with the 'quantitative' and practical concerns of the rank-and-file—permit fewer doctors and provide more secure incomes . . . While blacks and women, as well as the lower middle class and sons of workers, found themselves increasingly excluded from the reformed profession, the status of the average physician was considerably improved, as was his income, by the rapidly attained reduction in numbers."[39]

A second effect was also unforeseen. The restriction of entry into the medical profession accelerated the movement by doctors from poorer to richer areas of the country. Paul Starr cites the following:

"a study by AMA President William Allen Pusey [showing] that more than a third of 910 small towns that had physicians in 1914 had been abandoned by doctors in 1925. 'As you increase the cost of the license to practice medicine you increase the price at which medical service must be sold and you correspondingly decrease the number of people who can afford to buy this medical service.' He [Pusey] expressed particular concern about data he had collected showing that irregular practitioners were settling in the counties abandoned by physicians."[40]

What can be learned from the medical profession about how to reform teaching is therefore much more complex, halting, and qualified than many want to admit. As we will see below, the legal profession, too, has an underside that deserves examination.

## LESSONS FROM THE LEGAL PROFESSION

Both Carnegie and Holmes have advocated formal differentiation of the teaching force that conforms roughly to stages of professional preparation. Analyses of the history of the legal profession suggest that the differentiation of roles and responsibilities may not be able to proceed without also creating some sort of hierarchy that will not reflect merit as much as existing inequalities in access to educational opportunity. In 1933, one scholar of the American bar noted that, despite the professional ethic of "omnicompetence" (the idea that lawyers should be competent in all areas of the law), "most of the best brains, most of its inevitable leaders, have moved masswise out of court work, out of a general practice akin to the family doctor, into highly paid specialization in the service of large corporations."[41] While differentiation and specialization may make for a more efficient practice of law, recent evidence suggests that *who does what* is not determined by skill, aptitude, or special competence, but by socioeconomic origin and by the type of law school attended. Heinz and Laumann's study of Chicago lawyers confirmed that top jobs in top law firms go to graduates of elite law schools, while graduates of local law schools are overwhelmingly concentrated in low-prestige, lower-paying work in criminal, personal injury, general, and routine divorce law. The effect, they say, "is that there is a rather strict and precise correspondence between the suppliers of trained personnel (i.e., the law school) and of the buyers (the employers or employment context)."[42] Elite schools train elite members for elite work.

We are already hearing echoes of a similar division of labor in the emergent teacher-professionalization movement. The composition of The Holmes Group, combined with its expressed objective of specializing in the professional preparation of Career Professionals/Lead Teachers, already suggests hierarchical ordering of access to teacher preparation. Some might argue that lawyers trained in elite law schools may well be more effective at representing elite corporate clients. But the production of a cadre of elite teachers to serve as instructional leaders of a reformed American school system whose principal clients are black, Hispanic, Asian, or poor would be nothing less than social dynamite.

## SUMMARY AND CONCLUSIONS

*The "Voluntary" National Standards Board*

When medical practitioners first tried to organize a medical association in the late 1800s, "one prominent doctor called it 'a purely voluntary organization, without any chartered privileges and with no authority to enforce its own edicts.'"[43] Of course, the American Medical Association did not remain "purely voluntary" for very long, and neither will the National Professional Standards Board if it expects to have any significant impact on the teaching profession. In view of this:

- A careful reading of the two reports discussed earlier makes it obvious that special attention must be directed to the existing and potential pools of minority teachers. The majority of black teachers are educated in the historically black colleges and universities. Yet, not one of these institutions was represented and scant attention paid to their role in preparing the new elite corps of "professionals." We cannot afford to leave the preparation of Career Professionals/Lead Teachers to elite institutions; some HBCs must be among those assuming this function.

- Establishing the Masters degree as a requirement for entrance into the profession has profound implications for minorities, the poor, and the HBCs. Unless the resources for students who must now spend an additional year in college are made available, and unless the HBCs are provided the resources for strengthening their programs, there is little likelihood of providing an adequate supply of black teachers who can qualify for entering the Masters degree programs or who will be equipped to pass the National Board examinations.

- The reports both mention the need to improve schools with minority populations and there is passing reference to the need to bring talented blacks into the teaching profession. One notes, however, that there is a lack of specificity and a pervasive vagueness in the recommendations for improvement in these areas. Great stress is placed upon the need to improve quality; there is a failure to place equal stress on the need for equity.

- There is little attention paid to the need for multicultural education and cross-cultural experiences . . . All teachers—black, white, Hispanic, Asian—must be prepared to understand and teach the student populations of the future.

*The Potential for Chaos and Friction in the System*

There are a host of concerns about potential conflicts between newly-professionalized teachers and other elements of the system. The literature on professional work debunks the notion that there is a rigid and neat distinction between making policy and carrying it out. As one scholar recently put it, "the capacity to make policy is created by the . . . exercise of discretion in work."[44] Much more careful consideration must be given to how a corps of professional teachers will relate to and impact on other elements of the system. For example:

- Too little attention is paid to the shortcomings of the market model as it relates to the delivery of services. We must learn from the experience of medicine when it was newly professionalized and from the legal profession when it became specialized and professionalized. As the market model operates in education today, it is most often to the detriment of the poorer and predominantly minority districts and schools, where too many teachers teach in subject areas in which they are not certified or in subject areas where they have had limited or no training. Working conditions, including salaries, are often less than optimum.

- Too little attention is given to the organizational and political implications of the new Career Professional/Lead Teachers. Here are just a few areas for concern:
  - teacher autonomy vs. parental involvement
  - increased teacher discretion in assessing the educational needs of children vs. the policy goal of equality of educational opportunity
  - teacher judgment vs. public accountability of school districts
  - teacher autonomy vs. supervision by principals
- The presence of Career Professional/Lead Teachers may eventually force the reorganization of elementary education. Principals who formerly functioned as instructional leaders (although there is evidence that too little time was spent on this responsibility) might eventually become more like their high school counterparts. The elimination of the undergraduate education major along with the creation of the career ladder for teachers may cause elementary teachers to specialize in subject areas, which most do not do now. In the meantime, however, there is likely to be considerable conflict between principals or other administrators and "new breed" teachers over the boundaries of their roles. In Rochester, New York, the one place where professionalization proposals are being implemented through a collective bargaining agreement, signs of strain have already emerged.

## RECOMMENDATIONS

1. Organizations of minority educators, along with others, should immediately begin to develop specific strategies which will ensure that equity and excellence are of equal importance; that they are inseparable. The President and Chief Executive Officer of the National Urban League John E. Jacob has said: "Our schools won't become excellent unless all of them are excellent. We can't have a system in which some schools—those with minority populations—are allowed to be less than excellent."[45]

2. Organizations of minority educators, along with other interested groups, should insist that "professional teachers" certified by a national board be required to demonstrate their ability and competence to teach students of diverse backgrounds and special needs. Moreover, they should demonstrate their commitment to high expectations and high performance goals for all

students, not just majority students from more advantaged backgrounds. These "qualifications" must be reflected in the evaluation instruments now under development at Stanford.

3. Elite colleges and universities, which will likely prepare many, if not most, of the new professionals, must accept the responsibility to teach their students how to teach black and other minority young people. If this means hiring minority faculty members who are knowledgeable and experienced in the area, this should be done. In other instances, the predominantly white institutions should work out coordinated and cooperative agreements and programs with the HBCs. Such programs could include exchanges of students over the summer, exchange semesters for students or faculty or both, joint degree programs, and a host of other possibilities.

4. Elite and high status institutions engaged in the preparation of the new professionals should, by whatever means necessary, establish programs of recruitment, financial aid, retention, and motivation for talented black and other minority students. Such programs need to be sustained over time.

5. The HBCs, which prepare more than two-thirds of black teachers, should insist that they be adequately represented on the National Board and on groups convened to upgrade teacher preparation programs. Moreover, the knowledge and experience they represent must be a part of deliberations, program design, the establishment of standards, and the certification criteria for the new professionals.

6. Because of their expertise and experience, and because they attract a disproportionate number of blacks who enter teaching, public and private funds to strengthen teacher education programs in the best of the HBCs should be made available for such purposes.

7. As in the past, organizations of minority educators, along with organizations committed to equity as well as excellence, must not become mesmerized by the rhetoric of excellence and professionalization in the various reports. John Jacob has warned us that based on experience: " . . . when ideas are translated into reality, black people wind up being shortchanged."[46] As the professionalizing and upgrading of medicine and law did not ensure that disadvantaged people received quality medical care and legal representation and protection, neither does the upgrading and professionalizing of teaching ensure that disadvantaged, and particularly black and other minority, youngsters will get quality education.

It will be up to organizations at the local, state, and national levels to participate in the political process which will eventually translate the various recommendations and proposed programs into a reality that serves minority and disadvantaged youth. We ignore that responsibility at our own peril. It may be a cliche, but it is nonetheless true—our children and our own future are at stake.

The struggle goes on.

# Civil Rights and the Future of the American Presidency

Dianne M. Pinderhughes, Ph.D.

## INTRODUCTION

In this article I want to evaluate the role of the presidency in achieving civil rights for black Americans. In recent *The State of Black America* articles, I have considered the potential of the black vote and examined the strategic choices that can enhance the existing black vote potential (1984). I have also considered how blacks might reshape their partisan political behavior to enhance their political strategy (1986). In this year succeeding the Bicentennial of the Constitution, this year which precedes another presidential election, I wish to consider what past presidents have done to further the political and economic status of black Americans. What difference has it made when they have taken strong, aggressive postures rather than "moderate" or weak positions on racial public policy. What were the consequences of their civil rights policy positions for them as individuals, and what were the consequences for their presidencies; that is, for the presidency as an institution, and for national politics.

I propose that presidents strengthen their own offices, as well as strengthen the institutional presidency when they take an aggressive liberal stance on civil rights reforms broadly defined to include civil and political citizenship rights, economic and social issues. I have included economic protections under the area of civil rights for reasons I will articulate more fully toward the end of this article. In other words, exercising strong liberal reformist leadership in civil and political rights for blacks, and for any other group subject to political or economic discrimination, enhances their exercise of power and authority as president at the national level. A president who takes a liberal reformist leadership role on civil rights issues is assumed to be morally courageous but politically suicidal; I am going to argue that it is institutionally beneficial for presidents to act aggressively on civil rights.

When political commentators evaluate the changes that have occurred in civil rights in the past few decades, they often locate the origins for these changes in the moral dimensions of politics. The American people were moved by the legitimacy and the values represented by civil rights demonstrators in Montgomery, in Birmingham, at the March on Washington, at Selma, Alabama. Religious organizations, members of Congress, the president, and many ordinary people responded to the horrible scenes often brought into their living rooms via the nightly news with a conviction to press for social and political change. The crises generated by protests collectively organized by Martin Luther King, Ella Baker,

Stokely Carmichael, Rap Brown, Rev. C.T. Vivian, Rosa Parks, John Lewis, Septima Clarke, Diane Lewis, and many others involved in the Civil Rights movement focused on the moral imperatives for change.[1]

Significant changes have occurred in electoral politics since the late 1960s. The 1964 Civil Rights Act and especially the 1965 Voting Rights Act (with its subsequent extensions in 1970 when the 18-year-old vote was legislated, in 1975 when protection for Hispanic Americans was included, and in 1982 when the act was broadened to include a results, rather than an intent, test as a proof of discrimination), have significantly integrated the American electorate. Additionally this legislation has led to the gradual increase in the number of black elected officials in the Deep South, in the urban North and now even in small- and middle-sized cities in the midwest with small black populations (L. Williams, 1987; Joint Center for Political Studies, 1987). In the last decade cities such as Chicago, Philadelphia, Birmingham, Hartford, and New Orleans have elected black mayors. Black state legislators and members of Congress have increased incrementally. At the national level, the Reverend Jesse Jackson ran for the Democratic nomination for president in 1984 and is running again for the nomination in 1988.[2]

Most of these gains in what Hannah Pitkin (1972) called descriptive representation, however, have come in areas where blacks are a significant part of the electorate or even dominate it. Blacks are rarely elected to office in areas where they do not reside in sizeable numbers. There are exceptions including the eighth congressional district in northern California covering parts of Oakland and Berkeley whose overall population is 43 percent black, but whose voting age population is only 24 percent black, and where black Congressman Ronald V. Dellums has been in office for 17 years. Los Angeles has elected Tom Bradley mayor four times even though blacks are less than 25 percent of the total population; nevertheless, Bradley lost two successive races for governor of the state of California. Dellums and Bradley are unusual; it is much more common that black officials do not win office in predominantly white districts (Barone, Ujifusa, 1987).

To protect the reasonable right of representation, many cities in recent years have moved from at-large electoral systems to district systems.[3] Research has shown that it is more difficult for a minority group to elect its representatives in an at-large rather than a district system (Davidson and Korbel, 1984; Blacksher and Menefee, 1984). The federal courts have also concluded that at-large systems, in combination with polarized voting and consistent failure of geographically distinct minority groups to elect a representative of their choice, lead to a denial in black voting rights and therefore deserve protection under the 1965 Voting Rights Act and its extensions. The Supreme Court decision in *Thornburgh* v. *Gingles* in June 1986 concluded that state multimember legislative districts in North Carolina, combined with other factors, had impeded blacks from electing the representatives of their choice.[4] Cities such as Mobile, Ala.; Cairo, Ill.; Springfield, Ill.; and Boston, Mass. under federal court direction have changed from at-large to district systems. In most instances for the first time since the at-large systems were initiated, voters there have begun to elect black officials. In other cases, cities such as Danville, Illinois have chosen to settle out of court rather than face a long, expensive suit in defense of an at-large electoral system. The city has already held its first election with a district system and has elected two black representatives.

The presidential race however would seem to be the ultimate at-large election. In a strict numerical sense blacks are very much a minority in this contest, but because of the intricacies of the electoral system, their importance is not at all insignificant. As of 1986 blacks constituted 10.9 percent of the over 173.8 million people of voting age taken as a whole, but range from five to over 32 percent of the population in 20 states in which they are concentrated.[5] A successful presidential candidate must win 270 of 535 votes in the electoral college and must do so on a state-by-state basis. Winning all of a state's electoral votes requires only that a candidate win at least a plurality of the popular vote. The most populous states as of 1984 with the most electoral votes such as California (47), New York (36), Texas (29), Ohio (23), and Illinois (24) happen to be in the Northeast-Midwest, where the black population is most heavily concentrated, or in the West-Southwest where blacks and Hispanics are the largest "minorities" (Watson 1987: 65). Blacks are also a critical part of the southern electorate, ranging from a low of 14.6 percent in Florida to a high of 29.6 percent in Mississippi (L.Williams 1987, 102). This influence will be especially heightened by the combined regional southern primary; that is, many of the southern states will hold their primaries on the same day for the first time in 1988.[6]

Under certain circumstances candidates with policy appeals that evenly divide the white vote and strongly attract the black vote make black voters the deciding factor in a presidential election; that was the case in 1960 and 1976 (P. Robinson, 1982; Pinderhughes, 1984). When a candidate appeals strongly to a large portion of white voters, black voters add to the victory margin (as in Johnson's 1964 election) or disproportionately oppose the winner (as in 1972, 1980, 1984 against Nixon and Reagan). Unless the white electorate is evenly split between the Democratic and Republican candidates, black voters must rely on the willingness of the Democratic candidate to bid for their votes when there is typically no incentive to do so. Jesse Jackson's race in 1984 was born at least partly out of his perception that Democratic candidates would offer no congenial alternatives and that black voters would be forced to support the Democratic candidate, as long as Republicans choose not to compete for black votes (Barker and Walters, forthcoming; Smith and McCormick, 1985).

The existence of racially polarized voting in which most whites vote for white candidates and/or most blacks vote for black candidates suggests it is unlikely white voters will help blacks elect the black presidential candidate of their choice. The partisan distribution of the electorate, with most white voters more conservative than most black voters, also means that a white candidate of the latter's choice seems free not to formulate and implement the civil rights policy they find attractive (Petrocik, 1981; L. Williams, 1987). The Carter administration was one which many black activists criticized for having positioned itself to draw black votes in the 1976 election, but forsook a compatible policy agenda once in office. In some ways the Jackson campaign can be seen as a reaction to blacks' dissatisfaction with Carter. Paul Light (1982) shows despite the central role of black voters in Carter's election, civil rights did not appear on White House staff members' ranking of the most important domestic policy issues (Henderson 1987; Barker 1987).

I think therefore that it is time to move the focus of analysis to another level by evaluating the benefits and costs of presidents as independent actors altering their behavior relative to civil rights policy formulation. If presidential candidates or sitting presidents assume there are severe penalties for taking strong reform positions on civil rights, then it is altruistic rather than politically advantageous for them to do so. However I propose the following hypothesis for examining presidential leadership in civil rights policy.

**Hypothesis:** Presidents have more to gain than to lose by exercising strong reformist leadership in the area of civil rights.

The assumptions about political consequences shift if presidents presume they will not be harmed by taking strong action on civil rights, or that they will be harmed by *not* taking action, rather than that they *will* be harmed. The possibilities of presidents taking stronger positions on civil rights increase, the areas of public policy in which the extension of rights is supported will expand, and eventually, the possibility of creating a political environment in which presidential candidates from both parties will compete for black votes also increases.[7]

This involves two assumptions. The first requires the creation of support for the political inclusion of the entire population and/or opposition to the political exclusion of any portion of the population. The inability or unwillingness of presidents otherwise seen as liberal, such as Franklin D. Roosevelt, or seen as fair — Eisenhower, to state their positions in this area was related to the character of the electorate before 1965 and its representation in the Congress.

The second requires a discussion of the meaning of strong leadership, including the kind of actions which are involved. There is a large volume of political science literature on the concept of power as it is exercised by presidents: command and control, power through institutional advantage and persuasion, power through effective bargaining, and exceptionally high expectations of presidential power. Whatever the definition, presidents have rarely exercised strong reformist leadership in the area of civil rights. Truman's decision to desegregate the Army, Lyndon Johnson's role in the passage of the 1964 Civil Rights and 1965 Voting Rights Acts, and Nixon's creation of affirmative action are notable exceptions (Barnett and Williams, 1986).

*The Creation of a Nationally Integrated Electorate*

The exclusion of blacks from the national electorate created enormous constraints on the exercise of legislative-executive leadership, The exclusion allowed for the development of a distinctive electorate. With the brief exception of the years from 1870 through the early 1890s, the American Presidency and the entire American electoral system have operated within a political framework that gave exceptional power to the South and to its elected leaders. In the 18th and the first half of the 19th centuries, the three-fifths clause of the Constitution meant that economically entitled southern voters elected representatives in larger proportion than their numbers would otherwise have allowed because of the black slave population which could not vote (Litwack, 1961: 33-55, 64-112; Walton, 1972: 84-140; Woodward, 1957; Bunche, 1975). Article 1, Section 2 of the Constitution specified:

"Representatives and direct [Taxes] shall be apportioned among the several States which may be included within this Union, according to their respective numbers which shall be determined by adding to the whole Number of free Persons, including those bound to Service for a Term of Years, and excluding Indians not taxed, three fifths of all other Persons."

This permitted the South simultaneously to use a proportion of the slave population within the electorate for purposes of increasing white southern representation in the Congress, but to deny political privileges to its slave population.

The institutional consequences of these arrangements were not as important for the Congress and for the president in the nineteenth century because of the relatively high rate of turnover which prevailed and the unstructured character of the institution. By the twentieth century service in the House and/or the Senate became more career-oriented and members stayed for a succession of terms (Polsby, 1968, 1969). Turnover declined in all regions of the country, but especially in the southern states where the exclusion of blacks and of significant portions of the white population from the electorate in the late 19th and early 20th centuries reduced electoral competition, increased the return rate of southern House and Senate members to office, and — in light of the growing importance of the committee system and the role of seniority in it — enormously increased the power of southern representatives.

V.O. Key (1949) compared the proportions of the population eligible to vote in southern senatorial Democratic primaries, in which there was some competition for office, with the proportion of citizens 21 and over in the Ohio and New York general elections, from 1920 through 1946 — well after voting restrictions were in place. Sixty percent of the population 21 and over voted in New York and Ohio, but only twenty to thirty percent of the same population voted in South Carolina, Texas, Florida, Louisiana, Arkansas, North Carolina, Tennessee, Georgia, Mississippi, and Alabama (p. 497). Key also used statistics reported by the NAACP and Luther Jackson to estimate the proportion of the black population eligible to vote in the southern states in the late 1940s *after* the Supreme Court's 1944 decision in *Smith* v. *Allwright* had invalidated the use of the white primary and incrementally opened up the franchise to black voters (p. 523). The respective percentages of blacks eligible to vote were 0.9 percent in Mississippi, 1.2 percent in Alabama, 2.6 percent in Louisiana, 13.0 percent in Sc ith Carolina, 13.2 percent in Virginia, 15.2 percent in North Carolina, 15.4 pe.'cent in Florida, 17.3 percent in Arkansas, 18.5 percent in Texas, 18.8 percent in Georgia, and 25.8 percent in Tennessee. Thus the southern congressional electorates were much smaller, structurally noncompetitive, and virtually if not actually all-white.[8]

One measure of the power of the southern white electorate is shown by the number of southerners who chaired House Committees from 1920 through 1984. Table 1 reveals the impact of the disfranchisement movement within the Congress of the late nineteenth and early twentieth centuries on Congressional structures of power (Key, 1949). By the late 1970s and 1980s southern committee heads, like Strom Thurmond or John Stennis in the Senate or others in the House, might have been holdovers from the old system, yet their constituency bases have radically changed as President Reagan recently discovered on the nomination of Judge Robert Bork to the Supreme Court (Lawson, 1976; Ladd, 1969).

---

**Table 1**
**Southern Committee Chairs in the U.S. House of Representatives**

|      | Committees | Southern Chairs | Percent |
|------|------------|-----------------|---------|
| 1921 | 60         | 0               | 0       |
| 1941 | 46         | 19              | 41.3%   |
| 1961 | 20         | 13              | 65%     |
| 1979 | 22         | 7               | 31.8%   |
| 1984 | 20         | 6               | 30%     |

Source: Congressional Directories for respective years.

---

The peculiarity of concerns of this set of representatives and their attentiveness to matters of race is also reinforced by Key's analysis of southern voting patterns from 1933 through 1945 in which there was a very high degree of voting cohesion among southern Democrats. The highest levels of cohesion on which southern Senate Democrats were not also aligned with northern Democrats and Republicans came on nine roll calls; seven dealt with race in one form or another: antilynching, federal aid to state educational systems, and the appropriation for the Committee on Fair Employment Practices (Key, 1949: 351-2). In the House, similar levels of cohesion were again attained on eleven roll calls of which seven dealt with racial issues (Key: 372). On the southern senators' voting patterns, Key concluded "On the race questions, and on that question alone, does a genuine solidarity exist . . . Thus the inference to be drawn from House behavior is similar to that deducible from Senate voting: southern attitude [sic] toward the Negro provides the bedrock of southern sectionalism" (Key, 359: 372).

A second measure of the power of this electoral structure in which southern members chaired committees such as Education and Labor, and the Judiciary (through which reform legislation would have to pass) is indicated by a summary of the "Bills and Proposed Resolutions Relative to Afro-Americans" introduced in the 57th through the 80th Congresses, covering 1901 through 1948. These are bills and resolutions which "deal *expressly* with the status of Blacks in America" (Holden, 1987). By my count 370 bills were introduced and referred to committees. Of these approximately 34 had some kind of hearing, eighteen of them positively so, and five negative. Eleven were debated and voted on. Nine passed the House and six the Senate, but only two passed both houses. The first was passed in 1928-29, during the 70th Congress, to create a commission to secure plans for a building for a National Memorial Association as a tribute to Negro contributions to the United States. President Hoover appointed "Mary McLeod Bethune, president of Bethune Cookman College [later a member of Roosevelt's so-called "kitchen" cabinet], to the National Monument Committee to direct plans for a Negro memorial in Washington, though, unfortunately, the Federal government did not provide the money which was requested to construct the monument" (Garrett, 1982: 262).

The second, passed in 1940-41 during the 76th Congress, was a bill to defray the expenses of the American Negro Exposition in Chicago in 1940 (Holden, 1987). For half a century, this was the entire legislative history of enactments specifically related to the status of blacks. As the numbers introduced suggest, there were significant numbers considered, if referral to committee can be considered discussion, especially in the mid- and late 1930s. Thirty-three bills were introduced in 1935, 61 in 1937-38, and 28 in 1939, most proposing federal legislation dealing with lynching, some attempting to outlaw the poll tax. All of these failed (Bunche, 1975; Sitkoff, 1978).

Democratic and Republican presidents alike were constrained by this electorate and the institutional structures arising from it at the local, state, and national levels for nearly seven decades. For conservative Democratic presidents such as Woodrow Wilson, this was not a problem as it reinforced his own predilections. He courted black leaders during the closely fought election campaign of 1912; afterwards, he failed to respond to a delegation of black leaders including one of the founders of the NAACP, W.E.B. DuBois, who appealed to him for a more liberal posture on civil rights (Kellogg, 1967: 155-60). Segregation in lunchrooms was introduced into the federal government during his administration. Wilson commented favorably on D.W. Griffiths' *Birth of A Nation*; these remarks were quoted in the cards describing events or presenting dialogue in this silent film, although one of Wilson's spokesmen denied he had endorsed it[9] (Garrett, 131).

For moderate or liberal Democratic or Republican presidents, the structure of the Congress created a serious political problem for any attempt to deal with race, or with policy areas affected by race such as labor or employment issues in the South, federal aid to education or any other policy area in which the South feared regulation of its social and political mores. Fear of offending the white southern electorate and its elected representatives seriously hampered the legislative behavior of presidents from Franklin Roosevelt through Kennedy, each with a somewhat more liberal set of preferences than the southern electorate would support. Eisenhower and Kennedy kept extremely low profiles as they developed racial policy. When Eisenhower acted — and Robert Burk (1984) suggests he did so in helping to initiate desegregation in the District of Columbia after the *Brown* decision — he sought only nonpublic, low-key action which did not include the force of law.[10] This was not only because he wanted to avoid public conflict with southern conservatives; he also felt it inappropriate for the federal government to be involved in a leadership role in this area. "More than once, in fact, his statements seemed to imply reservations about the wisdom of the decision and the pace of even such modest change as it had generated" (Fleming, 1965: 924).

Kennedy had only a narrow majority in the Congress — especially in the House — and that included an important southern component whose support was critical for him to maintain. By Light's analysis of presidential capital, Kennedy scored strongly only on one of three possible categories: public approval. His own lack of seniority, prestige, and experience in the House and the Senate and his 49.7 percent level of electoral support in the 1960 election left him with very little expertise and few resources he could employ to mobilize southern support for civil rights legislation (Light, 1982: 32). He therefore avoided confronting the Congress until late in his term, and he sought to increase his southern support by appointing a large number of southerners to the federal judiciary in the South. Because they were also conservatives, implementation of the 1957 Civil Rights legislation was made considerably more difficult.

For each president it was individually rational not to challenge this southern structure of power in the Congress; for this institution, Lyndon Johnson's leadership was seemingly courageous. It significantly increased the power of the Democratic party; it also increased the power of the presidency itself when Johnson supported black voters' inclusion in 1964 and 1965. The complete transformation of the southern electorate has taken 20 years to effect. As mentioned previously, federal civil rights legislation and its implementation helped transform voting participation in the South.[11]

Finally voter mobilization organizations such as the National Coalition for Black Voter Participation, the Campaign for Full Political Participation, and Human SERVE have grown and developed over the last ten years and created new tactics for voter registration. The combined impact of these groups has helped bring black voter registration to levels that exceeded white registration in Mississippi, South Carolina, Louisiana, Arkansas, and Tennessee in the South, and in California, Illinois, Michigan, and Ohio in the North and West, using

1984 census figures[12] (L. Williams, 1987: 103). Table 2, based on 1986 census estimates, reflects an even more recent picture of this increase.

Of the states with more than five percent black voting age population, twelve have *higher* black than white registration figures (California, Florida, Illinois, Indiana, Louisiana, Maryland, Ohio, Pennsylvania, South Carolina, Tennessee, Texas, and Virginia). Four have *less than a two percent difference* in the registration rates of whites over blacks (Alabama, Arkansas, Mississippi, and Missouri). Four have between two percent and five percent of white over black registration (Georgia, Kentucky, Oklahoma, and North Carolina); and five including the District of Columbia have surpluses greater than five percent white over black registration (Kansas, Massachusetts, New Jersey, and New York) (Barone and Ujifusa, 1987; Jennings, 1987: 25-28). Of the seven states (Alabama, Georgia, Louisiana, Mississippi, North Carolina, South Carolina, and Virginia) covered in whole or in part by the 1965 Voting Rights Act, five have higher black registration or nearly equal black and white voter registration levels, and only two, Georgia and North Carolina, have significantly different registration levels. The highest differences in registration of whites over blacks appear in northern states such as Massachusetts (18.6 percent), New York (11.5 percent), and New Jersey (10 percent). Black politicians, community groups, and clergymen in New York City recognized their paradoxical situation recently: "In New York City's black community alone, there are more unregistered voters than there are in all the Southern states combined" (French, 1987a).

The change in the racial composition of the electorate has significantly reduced the numbers of southern committee heads who are also racial and social conservatives. Such individuals of the traditional Southern Democrat mold exist in much fewer numbers, and they rarely sit at the heads of the most critical points of social change. When they do, they can no longer vote as classic Southern Democrats, thereby freeing the president to act with much greater discretion in the area of civil rights reform than has been the case in the past for two reasons. Combs, Hibbing, and Welch conclude an evaluation of southern black constituents and congressional voting with the observation that

> "As the proportion of [southern] urbanized population increases, the relationship between the number of black constituents and conservative/ liberal voting of the representative reverses itself. In the urbanized South, the relationship is very much like what we find in the North: the more blacks, the more liberal the voting record of the representative. In the urban South, representatives are as responsive to blacks as representatives in urban areas in the North; in fact, if anything, urban South representatives appear slightly more sensitive to the number of blacks in the district than their northern counterparts. The rural South remains an anomaly, still reflecting — in spite of major changes in the political activity levels of blacks — the relationships found by V.O. Key 35 years ago."[13]

## Table 2
## The Black Electorate By Region

| Northeastern-Midwestern States | % Black | %White-Black Diff. | Electoral Votes |
|---|---|---|---|
| New York | 12.2 | -11.5 | 36 |
| Ohio | 8.3 | +1.3 | 23 |
| Illinois | 14.5 | +7.3 | 24 |
| Indiana | 6.8 | +3 | 12 |
| Michigan | 13.1 | -2.4 | 20 |
| Pennsylvania | 7.5 | +3.6 | 25 |
| Regional Subtotal | | | 128 |
| **Southern States** | | | |
| Florida | 13.2 | +1.4 | 21 |
| Georgia | 29.7 | -5.1 | 12 |
| Louisiana | 27.3 | + .5 | 10 |
| Maryland | 23.3 | +5.6 | 10 |
| Mississippi | 37.1 | -1.4 | 7 |
| North Carolina | 20.1 | -8.7 | 13 |
| South Carolina | 28.8 | +2.4 | 8 |
| Tennessee | 16.3 | +8.0 | 11 |
| Virginia | 18.9 | +3.2 | 12 |
| Alabama | 23.0 | - .9 | 9 |
| Arkansas | 16.3 | -1.0 | 6 |
| Kentucky | 6.0 | -5.2 | 9 |
| Missouri | 9.3 | - .7 | 11 |
| Regional Subtotal | | | 139 |
| **Western-Southwestern States** | | | |
| Texas | 11.0 | +8.4 | 29 |
| California | 6.1 | +5.9 | 47 |
| Regional Subtotal | | | 76 |
| TOTAL | 21 states | | 355 |

Sources: Jerry T. Jennings, *Voting and Registration in the Election of November 1986*, Current Population Reports, P-20, No. 414, Bureau of the Census, 1987, 25-28. For similar figures for 1984, see Linda Williams, "Black Political Progress in the 1980s: The Electoral Arena," 97-136, in *The New Black Politics*, edited by Michael B. Preston, Lenneal J. Henderson, Jr., Paul L. Puryear, New York: Longman, 1987. (The " + " symbol indicates that the percentage of black registration is higher than that of whites; the "-" symbol indicates that the percentage of white registration is higher than that of blacks.)

Thus the president is free to act if he seeks to enlarge the political or economic privileges of this constituency. If he seeks to constrain this new constituency and its congressional representatives, the president is likely to encounter resistance. Given the current electorate, the president either must not oppose this group, or he must seek to disfranchise significant portions of the electorate, which is not a credible strategy.

Not all southern conservatives in the "Solid South" sense of the term have left the Congress; and some southern conservatives of a new generation have been elected to office in recent years, but none of their electoral constituencies is all white and not all of their white constituents are Democratic. Alabama, Louisiana, Georgia, Mississippi, Florida, South Carolina, North Carolina, and border states such as Texas, Arkansas, and Tennessee have significant proportions of blacks in their electorate, as Table 2 shows:

"None of the 16 southern Democratic Senators can expect to be supported by a majority of the white voters of their states; too many of those whites have migrated into the conservative Southern Republican party, or will support more conservative Republican candidates in a general election. These Democratic Senators like all five of those first elected in southern states last year, each of whom was strongly opposed by Ronald Reagan, must depend on black voters if they are to put together winning majorities."[14]

Presidents who did not take the strong stand of Lyndon Johnson, in the days before the 1965 Voting Rights Act, did not exert especially strong supportive leadership in civil rights or in large areas of domestic policymaking; they feared enraging the conservative white South. Today presidents who want to win in the Congress, especially in the Senate, *must* take into account the interests of black southerners and the new white southerners, who have also registered for the first time in recent decades (L. Williams, 1987; U.S. Commission on Civil Rights, 1981). Significant numbers of whites have also registered to vote in the South in the years since the Voting Rights Act was first passed. Presidents must therefore take a strong supportive posture if they want to be influential as individuals and if they want to enhance the power of the presidency. Otherwise they face defeat in midterm senatorial elections in the South. This posture lost the Senate for President Reagan in November 1986. He campaigned for an ideologically responsive, that is, a Republican Senate. All six of his Republican candidates in the South lost in the face of very high black turnout in support of the Democratic candidates (L. Williams, 1986: 5-7). Reagan also lost his campaign to appoint the nominee of his choice, Judge Robert Bork, to the Supreme Court. Even Senator John Stennis of Mississippi, a member of the old solid Democratic South since he was first elected in 1947, voted against Bork.

## THE CONCEPT OF STRONG PRESIDENTIAL LEADERSHIP

For a president to be regarded as a strong leader, he must be willing to place the prestige of his office on the line for civil and political rights.

As I was completing this article, Chicago's first black mayor, Harold Washington, died suddenly of a heart attack on November 25, 1987. Washington's passing and the swift disintegration of the newly forged coalition of black, Hispanic, and white aldermen into four or five disparate competing groups shows just how strong a hold he had on the institution of the mayor's office and on the network of relationships within the complex political environment of the city in less than five years in office. As I initiated research on this paper, I did not include examples from urban politics nor had I thought about Mayor Washington as an example of strong leadership. I had been concentrating primarily on the presidency; but a brief summary of the sources of Washington's strength, and his willingness to use his prestige to get what he wanted may offer some insight into national leadership. Washington is an appropriate example because his very accession to office incorporated some of the patterns of institutional resistance presidents have confronted on civil rights issues in Congress which I discussed in the previous section.[15]

Washington faced a strong bloc of legislators opposed not only to his program, but to his very presence in the office (Preston, 1987). He dealt with them not by cooperation or avoidance but by confrontation in the city council and in the courts; by challenges to them on their own constituency grounds; by attempting to generate support for himself and his policies in white ethnic neighborhoods; and by carefully monitoring city council elections. Finally Washington reshaped the political domain by proving his own vote-getting ability not just in one season — in the 1983 primary and general elections, which many council members regarded as a fluke growing out of the divisions in the white leadership — but a second time, in the 1987 primary and general elections. Although the proportion of his electoral support was not substantially greater in the 1987 elections, the fact that he won virtually unanimous electoral support from his black constituents created a dramatic and immediate response within the city council. Instead of facing a bloc of white ethnic opponents large enough to slow or stall his proposals, Washington's first efforts in the new 1987 council produced 40 votes to nominate his own candidates for committee chairs, an increase of fourteen from the end of his first administration.

Aggressiveness, domination, and sheer force of will characterized some of Washington's leadership skills and talents, especially with regard to his opponents among traditional white ethnic city council members and party leaders. Among blacks force of will was not unimportant, but was combined with bargaining, negotiation, and camaraderie with black leadership groups. Washington held together old machinists, community organizers, black nationalists, leftists, and the black middle class for most of his first term. The differences within the black community stand in clear, poignant contrast only days after Washington's death in comparison to the appearance of unity under his leadership. He won all of these groups' support in 1983 and in 1987; he also generated direct popular admiration and approval from the black masses (Alkalimat and

Gills, 1984).

While I have emphasized the personal characteristics of the man Harold Washington, his personal interests also helped accumulate enormous political influence for the institution of mayor of the city. That in turn gave him statewide and national clout. Some commentators recently suggested his power resources had developed even more quickly than had those of the late Mayor Richard J. Daley (*Chicago Tribune*, November 29, 1987). Next spring, Washington had been expected to lead a statewide coalition supporting a tax increase in the state legislature. His strong command over black voters, over black community organizations which had become important voter mobilization forces, and over city councilmen in black and white wards, meant his endorsement of Jesse Jackson for the Democratic presidential nomination imposed a significant constraint on Senator Paul Simon's presidential campaign in the state.

The office of the mayor of Chicago is distinct in its power formulations from the office of the presidency. There is no limit on the incumbent's terms in office; in fact, the office formally has much less power than either Washington's or Daley's last years suggest. Yet Washington's ability to nurse support from a highly resistent constituency and to expand his powers significantly in short order was no more apparent than on the days after his death: black and white city council members looked for a successor who had his personal charisma, vote-getting abilities, broad political experience, intellectual talents, personal integrity, and expansive presence. The political vacuum created by his death revealed just how much the person Harold Washington brought to the office and how effectively he influenced city, state, and national politics.[16]

Some direct examples of strong presidential leadership may be selected from the political science literature on the institution. Cronin identifies the "cult of the Presidency," the tendency in American political textbooks for scholars to elevate the institution and its incumbents beyond all reason:

"If the President is a king, it is equally clear that he is no mere constitutional monarch. . . . [as] the power of kings has declined, the power of the President has enormously increased . . . The Presidency is like a family dwelling that each new generation alters and enlarges . . ." (Cronin, 1975: 27).

He identifies Richard Neustadt (1960), Clinton Rossiter (1956), and others who describe presidents and the presidency as the keepers and the repository of enormous power. Cronin suggests some of the constraints under which presidents operate, but few students of the institution offer any advice about presidential roles in the area of civil rights and race relations.

In the decades since the 1960s, Barger (1984) and Edwards (1980) emphasized the complex political environment in which presidents must negotiate and the difficulties that often arise as they seek to shape their environment. During the Roosevelt era, Harold Laski (1940) also discussed the inherent constraints in a system of divided power but concluded that "leadership can come from the

President alone; . . . there is no other source of direction which can secure the attention of the whole nation" (p. 16). Yet the separation of powers and checks and balances inevitably minimize the president's absolute power. " . . . The Congress is not a body capable of constructive leadership; the functions it performs most effectively are those of criticism and investigation rather than responsibility for the direction of affairs" (pp. 19-20). As Chicago politics between 1983 and 1986 and Washington's death in 1987 show, there must be strong leadership and cooperation between the executive and legislative branches. That cooperation must be generated structurally, or elicited through positive or negative incentives; in either case, it is required for coherent governance.

Paul Light argues that a president's ability to succeed is based on a number of factors: the individual's expertise; his political capital earned from the electoral margin, giving him an edge with which he can elicit political support from party members in the House and Senate; and popular opinion. The first and last are important, but Light argues "Though power may remain undefined in the presidential literature, among the presidential staffs it is generally understood to be equal to the President's party support in Congress" (Light 1982: 26). While public approval and electoral margins are important, the core of a president's power is always the margin of seats loyal to the president based on the party in power.

As Light evaluates presidents based on their political capital in these three areas — electoral margin, popular opinion, and party support, Lyndon Johnson had the greatest resources of political capital; Gerald Ford, the least. Jimmy Carter was strong in two of the areas, but his narrow electoral margin made it difficult for him to establish his credibility with the Congress. Surprisingly Richard Nixon was only somewhat more well endowed with political capital than Ford, especially in his first administration (Light, 1982: 32). These rankings are also somewhat indicative of their aggressiveness in civil rights policy areas.

Placing the prestige of the presidency on the line in public view involves using a variety of actions available to the president. They range from low to high status and involve private and public actions. When a president commits to a policy, he uses prestigious occasions to communicate a message about that policy to his relevant publics — the Congress, the media, interest groups, executive agencies, and the courts. The president will also make every action on the topic as visible as possible, thereby making his commitment public. And he will take the initiative in attempting to create an interest in the policy in Congress by making his commitment to the subject known in a direct personal way to the congressional leadership.

Many specific examples exist of ways in which these actions might be accomplished. The president may indicate his interest in civil rights by *direct contact* with representatives of black or other minority groups. President Theodore Roosevelt, who met with Booker T. Washington over breakfast, found that even individual contact in the White House was viewed as highly controversial at the time (Holden, 1986: 11). Others might seek to prevent black leaders from demanding highly prestigious actions, or more public displays of support by agreeing to meet with leaders directly. Representatives of groups often find this kind of contact rewarding, although it is not in and of itself meaningful for policy reform.

*Public appointments* of blacks are comparable to the previous type of presidential action. They can be viewed as highly controversial or far too radical; as a sign of a president's position on policy, or as a substitute for policy. On the other hand, a strong commitment to liberal civil rights reform, even in private, combined with numerous political appointments can be an effective strategy for broadening the base for policy change. John F. Kennedy is an example of the latter; he was not willing to take highly prestigious action, or to make that action public. He appointed a number of blacks to public office at levels which had not been typical (Garrett, 1982). Eisenhower was credited with appointing the first black to the White House staff, but E. Frederic Morrow faced a difficult time just "recruiting an office staff" (Morrow, 1963: 17; Burk, 1984).

If direct contacts and public appointments are part of the process of executive agency leadership, or of the effort to generate public support for a legislative campaign, then they are meaningful. All too often they may be used outside of any larger plan. These two areas conform to Pitkin's concept of descriptive representation.

Issue formulation is developed and presented in three main areas: public statements, legislative contact, and executive agency leadership. The President conveys concerns through *public statements*, communication with the people through the mass media. Any number of ways exist for a president to indicate support for reform or opposition to racial violence, for example. But a high-prestige event, which by definition also has maximum publicity and visibility associated with it, much more effectively communicates one's interests than a low-key statement on a subject. During the Wilson administration, for example, there were numerous incidents of mob violence against blacks and the NAACP asked for Wilson to make public his opposition to racist violence, specifically to lynching. After many requests Wilson "issued a strong denunciation" of mob violence, without using the word "lynching" (Garrett, 1982: 236; St. James, 1980: 164-165; Kellogg, 1967: 227-228). The NAACP itself reproduced and disseminated 50,000 copies of the message (Holden, 1986: 19-20).

This language suggests only a press release; it contrasts dramatically with Lyndon Johnson's decision to use an extremely prestigious occasion — a special address before both houses of Congress — to convey his support for civil rights legislation which became the 1964 Civil Rights Act (Cronin, 1975:

144; Miller, 1980: 338-339). Presidents can use any and all highly prestigious, highly public occasions to indicate consistent support for reform, including speeches to major organizations, news conferences, his State of the Union addresses, and budget messages to Congress. Placing civil rights in these public arenas significantly increases its importance. Securing cooperation based on the president's interest does not guarantee support from all quarters, but it makes the opposition, especially by members of his own party, considerably more difficult and costly.

In the second area, *legislative contact*, the president can affect policy by issuing executive orders, which do not require confrontation with his legislative opponents. Several presidents used this strategy when there was great opposition to change within the Congress: The Fair Employment Practices Commission created by Franklin Roosevelt through executive order 8802, the desegregation of the Army by Truman through order 9981, of armed forces housing and other actions by the Kennedy administration, and the creation of an affirmative action program in the Johnson administration (Holden, 1986). These actions have the force of law, but did not necessarily generate the same political support of legislation passed by the Congress. On the other hand, they *were enacted*, which might not have happened had they been brought before the House or Senate (Morgan, 1970; Garfinkel, 1969; Binkin and Eitelberg, 1982; DeFranco, 1987).

Presidents use other strategies when they wish to draft legislation but seek broader institutional support, making the impact of the action more significant. The State of the Union address is the president's annual opportunity to convey to the Congress those priorities he feels are most important for it to know as it begins another year. An issue presented in this speech, placed prominently within it, derives considerable prestige from this status. This speech is an opportunity for the president to let Congress see and hear directly how he feels about important issues. It is a very important opportunity and a rare one.

The President's budget message is another such opportunity which has the added weight of prestige, visibility, and some indication of how the chief executive is willing to translate verbal commitments of support into financial expenditures, whether for new programs, for expanded support for existing programs (in both the authorization and appropriation phases of congressional action), or for implementation of policy.

Finally, the president's personal message included in the State of the Union address can be significantly reinforced through personal contacts with the legislative leadership in both houses. Johnson knew how to effect such contact, while Carter had great difficulty in making such appeals. Presidential attention to legislative affairs on a consistent basis also has a strong positive impact.

These events concentrate on the start-up phases of legislation. Proposals in which the president is directly interested also require carefully monitoring the specific topic through his own contacts and on a day-to-day basis through the interaction of his congressional liaison office. The president's effectiveness on his specific legislation can also be advanced or hampered by the general tenor of the relations developed by his liaison office with the Congress. President Carter's legislative liaison rapidly developed a very poor working relationship with the Congress, significantly reducing the president's ability to shape policy in a variety of areas (Light, 1982: 156). In contrast, the late Clarence Mitchell, the NAACP's Washington lobbyist, reported immediately after passage of the 1964 Civil Rights Bill in the House that he and Joseph Rauh "were in a footrace over to the Senate to start work there. The phone rang in one of those pay phone booths over in the House wing, and to our amazement it was the president calling — I don't know how he ever managed to get us on that phone, but he was calling to say, 'All right, you fellows, get on over there to the Senate because we've got it through the House, and now we've got the big job of getting it through the Senate!' " (Miller, 1980: 368).

*Executive agency leadership* is realized in a variety of ways, beginning with appointments; the person selected is important, but the mandate passed on to him or her has equal priority. Personal reinforcement of commitment to policy is important, whether the president is interested in maintaining existing programs, initiating new ones, or carefully monitoring responsibility for administration. Finally the agency must be effective in the way in which it expends the financial and other resources at its command.

Action on civil rights issues was viewed as a highly risky enterprise by many, including Presidents Eisenhower and Kennedy. According to Harold Fleming, Eisenhower was unwilling to undertake aggressive public action as president to attack racial segregation:

"Throughout his eight years as chief executive, Dwight D. Eisenhower reiterated his essentially *laissez-faire* views on civil rights. He held that this was an issue to be resolved at the local level and at an evolutionary pace, that laws in this field were of dubious value, that alteration of 'the hearts and minds of men' was a precondition of change, that local intervention by the federal government was to be assiduously avoided" (Fleming, 1965, 924).

For most of his administration, Kennedy's posture on civil rights was low-profile and limited to executive rather than to legislative action; that was to be exercised only where federal authority was most dominant, as his own presidential prestige would not be risked. In short, he avoided conflict until the end of his administration. In contrast Lyndon Johnson — despite his southern origins and his long-term membership in and leadership of the Senate (an institution decisively shaped by the power of southern/racial conservatives), strongly supported passage of the civil rights legislation introduced by President Kennedy at the end of his administration. He said in his first address to Congress: "No memorial oration or eulogy could more eloquently honor President Kennedy's memory than the earliest possible passage of the [1964] civil rights bill . . . I urge you . . . to enact a civil rights law so that we can move forward to eliminate from this nation every trace of discrimination and oppression that is based upon race or color" (Miller, 1980: 339). When Johnson announced his support to the nation for a Voting Rights Bill in a special joint session of Congress the next year, he framed his support for it using the language and the passion of the Civil Rights movement, "We Shall Overcome," so that no one would misunderstand the depth of his commitment or the significance of his language.

In the future, presidents will have a strong core of support from the Democratic electorate and from within the Congress, but also from the business community. As demographic shifts in the racial and ethnic balance of the American population significantly increase the proportions of blacks, Hispanics, and Asians entering the work force, the political consequences of support for affirmative action policy will fall. An example was recently reported in reference to graduate education in business administration:

" 'If you look at the year 2000, 28 percent of the college-age population will be black and Hispanic,' said Charles Hickman, an official with the American Assembly of Collegiate Schools of Business, which accredits graduate business schools. That key block of minority people as part of the total student population 'clearly means that either business school enrollment will drop, or we will have to find a way to attract more students' " (French, 1987b).

The president of the Graduate Management Admissions Council, William Broesamle, estimated that by 2003

"one-third of the workforce would consist of members of minorities . . . and said 'even with a reduction of affirmative action pressures, corporations continue to request more minority graduates' " (French, 1987b).

This does not mean all opposition to black and Hispanic hiring and promotion will evaporate, but the nation is entering a period similar to the economic climate of the early 1960s when shortages of white labor made affirmative action policies highly attractive to some sectors of the business community (Barnett and Williams, 1986).

## INSTITUTIONAL CHALLENGES TO THE PRESIDENCY

One of the consequences of presidential administrations that do not take strong positions in support of civil rights is institutional challenges to the office. These challenges can come in one of two ways.

First, individual incidents of racially motivated violence may increase. The population may feel that expressions of racism and racist violence are permissible. There is a tradition of exercising social control of blacks through "formally informal law." "Formally informal law" means *lynching*. Lynchings frequently occurred from the late 1800s through the mid-twentieth century. The record is incomplete; thus, we cannot easily say whether there were as many or fewer such events before the Union army withdrew from the South and before

Republican presidents abrogated their responsiblity to implement the 14th and 15th amendments. (Their failure to do so ended strong support for Republican reconstruction governments in the South in 1877.) Five years later, the number of lynchings (including whites from 1882 through 1903) began at 114 and rose rapidly (Ming, 1947: 58-61; Holden, 1986; Zangrando, 1980).

Some would say that President Reagan has taken a very strong role in the area of civil rights: he has indicated his opposition to governmental involvement in civil and voting rights issues including affirmative action, minority set-asides, comparable worth, and a variety of other areas. However, the posture of the Reagan administration — to withdraw support for previous civil rights legislation or to implement it differently from prior administrations including that of President Nixon — has created a very different civil rights environment in the 1980s.

There was an apparent increase in incidents of racial violence by the second year of the Reagan administration. These incidents of racially motivated violence suggest a challenge to the rule of law, something with which public officials were comfortable in the past — when it applied to blacks. The figures shown in Table 3 are reports of serious problems requiring conciliation and mediation, involving administration of justice problems, and other racial and ethnic conflict issues as reported by the Community Relations Service of the Department of Justice (Annual Reports 1965-1984). All show increases during the Reagan administration. Not all of the incidents listed above are necessarily evidence of racially motivated violence; further, there is no agreed-upon source of data which shows conclusively the levels of racial violence in the recent past, or whether they have increased over time (Oehlsen, 1987)[17].

The second type, more directly related to the institutional challenge I am describing, is of a kind led by or tolerated by state and local elected officials. As national institutions reordered the racial laws and priorities of the previous two centuries, public officials who represented only their white constituencies felt it necessary to resist any challenges to their authority, which until then had included the right to subordinate their black populations. Some examples of this type include the Little Rock, Arkansas conflict over the integration of Central High School. Eisenhower eventually sent the 101st Airborne Division to restore control. He reportedly conveyed a lack of resolve to Governor Orval Faubus, who proceeded to encourage local resistance to the integration of the high school (Burk, 1984). When Faubus took such action, Eisenhower was forced to commit federal troops, lest he be seen as not enforcing the law. However, once the situation had reached this stage, it took considerably more political resources and exercise of federal authority than might have been the case if Eisenhower had assumed a more forceful position earlier in the conflict.

Some other examples include the racial warfare at "Ole Miss," the University of Mississippi at Oxford, where during the Kennedy administration, Assistant Attorney General Nicholas Katzenbach helped James Meredith become the

**Table 3**
**Incidents Handled by the Community Relations Service, 1978 – 1984**

|                                    | 1978 | 1979 | 1980 | 1981 | 1982 | 1983 | 1984 |
| ---------------------------------- | ---- | ---- | ---- | ---- | ---- | ---- | ---- |
| New Alerts Processed               | 1353 | 1315 | 1404 | 1548 | 1996 | 1741 | 1771 |
| Total Dispute Activity Processed   | 1635 | 1757 | -    | -    | -    | -    | -    |
| Assessments Processed              | 1257 | 1315 | 1077 | 1219 | 1476 | 1382 | 1419 |
| Conciliation and Mediation         |      |      |      |      |      |      |      |
| Cases Conducted                    | 702  | 746  | 924  | 1022 | 1096 | 1052 | 974  |
| Cases Concluded                    | -    | -    | 684  | 812  | 855  | 815  | 734  |

Source: Community Relations Service, *Annual Report*, 1979, p. 14; 1980, p. 3. The Service added cases conciliated and mediated as separate categories in 1980. In some instances the categories are not precisely comparable. 1981, p. 14; 1982, p. 23; 1983, p 21; 1984, p. 18. Furthermore, the 1983 figures as reported in the 1984 *Annual Report* vary with the figures shown in this table. The administration claims incidents of racially motivated violence have not significantly increased; other organizations disagree.

first black student to register — but only under military protection (J. Williams, 1987: 213). In Birmingham, Alabama black demonstrators challenged segregation in downtown stores, denial of voting rights, and a variety of other problems. Here the conflict was precipitated by black protesters challenging the legitimacy of local authority figures such as Sheriff Bull Connor who resisted federal efforts to mediate the situation. To thwart integration efforts, Governor George Wallace of Alabama stood in the door of the University of Alabama. Other officials resisted Charlayne Hunter's and Hamilton Holmes's ultimately successful efforts to enroll at the University of Georgia.[18]

President Reagan is an interesting case. He would be classified by many observers as a strong president. He certainly has been perceived to be. In terms of Light's resource categories he is only moderately strong as he narrowly controlled the Senate in his first term, and controlled neither house during his second. Reagan has strong public approval ratings, but they fall well below Kennedy and Johnson in his early years. He scores best on his electoral margin.

Despite these power resource limitations, Reagan has taken very clear stands on civil rights issues, seeking to dissipate the impact of voting rights legislation prior to its 1982 renewal deadline by seeking to apply it to the entire nation. He reconstructed the U.S. Civil Rights Commission, appointing its members with some attention to their partisan affiliation in a fashion that was distinct from its previous history in Democratic and Republican administrations. He named William Bradford Reynolds as Assistant Attorney General, although Reynolds had no experience with civil rights law prior to his appointment. He has significantly expanded the size of the federal judiciary and filled it with white male conservative jurists. Most importantly, the administration reduced spending on social welfare programs.

By the late 1980s, in the post-civil rights era, the southern electorate is now fully integrated (see Table 2). A fully integrated electorate means that southern members of the House and Senate as well as the President must pay careful attention to black voters, who are much more intensely loyal to the Democratic party than almost any other sector of the population. In thirteen broadly defined "southern" states, blacks roughly equal or exceed white registration figures in ten of them, and constitute up to one-third of the voting age population. In the North blacks range between seven and fifteen percent of the population, and also compare favorably in voter registration rates although not as closely as in the South. When the electoral votes are totaled in the states in which blacks equal five percent or more of the population, they equal 355. This is a very comfortable margin of victory in the electoral college, but only under the highly specified conditions, requiring evenly divided support among white voters and unified support for one candidate by black voters. President Reagan has lost — and lost *badly* — each time he has taken a public position on civil rights diametrically opposing that of the new southern black electorate. This bloc has developed considerable clout, especially when it merged with the fully mobilized northern black electorate and national civil rights groups. This was demonstrated in 1986 senatorial elections and in the voting behavior of southern Senate members during the Bork nomination fight.

Is this important to the president as an individual and to his presidency? Before the Bork vote, President Reagan said that the nomination would go down "over his dead body," and brought the issue to a vote on the Senate floor even after the Judiciary Committee voted nine to five to recommend against the nomination. What was revealed by the outcome of the vote was the full extent to which the Congress has been reshaped by more than two decades of efforts to develop black voting rights. Unless the president is strongly supportive of civil rights reform, which by now means protection for the status quo, the institution will find itself under considerable attack. Put another way, presidents have more to gain than to lose by exercising strong, reformist leadership in the area of civil rights.

## CONCLUDING OBSERVATIONS

The presidency was seriously constrained by the exclusion of black voters from the electorate from the 1890s through the 1960s. Presidents rarely took aggressive reform postures on civil rights; but when President Johnson helped reform the southern electorate, the institution was strengthened by opening up pathways in the Congress for racial and social change. Once opened, presidents who do not also offer policies consistent with this new constituency face constraints on their leadership.[19] A critical subject that deserves comment is the celebration of the Bicentennial and the popular observation that the American Constitution is a triumph for individual liberty. One can argue that is *especially*

59

true when the three-fifths clause and other recognitions of the politically subordinated status of slaves, indentured servants, Indians, and women are included. The triumph of individual liberty, that is of *private power*, in the unamended Constitution meant the stillbirth of black political and economic rights for nearly two centuries. It was not until the federal government, the public sector, was constitutionally strong enough to specify to the states and to private individuals that African slaves and their descendants could *not* be considered the property of whites, that black people could begin to be treated legally and politically as human beings.

The national government including the president had to acquire enormous political power in order to incorporate blacks into the polity for the first time, in the nineteenth century. For that incorporation to occur again after nearly three-quarters of a century of national nonintervention into the affairs of the South, the national government including the president had to acquire these powers a second time.

Strong presidential leadership and strong federal and executive authority have been required for blacks to attain their current political status; that is, to be considered full citizens of these United States. Strong presidential leadership in preservation of these rights will be required for blacks to retain their political status and to acquire equal economic status.

# Critical Perspectives
# On The Psychology of Race

Price M. Cobbs, M.D.

## DEFINING RAGE

As I reflect on a turbulent and instructive generation of work as a psychiatrist, my thoughts reflect a broad synthesis of views, concepts, and insights about human behavior and race. Yet, however broadly these thoughts range, I always return to a seminal formulation. The formulation crystallized in the mid-nineteen sixties when William Grier and I decided to collaborate on a book, and thus began an exciting and methodical process of examination.

Over a period of several years, we dissected in minute detail the case histories of hundreds of patients, affluent and indigent, from brief evaluations to long-term therapy. We pored over notes taken after seeing proud welfare mothers, embittered unemployed laborers and confused and frightened professionals. The people who visited our offices came in all sizes, shapes, ages, sexes, and colors, and this diversity contributed breadth and depth to our conversations.

Our discussions ranged from a comparison of different clinical approaches and teaching methods to a minute dissection of the themes and theories of Freud, Jung, E. Franklin Frazier, and W.E.B. DuBois. Occasionally, we argued long and loud over differing interpretations of books, articles, and research. At times, we swapped long-forgotten stories, and shared gossip and delicious secrets from our family lives and personal experiences. The incidents we recalled were sometimes rollicking and tear-producing in uncovering some hidden, ironic humor. At other times, they were gut-wrenching and thought-provoking in revealing a glimpse of some long-suppressed pain.

Underlying all discussions was an unyielding curiosity, indeed a barely contained passion, which focused our energies and intellect on understanding the deeper psychological mysteries and vicissitudes of race. We wanted to know more about the influence of race on psychosexual development and identity formation. What were the deeper understandings of how it affected self-image and self-esteem? Why did it influence so powerfully both lovemaking and mythmaking?

In delving deeper, we searched for questions and answers about the influence of race and its effects on how intellect was formed, how it was used, or not used. In this, we were not looking for genetic answers. A critical study of the writings of researchers such as Shockley, Jensen, and others convinced us that these works were based on cleverly contrived research questions bent on proving once again a historic racist formulation of white superiority and black inferiority. None of these researchers attempted to understand a world that was, for a black American, at best tortuous and ambiguous and, at worst, implacably hostile.

Finally, at the end of a long and draining evening, something clicked for both of us. The puzzle came together, and we struggled with completing a formulation. The rage of blacks then being expressed so explosively, we concluded, was their response to the hatred of them by whites: Hatred that could be masked, denied, and otherwise not consciously experienced, but hatred, nonetheless. At a deep, complicated, and only faintly understood psychological level, hatred based on a series of often automatic value judgments about physical differences—skin color, hair, the shape of noses, lips, and the vast range of facial and body features that distinguish people of different racial groups. Contributing to this was a lack of knowledge about group history, about how different groups and individuals came to this country, and how they developed their own culture and unique niche as Americans. This formulation became the foundation of our book, *Black Rage,* where we set down our views about the inner lives of black people in America.

We defined rage as expressing outwardly or experiencing inwardly a violent anger. It is volatile and can be released explosively as a response to a wide range of long-term frustrations. If these frustrations are similar and deeply felt by a group of people, rage can be contagious as individuals within that group get in touch with their own long-repressed and suppressed feelings about who they are and who they want to be. Rage is experienced as people come in contact with being perpetual victims and try, however antisocially, to redefine themselves and escape victimhood.

Rage occurs for individuals in a world where one is constantly the object of abuse, assault, and oppression. It builds in people as a result of cumulative personal insults, consistent devaluation, and individuals being treated as a deficit model. Rage can be turned off and on, responding directly to the interaction. Most feel rage when they are viewed as part of a group or category rather than as an individual. As a final caveat, this interaction is based in many cases on a response to physical characteristics that one cannot change.

In addition, we found rage in black people more frequently focused inward. An example of rage directed inward is that of an individual not appearing angry, but rather feeling angry and not dramatically showing it. Such a person can be, by turn, intellectually shut-down, emotionally withdrawn, or sullen. At all times, rage is a struggle with inner turmoil.

We saw then, and I see now, black rage occurring on a continuum. At one end, it is known, visible, and observable. At the other end, it is unseen, silent, and all-consuming. Every black person in America experiences rage, and exists somewhere on this continuum.

## REALITY OF RACE

The passage of time, coupled with an ongoing examination of many experiences, helps me understand more fully the subtleties and nuances of the psychology of race in America today. I have discarded long-held notions, added others, refined many thoughts, and grappled with ideas, new and old. Certainly, as a nation, we have progressed in how we people are treated based on race. There has been an expansion of legal rights and protections, more political participation, broader representation, and greater access to education and employment opportunities. In addition, black Americans are much more visible and maintain a more vital presence in the tapestry of both national and international affairs.

However, a singular focus on progress denies and therefore misses the underlying emotional conflict which grips so many Americans when this country and individuals within it have to deal with the reality of race. These conflicts can involve a minimum of overt bigotry and conscious intolerance or they can be blatant in their racism. In many ways those which are overt are easier to deal with, if harder to accept. Conflicts based on race perpetuate misunderstandings and devalue differences.

The reality is that Americans of this day are not completely comfortable in moving beyond the myth of the melting pot. Even though we *seem* to accept people from all over the world, my contention is Americans refuse to understand and value differences thoroughly. In other words, deeper, if unknown, conflicts arise from not examining issues of superiority and inferiority. These types of conflicts are strongly embedded in the American psyche. The reality of race, then, is elitism based on a color line.

For many individuals and certainly for the nation, there is a long-overdue examination concerning unearned arrogance, whether it is based on race, religion, gender, or just luck. Understanding and resolving the above realities of race are the daily staple of my activities.

## UNDERSTANDING DIFFERENCES

In my work, I continue to see black rage and white hatred; however, one might be muted and the other might be unintended. The continued reduction of both remains my overarching clinical and theoretical challenge. Moreover, this conundrum serves as a metaphor for understanding a much broader set of issues concerning difference.

The breadth of my work with individuals, groups, and organizations of all sizes and degrees of profitability allows me an unparalleled view of a varied America. One day, I am in the elegantly furnished boardroom of a Fortune 500 company, sitting with a group of white executives at a highly polished walnut conference table, engaging in an understated discussion about diversity in the workplace. This might be followed the next day by an energetic conversation about psychological empowerment with a young black couple who wants to start a Mom-and-Pop greeting card business armed mainly with grit, a fierce desire for upward mobility, and $1200 in start-up capital.

The next week could find me conducting a seminar on career development at an Ivy League college by day, and at night having an intense dialogue with the underpaid and overworked director of a non-profit agency dedicated to changing the self-image and behavior patterns of a group of drug addicts. My work bridges talking with recent inmates from a state prison to consulting with the leadership of a government agency about social policy for the nation. The diversity of these activities forces me as a social scientist to think about critical perspectives as I try to fathom the psychology of race.

Individuals of many races, creeds, and cultures have sat, stood, and paced in my office. Whatever other discomforts brought them to me, all were wrestling at some level with the contradiction and paradoxes of race in America or in the world. One might be a leader of a civil rights group coping with the anger, confusion, and grief unleashed by the untimely death of a revered leader. Another could be an introspective intellectual spending endless hours sifting and weighing each implication to determine whether one is a black or Afro-American or indeed an American at all.

Others are struggling with understanding their whiteness and how to expand it in order to hear, feel, and connect with what is different and heretofore alien. Working with diverse individuals and organizations has been crucial in stimulating the development of a theory and practice to understand and value differences better.

## LIKE A PERMANENT ACID RAIN

I have discovered significant and critical perspectives about the psychology of race. A primary one is my view that thoughts, feelings, attitudes, perceptions, and behaviors, as they pertain to race, are frequently contaminated by unseen cultural pollutants. The source of these pollutants can be likened to the fallout from a persistent acid rain. At times, it is a light drizzle or even a mist which affects us so mildly as to be unaware of its influence. At other times, it is a heavy storm, drenching and enveloping us with water and, in the process, distorting and greatly affecting our reaction and responses where race is involved.

In my view, the pollutants so deeply contaminate us that we have little awareness of how deeply we have incorporated them into ourselves. We deceive ourselves into thinking that something called the "race problem" has mostly been solved or, if thought about at all, is the fault and responsibility of someone else. Besides, only Ku Klux Klanners, crazy nationalists, and other radicals harbor negative feelings about those who are racially different.

Individually and collectively, Americans continue to be passive in acquiring any knowledge about the psychology of race. We underestimate its implications for how and with whom we conduct our lives. Most of us, when confronted with racial attitudes in any form, fall back on a comfortable intellectual laziness which elevates stereotypes to facts, and converts individual behavior to group characteristics. This, I believe, is normal human behavior.

Despite its normalcy, however, this behavior tolerates inactivity and condones negative stereotypes. It is one-sided and needs to be changed. Most people, particularly those who are not the historical objects of negative racial attitudes, rarely engage their intellect in any serious or disciplined manner to understand such attitudes. Whatever else, my work convinces me that without a sustained engagement of intellect and an examination of feelings, negative racial attitudes will continue to dictate behavior, to have an impact on decisions, and to prevent intimacy between people.

I invite the reader to examine several critical perspectives pertaining to the effects of this pollution. If we help create, however unknowingly, an acid rain, then we must assume responsibility for undoing its effects. This examination will help us, I believe, better understand the contaminants of racial pollution and their effect on us individually and on our nation.

## INCLUSION VS. EXCLUSION

For me, nothing crystallized more the contemporary perspectives of race in America than a story appearing in late September of 1987, in *The New York Times*. The story was written by Robert Pear and the headline read, "Blacks and the Elitist Stereotype." The opening line stated that the highest-ranking black official in the State Department had resigned recently after suggesting that he had been treated in a racially insensitive manner. The story went on to note other black employees in the department knew how he felt. They described events where they too were snubbed and talked over. Others mentioned that white subordinates were invariably consulted before these same issues were discussed with a black manager.

Much of my work as a consultant to organizations deals with trying to clarify many of the issues raised in the *Times* story. The article and direct quotes could serve as a case study which condensed what thousands of black men and women have said to me over a twenty-year period. The irony of the situation noted by Washington lawyer Mary Frances Berry is that the people complaining and mentioned in the story are among those most wedded to a view of the world as colorblind. They have been among those castigating civil rights leaders as being out of step with their constituencies and railing about issues which have been buried.

What is important here, and I add this briefly, is psychologically, blacks and other minorities, in order to be included, feel they must "buy into" or at least act as if they have "bought into" the attitudes, perceptions, and feelings of their immediate environment. They may collude in order to be a part of it. This is implicit in the *Times* article and ironically becomes a "Catch 22." If black managers refuse collusion, they may sacrifice an opportunity to be included. If they decide to collude, they may lie to themselves. Perhaps they think and hope this is better than exclusion.

My perspective is that many blacks have not carefully examined their marginality within their home, social, and work environments. In addition, the white counterpart does not understand this marginality. Therefore, assumptions from both sides create this "Catch 22."

From the *Times* article, the disputes and the numerous quotes read like a laundry list of what I encounter daily. As always when blacks or others who are excluded begin to question their status, the first issue usually confronted is one of inclusion versus exclusion. Various examples demonstrated how this particular issue was ever present in this situation. One statement mentioned that whites were "talking around and going past me and keeping me out of meetings."

Another statement by a black manager was "I am kept out of the loop and I am not consulted" even when the affirmative action program he was responsible for was being revised. Others described how whites in the State Department were indifferent to the views of blacks.

When a core issue in an organization concerns exclusion based on race, what is most important to understand are the reactions of those who are included. How do they explain this to themselves and remain intact and whole? In this case, those doing the excluding are only dimly aware of the accusation. They continue to function more or less the same as they and others have done for generations. Again, we see intellectual laziness. For them, who they include and exclude in most cases is not even a conscious choice.

For those who are excluded, the issues can be explosive. They are aware, most times painfully so, that they are excluded and in the process something about them is deemed unworthy. In this instance what is deemed unworthy and therefore felt to be devalued is the intellect of black people. We must understand this hollow feeling. If we realize the response to it, we can gain a better comprehension of the psychology of race.

If words like "manager," "executives," and "communication loops" are dropped, then one is compelled to ask, what else is new? Historically, have white Americans in or out of the State Department ever been sensitive to the views of blacks? Whether it is neighborhood control of schools, education on drug abuse, or information about housing for low-income people, when and where have whites in power ever been consistently respectful of black views?

Examining the interactions of blacks and whites in the workplace and trying to fathom their divergent, individual reactions is a daily challenge. Consulting in organizations and simultaneously trying to diffuse some of the tensions described above without ignoring the depth of the root causes allow me to place the issues in a historical context.

As a result, using examples from the State Department does not imply that I think it is any more or less racist than other institutions in this country; that its white managers are more insensitive or its black managers more aggrieved. It is merely that the interactions and reactions so clearly point out some critical perspectives.

## SUPER BLACK SYNDROME

At bottom, so much of the rage of black people, however it falls out on the continuum, is rooted in the perception that their intellect has been consistently and historically devalued. Many of the people mentioned in the article—

like their counterparts in other organizations—have spent a lifetime denying, fighting, overcompensating, or otherwise trying to account for this critical perspective.

Another issue mentioned in the story was how black people are in a never ending cycle of proving their credentials. Alluded to was what most integrating black people call the "super black syndrome", namely, the feeling that in a predominantly white setting one has to be a combination of Mary McLeod Bethune, Martin Luther King, Jr., and Booker T. Washington, just to be accepted as a social, not an intellectual, equal.

Again, the phenomenon of having to prove one's credentials just to gain bare acceptance is nothing new in American life. From Crispus Attucks to Harriet Tubman to Ron McNair, black people have given of themselves to realize the American Dream. And until the issue of inclusion versus exclusion based on race is understood more fully, dramas such as the one in the State Department will go on.

I once treated a young black man over a period of several years. Each week he would sit facing me while describing in vivid detail conflicts in his life which he attributed to being black. As we tried to sort out reality and illusion, his humor was deep-seated and infectious. Many times I would be unsuccessful in reflecting the poker face of the therapist while he unraveled in vivid detail some new facet of derring-do about his life in the city.

Whenever he described an event or series of events which evoked his reflectiveness or caused a loss of cool, he would describe an ever-present fantasy. In this fantasy he equated being black in America with lacing on boxing gloves, stepping into the ring at Madison Square Garden, and daily facing an unknown and ferocious opponent. As we unraveled this, he meant not necessarily having to defend himself in a championship fight, but rather a daily fight against a series of small, covert slights and insults. Chester Pierce labels these "micro-aggressions," and they are ubiquitous in the lives not only of black managers at the State Department, but pervade the lives of all black Americans.

Looked at another way, these micro-aggressions can be seen as assumptions about a person based on how that person looks or fits into a group rather than engaging in the critical thinking which makes a person an individual. Black Americans are the most historically present of all non-white groups in this country, save Native Americans. They are the group most insinuated into the American national character. After all, blacks are described as three-fifths of a man in the original Constitution. This characterization codified and further institutionalized a process of being scrutinized.

## AN ONGOING DRAMA

Most Americans, including those most recently arriving on these shores, carry a set of assumptions about how blacks think, feel, and behave. They are assumptions that rarely are tested in any way with reality. Indeed one can make a case that new groups of people such as the Hungarians in the

1950s and the boat people in the 1980s were finally Americanized when they incorporated the set of assumptions about blacks which are carried by most other Americans.

The recognition of being once again the object of a range of mostly negative assumptions is a frightening experience. At some level, it means a new assessment of the impact and subsequent distortions resulting from how one views and is viewed by the world; and make no mistake, the critical variable is skin color and the responses to it.

There is always the hope that something has changed and the assumptions, however subtle, have gone away. The reality of race, however, intrudes once again. When we psychologically deal with that reality, black people are most painfully in touch with their rage. For those with less latitude to express outwardly their rage, and this includes blacks at the State Department, it is a frightening experience.

To manage one's rage in any circumstance is difficult. It is compounded when one must survive in a climate of micro-aggressions, and among tenuous relationships with whites. In the interest of securing a kind of symbolic acceptance of both sides, it goes something like: "I won't point out that you treat me differently, that you tolerate but do not welcome me at the State Department because I'm black if, in turn, you won't point out that I'm more cautious, reserved, and constricted around you because you're white."

It is an ongoing drama and a form of racial detente that black people in predominantly white organizations participate in to get the job done or, in many cases, to get the job—period.

Expressing rage outwardly is to unleash the demons and risk a loss of control. For most black people a point is reached where it becomes more emotionally sound to hold back and avoid a confrontation. This point was reached in the State Department situation when a black manager stated that the problems were due less to racism than elitism. Immediately there was a chorus of black amens and agreement. One thinks: how neat, how clear. This maneuver immediately reduces the tension, avoids a confrontation, and most importantly turns the rage inward.

To point out that elitism by definition translates to racism when several conditions are met is to jar the neatness of the solution. First, elitist groups establish the rules of the game: who can play and who can't. Second, they reinforce their power to do this. Third, they deny that they give power disproportionately to members of other groups, in this case black Americans.

An observer can see quite clearly how all parties collude in avoiding an acknowledgement of a racial problem. The State Department can accept accusations of elitism; it cannot accept racism. Blacks and whites join a denial of color-consciousness.

This conclusion is particularly sad because if such an acknowledgement were made, several things might happen. One, people in the organization might discuss race and its implications in making choices and decisions. This could at some point lead to needed discussions about the impact of race in our foreign policy. Finally, as a country we could profit by gaining greater clarity in our relationships with all those who are different from us.

Before thinking of race and racism as solely involving black Americans, it must be recalled that for many 1987 was not a great year. Not only did we face the harsh realities of Howard Beach and Forsyth County, but the year also saw a rising tide of macro-aggressions directed against Asian Americans. From Detroit to California, they were the target as people unknowingly acted out racial prejudices and devaluation of differences. In uncovering racial memories in this country Asian, Hispanic, and Native Americans are also intricately interwoven.

## DO NOT SKIRT THE TRUTH

My model for unraveling and more deeply understanding the many critical perspectives on the psychology of race is to focus at three levels: personal, interpersonal, and global.

At the personal level, a more active examination of how values, particularly values about differences, needs to be done. What messages were received which helped define one's worth and self-esteem, both as an individual and as part of a group, however such group was defined? What comparables, messages, and judgments were received about others, particular those who were different racially and culturally? It means uncovering and examining the parts of oneself and one's experiences which are hidden and run away from because they are considered different.

Probing at the interpersonal level involves a thorough and more minute dissection of what goes on between people, particularly where there are racial, gender, or cultural differences. It involves more understanding of the traits and characteristics of who attracts and repulses an individual. Who is immediately thought to be smart, who isn't. Who has the look of intelligence, who doesn't. What traits, characteristics, and style are acceptable, which ones aren't. When is there tension in a relationship, fear, with whom, and what types of people.

At the societal or global level, one needs a comprehension of the role of race and difference in the world. What understanding do people have of poverty, of the haves and have-nots? Is there any systematic study of racism, of sexism, of presumed superiority and inferiority based on race, or other factors of difference? Does the individual understand elitism and power? Who has it, who doesn't, and why?

In my view rage, black and otherwise, erupts when one is the perennial designated victim. This is based on controllable factors where one is characteristically devalued and denied power by another. If, in this country, we are to move beyond the prison of racial denial, where we are able to drop stereotypes and unwarranted assumptions, we must develop and refine a language of differences. We must learn to identify, appreciate, and value our differences. We must truly take to heart a concept that differences are important in our daily lives, that they do not make one person better than another.

In an essay which appeared in *Look Magazine* in August, 1964 and will be published in 1988 as a part of his memoirs, George Leonard writes "A Southerner's Appeal." It is a white man's autobiographical account of his experiences living in a segregated society. Years later, he returns home on holiday. Metaphorically, he uses the eyes as an indication of the racial problem. Through his own eyes, we see an important view. The appeal today is as imperative as when he first wrote it:

"Up to now, we have skirted the truth. National leaders and experts have analyzed segregation and racial prejudice as a sociological phenomenon, a political gambit, and economic lever. In limited ways, it is all of those things. But we have got to go a step farther. If we of the white race are to move effectively against the malady that cripples us, we must see it for what it is, and call it by its true name. Start with those glazed, unseeing eyes. What you are looking at is not a political, sociological or economic phenomenon. It is dangerous, self-destructive madness."

# The Black Family:
# Striving Toward Freedom

Charles V. Willie, Ph.D.

Reflecting upon the bus boycott in Montgomery, Alabama, that launched the direct-action phase of the contemporary Civil Rights Movement, Martin Luther King, Jr. said that discrimination "scars the soul and degrades the personality": it creates within some whites a false sense of superiority and among some blacks a false sense of inferiority (King, 1958:37). These false beliefs encourage the dominance of one group over another.

The family life of black people in the United States can be classified as subdominant in the community power structure. Blacks are subdominant in most power relationships because of the preference for Caucasian ancestry in this nation. Add to this reality the fact that whites also control a disproportionate amount of the nation's resources, and the result is that the customs and conventions of whites are considered normative for the total society.

The subdominant people are therefore assigned the role of the scapegoat in contemporary America—the manifestation of that which is bad in the society at large. In Biblical literature, the scapegoat is an animal upon whose head the sins of the people are symbolically placed. Such an animal is then ceremonially sent out or exiled into the wilderness as a way of expiating the community of its evil deeds. In our contemporary communities, black families bear the blame of others as scapegoats, through the irrational hostility and guilt of whites.

We know, of course, that the practice of scapegoating is not only ineffective but unethical. Most major newspapers and television broadcasting systems in this nation have recently carried stories about the disintegration and failure of black families which, in general, have been little more than attempts to scapegoat.

These stories are the projections of whites about their own worries, fears, and pathological practices. A book authored by Kenneth Keniston for the Carnegie Council on Children states that the first white settlers in Plymouth colony "were afraid their children had lost the dedication and religious conviction of the founding generation." He adds that "today about one out of every three marriages ends in divorce . . . [and that] four out of every ten children . . . will spend part of their childhood in a one-parent family" (Keniston, 1977:4). In general, he states that there is a "splitting up of nuclear families." Unable to reverse effectively these trends and to counter the rising

71

rates of family violence and child abuse, whites have projected their own fears upon blacks and black families.

A more objective analysis of the status of black families is possible when we recognize that the increasing concern about black families represents not so much a new and unique pathological adaptation of blacks as it does a projection upon blacks of the concerns about the pathological adaptations increasingly found among whites and all families.

## SOCIOECONOMIC DIFFERENTIATION

The first and fundamental fact about black contemporary family life is the increasing socioeconomic differentiation found among such households in the United States. This is a fact that should be celebrated. E. Franklin Frazier reported in an article published near the midpoint of the twentieth century that only approximately one-eighth of black families were able to maintain a middle-class way of life (Frazier, 1968:207). My studies of black families during the 1970s and 1980s reveal that about one-fourth to one-third had an annual income at or above the national median (Willie, 1981:208). Growing affluence is a fact of life within the black population that has been recognized by a range of scholars, including William Wilson (1978) and Reynolds Farley (1984).

In income, occupational opportunity, and educational attainment, Farley reports definite improvement among black households. The gap in median school year completed between black and white groups has been substantially reduced; the proportion of blacks in prestigious and higher-paying jobs has increased; and black earnings have improved (Farley, 1984:194-195).

Some social scientists such as Wilson assert that race-specific policies to ameliorate the problem of poor blacks have disproportionately profited more advantaged black families. In effect, he links "the improving position of the black middle class" to "the worsening condition of the black underclass" (Wilson, 1987:ix, vii). The Wilson analysis is flawed on two counts: it does not demonstrate that poverty among blacks is increasing, and it does not provide a logical explanation of how help for one sector of the black population is harmful to another.

We know from an analysis of data published by the U.S. Bureau of the Census over the years that the proportion of black and of white families below the poverty line has been reduced. Three decades ago, approximately 56 percent of all blacks in families were poor. Today, the proportion is about one-third. Three decades ago, one-sixth of all whites in families were poor. Today, the proportion is approximately 10 percent (U.S. Bureau of the Census, 1985:455). The ratio of the poor in these racial populations has remained more or less constant over the years, although the proportion of the poor has diminished. The proportion of black poor was 3.4 times greater than the proportion of white poor three decades ago, and is 3.3 times greater today. These data indicate that although the size of the poor population in both groups has decreased, the condition of the black poor with reference to the white poor has not worsened.

Neither has the condition of the black poor with reference to the white poor improved over the years. As stated above, the ratios for the two different time periods have remained more or less the same. Thus, there is no decline in the significance of race as a circumstantial factor in poverty.

Even when the analysis is limited to an examination of indicators for blacks only, Farley states that "it is an oversimplification to claim that the black community is now split into an elite and an underclass" (Farley, 1984:190). With reference to education he found that "lower-class blacks are not falling further behind upper-class blacks" (Farley, 1984:177). Moreover, Farley reports that the distribution of family income within the black population has changed very little over the last 30 years: "the richest five percent of black families have received about 16 percent of all the income obtained by black families, while the poorest 20 percent of black families have received about four percent" (Farley, 1984:191). These data indicated that racial discrimination is a constant experience in the United States and probably accounts for continuing differentials in status position between blacks and whites, that the proportional size of the poor population has declined among both racial groups, and that improvements among some sectors of the black population have not contributed to a worsened condition among other sectors of the black population.

The analysis thus far confirms the assertion by Martin Luther King, Jr. that "we are caught in a network of inescapable mutuality" (King, 1958:199). An analysis of the Civil Rights Movement reveals linkages between affluent and poor blacks have been helpful rather than harmful. Based on an examination of successful educational reform initiatives among blacks such as those for school desegregation, it appears that "a subdominant population is likely to intensify its press for affirmative action with reference to equal access and equitable distribution of community resources when it grows in numbers from a small minority to a large minority, and when it changes socioeconomically from a homogeneous to a heterogeneous population . . . . The size of a population and its socioeconomic differentiation are interrelated phenomena that must be examined to determine their joint effect, if the pattern of the press for social action by a subdominant population is to be understood" (Willie, 1983:197).

If a diversified population is essential in social action efforts among blacks and other subdominant populations, then a one-sided analysis that focuses only on the poor or lower class or underclass among blacks is a perspective that is too limited for the formulation of adequate public policy.

Missing from most analyses of black family life are black positive adaptations and contributions to American society. Moreover, many studies of black family life stereotype blacks as if all were poor. Finally some studies do not link descriptive findings to any theoretical framework that facilitates an explanation of the data. The assessment of black families reported here attempts to overcome these problems.

First we examine the social standing of blacks in America. According to Richard Coleman and Lee Rainwater, "social standing is a complex compounding of the individual's position in different hierarchies" (Coleman and Rainwater, 1978:xii). In general, "people combine such factors as income, occupation, and education in assigning social standing" (Coleman and Rainwater, 1978:23).

With reference to income, the interracial distribution for black and for white families has manifested only a modest change over the years in a positive direction favorable to blacks. The ratio of black to white median family income was .54 in 1950 before the *Brown* Supreme Court decision that outlawed segregation, and .56 slightly more than three decades later (in 1983 constant dollars). This ratio represented a slight gain of only two percentage points in median annual income for all black families in comparison with such income for all white families (U.S. Bureau of the Census, 1985:446). With reference to the poor, 56 percent of black individuals in families had income below the poverty line in 1959 compared with 16.5 percent of white individuals in families. The proportion of impoverished blacks to whites in that year was 3.39. By 1982, poor people in both racial populations had decreased substantially from 56 to 34.9 percent for black individuals in families, and from 16.5 to 10.6 percent for white individuals in families. The 1982 ratio of the proportion of impoverished blacks to whites was 3.29. For this measure of income, only a modest interracial improvement in favor of blacks is seen. During nearly a quarter of a century, beginning in 1959, blacks—whose proportion of poor was three and two-fifths times greater than that for whites in 1959—continued at only a slightly reduced differential of three and one-third times greater in 1982 (U.S. Bureau of the Census, 1985:455).

Despite the more or less constant ratio of the association of black to white annual family income when studied by a central tendency measure like the median, analysis of the income range reveals substantial improvements favorable to blacks. A ratio of the proportion of black families with incomes in the lowest quintile of the range in 1954 was 2.17 times greater than the proportion of whites similarly situated. However, in 1977 (nearly a quarter of a century later), the ratio of the proportions for these two populations was down to 1.98. In the highest quintile of family income, the proportion of blacks at this income level was only .27 of that for whites in 1954. By 1977, the ratio of the proportion of blacks to whites in the highest fifth of the income range had increased to .47. The actual proportion of blacks and other races in the bottom fifth of the family income hierarchy decreased from 43.3 percent in 1954 to 39.6 percent in 1977; in the top fifth of the family income hierarchy, the proportion of blacks and other races increased from 5.3 percent in 1954 to 9.4 percent in 1977. Data were not analyzed for the 1980s but probably reflect the same pattern of the past two decades (U.S. Bureau of the Census, 1980:483).

While black families continue to have a higher proportion of their population in the low-income range and a lower proportion of their population in the high-income range compared with white families, the proportion of blacks in the bottom quintile has decreased while the proportion of blacks in the top quintile has increased. While these findings represent a severe judgment upon our society and its continuing discriminatory practice in the distribution of income among families of different racial groups, they also confirm that poverty among blacks and all families has decreased, and that affluence among blacks and all families has increased. Moreover, this analysis indicates the importance of studying the prevalence rate of families by race for the entire range of income categories rather than focusing only on measures of central tendency such as the mean, median, or mode. This analysis reveals that race has not declined but continues as a significant variable differentiating blacks from whites at all income levels, and that the proportion of poor black families has decreased while the proportion of affluent black families has increased. Thus, the condition of lower-class blacks has not worsened as the condition of middle-class blacks has improved, as claimed by Wilson in his book, *The Truly Disadvantaged* (1987:vii).

With reference to employment, the proportions of white males and black males who work in the most prestigious professional-technical, managerial-administrative jobs had only modest increases during the past decade. White males in these occupational categories varied from 28 percent of the white employed population over 16 years of age in 1972 to 30.5 percent of such workers in their race in 1979—an increase of 2.5 percentage points. Black males and those of other races exhibited a similar rate of change for these occupations; they increased from 13 percent of those employed 16 years of age or older who worked in these most prestigious jobs in 1972 to 17.4 percent in 1979—an increase of 4.4 percentage points (U.S. Bureau of Labor Statistics, 1980:46-48). The ratio of these proportions of blacks and whites at the top of the occupational hierarchy changed slightly in a direction that favored blacks and other races. The increase in the racial ratio ranged from .46 in 1972 to .57, the final year of the decade.

For the bottom of the occupational hierarchy, the decade of the seventies showed slight changes that also favored blacks and other racial minorities. While the proportion of white males 16 or older who worked as laborers, private household workers, and service workers remained constant at 15.9 percent in 1972 and 1979, the proportion of black males and employed males of other races in these least prestigious jobs dropped slightly from 36 percent in 1972 to 31.4 percent in 1979 (U.S. Bureau of Labor Statistics, 1980:46-48). The racial ratio of the proportion of black males to white males at the bottom of the occupational hierarchy moved from 2.26 in 1972 down to 1.95 in 1979.

Again, when racial difference is analyzed, it is shown to continue as a mediating force in inequitable distribution of jobs. At the close of the 1970s, for example, the proportion of professional and managerial workers among white males (30.5 percent) was nearly twice as great as the proportion of such workers employed as laborers and service workers (15.9 percent). The converse was true for black males: their proportion of laborers and service workers (31.4 percent) was nearly twice as great as the proportion of professional and managerial workers (17.4 percent). Nevertheless, there was a change for blacks both at the top and the bottom of the occupational hierarchy. The modest increase in the proportion of blacks who got high-income jobs during the 1970s was accompanied by a modest decrease in black workers in low-income jobs. Apparently help for affluent blacks did not harm poor blacks as claimed by William Wilson (1978, 1987).

The disadvantaged circumstances that black families have experienced as participants in the labor force in the United States is not simply a result of inadequate education, another Wilson contention (1978:104-109). A majority of all adults 25 years of age and over in black and in white racial populations are high school graduates. The median school year completed by blacks and whites differs by only a few months today compared to a difference of 2.5 years in 1950 (U.S. Bureau of the Census, 1985:134). Nevertheless, whites had a median family income that fluctuated from 40 to 45 percent greater than the median for blacks during the first half of the 1980 decade (U.S. Bureau of the Census, 1984:5; 1985:446). But the median education for these two populations as mentioned differed only 3.3 percent (U.S. Bureau of the Census, 1985:134).

To test the Wilson hypothesis that low-income black households are locked into the low-wage sector because of their inadequate education, a ratio was computed of the median family income of poorly educated blacks (those with less than a grade school education) and the median family income of poorly educated whites. Poorly educated blacks in 1982 earned 23 percent less than the income received by poorly educated whites. The same pattern persisted for highly educated blacks who are college graduates; they earned 22 percent less than the income received by highly educated whites. The ratios of .77 and .78, respectively, for these pairs of least- and most-educated households among blacks and whites are almost identical (U.S. Bureau of the Census, 1985:447). The diminishing gap in educational achievement between the races has not brought with it equitable employment and earning experiences; inequity that is racially based remains.

## THE QUEST FOR UPWARD MOBILITY

Despite their continuing experience of discrimination, black families are upwardly mobile. During the first half of the 1980s, 9.5 percent of blacks twenty-five-years old and over had graduated from college (compared to 18 percent for the total population), 13 percent of blacks 16 years of age and over were employed as managers and professionals (compared to 22 percent of the total population), and 2.6 percent of black households earned $50,000 or more each year (compared to 10.9 percent of the total population) (U.S. Bureau of the Census, 1985:134, 402, 445).

Education may be conceptualized as an input variable, occupation as a process variable, and income as an output variable. If these three are interrelated, then what one earns is a function of the kind of work one performs. And the kind of work one performs is based on educational attainment. High-level education as an input variable should beget high-level employment as a process variable, which in turn should result in high-level income. Blacks in families lag behind the population at large as participants in the highest levels of educational and occupational attainment; their participation rate is approximately 40 to 50 percent less than others. This means that the proportion of blacks in the highest income level also should be approximately 40 to 50 percent less than that for the population at large. Actually, blacks lag behind others in the proportion who receive highest income by approximately three-quarters. The penalty which blacks experience in reduced numbers who receive the highest income is disproportionate to their participation rate in the highest levels of occupational and educational attainment. This disproportionality is a sign of continuing racial discrimination.

Although the proportion of black families in the first income quintile (the lowest) is twice as great as it should be, and the proportion in the fifth income quintile (the highest) is one-half less than it ought to be—if such families were distributed equally (U.S. Bureau of the Census, 1980:483), blacks nevertheless have made progress as participants in the economy at all income levels. The black population is no longer homogeneously poor.

Some social scientists view with alarm this increasing diversity as having the possibility of polarizing the population. Actually, the opposite is likely to occur. A diversified population is more capable of cooperating and adapting to changing circumstances because of the presence of multiple resources and complementary talents.

From population genetics we learn that "a species [is] polymorphic if it contains a variety of genotypes, each of which is superior in adaptive value to the others . . . in the territory occupied . . . " Moreover, population genetics reveal that "polymorphic populations [are], in general, more efficient in the exploitation of . . . opportunities of an environment than genetically uniform ones . . . (Dobzhansky, 1951:132-133). Thus, the increasing diversity of black families in the United States is not a liability but a sociological asset.

In *Stride Toward Freedom*, Martin Luther King, Jr. described how a diversified black population worked together and eliminated segregated seating in the city public transportation system of Montgomery, Alabama, in the 1950s. He said the mass meetings associated with this movement cut across class lines. They brought together "working people" and "professionals." He described the Montgomery bus boycott by blacks as bringing together "men and women who had been separated from each other by false standards of class." They cooperated with each other in a "common struggle for freedom and human dignity" (King, 1958:86). The struggle continues for black families at all levels of social organization.

## THE EGALITARIAN FAMILY

There is one achievement, however, which black families have in common across all income levels and which is a major contribution to the society at large—the gift of the egalitarian or equalitarian family (Myers, 1982:63).

New family forms are emerging due largely to changing social circumstances. Andrew Billingsley has stated that "the family is a creature of society" (quoted in Myers, 1982:35). The family form in the United States under greatest attack is the patriarchal structure in which the husband-father is the dominant authority. D.H.J. Morgan has stated, "the patriarchal model of family and society is felt to be inappropriate" today (Morgan, 1975:211). "In most American families," according to Hector Myers, "the pattern of authority and power is differentially assumed by husband and wife in different areas, with different issues, and at different times" (Myers, 1982:57).

Blacks have been pioneers in the development of the flexible family form which distributes decision-making authority between husband-father and wife-mother. My own studies of middle-class and working-class black families "confirm the presence of equalitarian decisionmaking" and reject the notion of female-dominated or male-dominated households (Willie, 1983:159). Furthermore, black parents tend to identify with the aspirations of offspring moreso than parents in other families who prefer that offspring not forget customs and conventions of the past (Willie, 1985:154-156, 188-192).

In my study of dominance in the family, I found that a high proportion of nuclear families, among middle-class and working-class blacks were equalitarian in household decision-making (Willie, 1983:158), that the egalitarian pattern of decision-making prevails among whites as well as blacks, but that "more residual practices of matriarchal or patriarchal dominance" are found among whites (Willie, 1983:161). Therefore, the egalitarian family form is a contribution by blacks to American society.

## SUMMARY

*The New York Times* reports that "racial discrimination is a significant contributor to the disproportionate number of blacks in the underclass," but also quotes William Wilson, who states that "If you were able to wave a magic wand, and there was no more racism, the situation of ghetto underclass would not change significantly unless you did something about the economy and communities they live in" (Wilkerson, 1987:26). Walter Allen speculates about whether "there are norms in the black community which encourage marital breakup" (Farley and Allen, 1987:186).

One should determine whether the changing experience of living as married couples or otherwise is similar or different by race. During the span of nearly a quarter of a century (from 1960 to 1983), erosion in the proportion of white households living as couples was down 14 percentage points compared with an erosion of 21 percentage points among blacks (U.S. Bureau of the Census, 1985:41). These erosion rates of one-sixth to one-fifth for the two racial populations during a similar period are not substantially different. Proportionately, if black households were less predisposed to living as married couples during the 1980s than in earlier years, so were whites. Thus, there is little evidence in these statistics of a cultural norm of family breakup that differentiates black and white populations in the United States.

There is ample evidence, however, that family income varies by race, on the one hand, and that family stability correlates positively with household disposable income, on the other hand. A plausible explanation of the different rates of family stability found among blacks and whites, therefore, would seem to be the different economic circumstances experienced by the two racial populations. And their different economic circumstances, according to economist Herman Miller, are due largely to racial discrimination. He said "the average [black] earns less than the average white, even when he has the same years of schooling and does the same kind of work" (Miller, 1964:21).

Well into the 1980s, the median income figures for blacks and whites demonstrated the absence of parity. The median for blacks hovered around 55 percent of that received by whites (U.S. Bureau of the Census, 1985:32). Thus, the difference between the proportion of white families (84.7 percent in 1983) and the proportion of black families (53.4 percent in 1983) who lived in married, two-parent units is probably a function of unequal income rather than different cultural norms.

We know, for example, that affluent households have a higher probability of being two-parent families than poor households. More than three-fourths of black as well as white households in the United States with incomes above $25,000 (in 1983) were husband-wife families. While half of the whites were in the top half of the income range and earned more than $25,000, only one-fourth of blacks had such income (Farley and Allen, 1987:174-175). It is reasonable to assume that if more blacks were in the top half of the economic scale, more would live in two-parent households.

Evidence also shows that a majority of poor whites as well as poor blacks with income below the federal poverty line live in single-parent or single-person households (Farley and Allen, 1987:174-175). However, only 10.6 percent of white persons are poor compared to 34.9 percent of black persons (U.S. Bureau of the Census, 1985:455). Since family instability is associated with low-income status, it is reasonable to assume that a higher proportion of white families than is presently seen would be unstable if a higher proportion of white persons were poor.

## CONCLUSION

On the bases of this analysis, one may conclude that racial discrimination and its negative effects upon the economic status of blacks make a substantial contribution to their higher rate of family instability compared to whites, and that cultural differences, if any, are of limited value in explaining differential rates of family instability among racial populations in the United States.

The black family is undergoing profound change in a society in great flux. We must recognize that—as an institution—the black family is under siege from a dominant culture that is alternately indifferent or hostile.

That black families survive is testimony to their strength, endurance, and adaptability. Survival, however, is not a goal, but a means. The challenge to the black community and the nation at large is to build upon survival strengths and continue to lay the groundwork for black achievement and full participation in all aspects of American life.

# Black Youth at Risk

Bruce R. Hare, Ph.D.

## INTRODUCTION

There comes a period in every person's life when the tasks of moving from childhood dependency to adult independence are to be accomplished. It is ideally at this time that a fusion of mental readiness and structural opportunity makes this passage possible. The continuous and smooth movement of youth from childhood to adulthood, from school to work, from parents' abode to their own abode, is essential both to the future well-being of the individual and society. Thus, it is in the interest of a society, then, to provide its young people *both* the training (aptitude) and the opportunities (structures) necessary to accomplish these tasks.

Were such conditions being optimally accomplished for black youth, they would be demonstrating a pattern of self-development, at the very least commensurate with that of their white and more likely middle class counterparts. They would be raised in psychologically and economically stable homes, successful in school, optimistic about their program and their futures, and successfully transitioning from school to work. They would furthermore as black youth demonstrate patterns of self-discipline, and commitments to self, family, and community, reflecting the legacy of struggle for equity and justice of which they are a part. Such does not, however, appear to be the case. Not only do our youth remain "disadvantaged" as regards other youth, but they are at greater risk than at any other time in recent history. Not only are they being denied their structural opportunity, as reflected in their highest high school drop-out and eviction rates, their lowest college attendance, and their well-beyond fifty percent unemployment rates, but are also reflecting alarming attitudinal formations as well.

These youth reflect a lower sense of control over their destinies and an absence of political and collective consciousness, as would be unfortunately expected of children of the post "civil rights," "black nationalism" eras. They are subsequently short on mentors, and long on rugged individualism. The soaring rates of out-of-wedlock births, "babies having babies" among increasingly younger black girls with irresponsible and abandoning black boys, the rising crime and drug abuse rates, and the increasing violence committed by our youth against each other and our elders also speak to a rising despair and declining discipline among our black youth.

While we recognize the role of dramatic change in the American economy and psychological climate in general that are causal to this shift, we cannot afford to be content with system blame and allow an entire generation of our youth to go down the drain. It is within this context that this detailed analysis of the state of black youth will be undertaken. Such an analysis, however, could not be undertaken in a theoretical vacuum and thus will be accompanied by an analysis of the workings of the American social system and the state of black people within America. Policy recommendations for increasing the life-chances of our youth will be suggested in the conclusion of this chapter.

## OVERVIEW: ON BEING BLACK IN AMERICA

It should be stated from the outset that this overview of the condition of black Americans begins from the premise that it is largely environment, rather than any mystical, within-group, biological, or cultural disorder which is responsible for the overrepresentation of black Americans among the losers in the society. Much as a slave may have been defined as ill- or maladaptive for failing to adjust to slavery, we have failed to adjust to poverty, racism, and discrimination.

For as long as recognition of the "disadvantaged" status of black Americans has existed, an assortment of explanations has been advanced to justify their disproportionate location in the lower slots of the social system. The notion of biological (genetic) inferiority is an example of the "bad genes" explanation for the inferior social position of black Americans. A revised and more liberal, although equally devastating, argument appeared with the emergence of cultural inferiority explanations. This justification of discrimination shifts the blame from the genes of the group to the culture of the group, while subtly retaining a victim-blame focus. While the second explanation does represent a kind of progress, under the assumption that culture can be improved, both perspectives serve to maintain the locus of blame within the group itself, while leaving the system unchallenged. In neither mode has it been posited as a tenable hypothesis that differential attainment is a requirement of the American social order and that processes are operative within the system that increase the probability that black Americans will be disproportionately allocated to the lower slots.

While acknowledging the relative underattainment of black Americans, this writer adopts a third ideological perspective in search of an explanation—that being that the relative academic and economic failure of black Americans in the American social order is functional, if not intended, given racism and the differential distribution of wealth, power, and privilege in the social structure. It is posited that both the biological and cultural explanations serve largely to justify current race, class, and gender inequalities. Furthermore, it is argued that the myth of equal opportunity serves as a smoke screen through which the losers will be led to blame themselves, and be seen by others as getting what they deserve. One might simply ask, for example, how can both inheritance of wealth for some and equal opportunity for all exist in the same social system?

Bowles and Gintis posit that the unequal distribution of wealth, power, and privilege is, and historically has been, the reality of American capitalism and that such a system must produce educational and occupational losers.[1] This writer further argues in what he terms a "class-plus" analysis, with classism as the engine and racism as the caboose, that black Americans have simply been chosen to absorb an unfair share of an unfair burden in a structurally unfair system.

As indicated in Figure 1, our structural determinism approach assumes that the character of the social system is preponderant as the determiner of the hierarchical arrangement of people within it, over either their biological or cultural dispositions. It is further argued that, in addition to the inherent intergenerational inequality caused by inheritance, the educational system, through its unequal skill-giving, grading, routing, and credentialing procedures, plays a critical role in legitimating structural inequality in the American social system. The triangles in Figure 1 represent the following: triangle 1, the assumed hierarchical distribution of intelligence—many low, few high; triangle 2, the assumed similar distribution of cultural readiness; triangle 3, the actual stratifying function of schools—many enter, few make it to the top; and triangle 4, the actual distribution of occupation prestige and power—many low, few high.

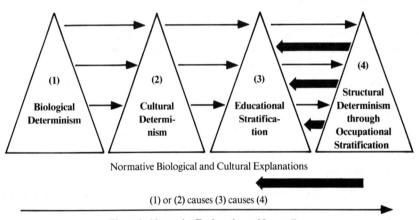

**Figure 1. Alternative Explanations of Inequality**

The biological and cultural deterministic traditions have argued that schools merely respond to innate genetic or cultural differences in ability when they receive and stratify youngsters. The occupational structure is further assumed simply to respond to the schools when it slots people into hierarchical positions on the bases of credentials and skills given in schools. The structural argument goes from right to left instead of left to right, and charges that the social system needs people to replenish its ranks at all levels of skill and credentials, and that in producing such differences the schools respond to structural needs rather than innate differences. It is further assumed that such ascribed characteristics as one's race, sex, and social-class background deliver differential treatment, consequently increasing the probability of lower educational attainment and lower occupational placement among people of color, women, and people of lower-class origin. The amount of inequality explained by biology or culture becomes notably minor in such an analysis, since such a system would theoretically be compelled to stratify a population of identical culture and biological characteristics.

The March 1986 issue of *Crisis* presents a series of dire statistics on black youth. For example, it was reported that "86% of Black youth live in poverty . . . , 1 out of every 22 Black American males will be killed by violent crime . . ., 51% of violent crime in the U.S. is committed by Black youth . . . , 1 out of every six Black males will be arrested by the time they reach 19 . . ., 40% of Black children are being raised in fatherless homes."[2] The magazine also puts the current high-school dropout rate at 72 percent. Given the structural issues presented, and the already known precarious state of the adults, one might wonder specifically how a people of equal innate childhood potential arrive at such a disadvantaged youth status. To be sure, early indicators do exist in the over 45 percent unemployment rate of black youth, but the process of structuring differential perceptions, access, and attainment among black youngsters is begun early on.

The cornerstone of the health of an adult is the capacity to take care of one's own, and one's own self. The mechanism through which this task is made possible is employment. As we enter 1988, not only do black Americans remain twice as likely to be unemployed as whites, but when they are employed they can expect to hold lower-status positions and to be paid less even if holding the same occupational positions as their white counterparts. The social and psychological consequences of job discrimination remain enormous both for the individuals and the relationships within the community and its families.

## ENVIRONMENTAL INFLUENCES

### The Role of Home

Ideally, the homes in which black children would blossom would consist of stable and successful parents who were capable of meeting their material and spiritual needs, providing discipline, and interceding on their behalf in the outside worlds of school, work, and community. They would be parents who would confidently challenge the school to teach their children. They would do the kinds of things that would facilitate their children's learning, such as reading to them, helping them with their homework, rewarding their successes, and exposing them to experiences and the world of knowledge. In short, such parents would provide their children with a safe, secure, and protected environment in which they would flourish with positive role models and develop both the skills and optimism necessary for a successful future.

While there are many black youth who, in fact, are blessed with such conditions, a significantly larger number find themselves in quite the opposite situation. It is important to emphasize that the existence of some privileged black individuals, be they children or adults, does not contradict or deny the aggregate endangered status of the black community as a whole. Black youth are four times more likely than their white counterparts to grow up in a poor household and are as likely to grow up in a one-parent household as not. They are, therefore, at high risk of exposure to the kinds of family instability and turmoil associated with deprivation. In such circumstances, they are also more likely to fall victim to child abuse, inadequate nutrition, poor health care, drugs, crime, and material deprivation. They are more likely to live in below-par crowded quarters, with relatives other than their biological parents, and in foster care. Given such possibilities as these, it is a wonder that they survive and thrive as well as they do. Fortunately, indicators are that they are loved and feel loved, but there is no denying that many black youth must also suffer the consequences of the pressure under which they and their parents live.

The significant absence of fathers both as successful role models and partners in the socialization of the youth is likely to have profound, although different, effects on both boys and girls. For example, there is evidence that this absence of fathers may be partially causal to reported differences in academic achievement, favoring black girls over black boys. Allen[3] suggests that since black parents are role models for their children and are harder on their same-sex children, the boys lose both the model and disciplinarian. Lewis reports that black mothers are in fact harder disciplinarians on their daughters.[4] Thus, to the extent that adolescent development requires boys to break from their mother's control, the absence of fathers is posited to contribute significantly to a loss of control as well as the increased probability that such boys will also reject school and be recruitable to, and controlled by, exploitive males of the peer and street cultures.

To the extent that poor, young girls see their mothers coping "successfully" as single parents, they may be led to believe that they can do the same. In fact, Mayfield[5] suggests "motherhood" as a road to recognized adult status. The rapid rise in the "illegitimacy" rate among young black girls, which is as high as 50 percent in some cities, who are literally abandoned by their children's young fathers and left to rear their children in poverty, speaks to the seriousness of this issue. It is worth emphasizing that acknowledging these negative possibilities neither denies existing strengths of black families nor removes the system from its responsibility for creating the conditions that are causal to these patterns. The fact, however, remains that socialization and control problems do exist among black youth, and particularly poor black youth.

*The Role of School*

It has been said that schools are places that people attend most and know the least about. Education to black Americans remains the symbolic key to advancement. The historic 1954 Supreme Court decision[6] declaring segregated schools inherently unequal represented what many hoped would be the turning point. Many believed it would bring an end to inferior education. However, over thirty years later the dream of the *Brown* decision remains to be realized, particularly in our cities. The underlying desegregation notions, that sprinkling a few black children in a predominantly white school would not depreciate the assumed higher quality of education and that sprinkling a few white children in a predominantly black school would appreciate the quality, are both racist and questionable. However, the fact that the wait for desegregation has allowed for significant "in the meantime" declines in predominantly black urban school systems is unquestionable. The education of our youth in urban systems has largely become an exercise in social control and babysitting by outsiders.

While much has been written about the achievement gaps between blacks and other ethnic groups on standardized tests, as through suggestions concerning the innate ability and motivational problems of the youngsters, less has been offered about the possible role of the school and teachers in the creation and forwarding of such differences. Nevertheless, there exists a body of literature on teacher expectations and differential treatment of children of different characteristics that might shed alternative light on the causes of these achievement differences.[7]

While conventional wisdom would have us believe that every child begins the greater quest for status at the same starting line, with the same track shoes, with only aptitude determining placement at the finishing line, there is ample evidence to suggest that such egalitarian theories are myths and distortions of facts. For example, Cicourel and Kitsuse, examining the egalitarian assumption in a study of educational decision makers, concluded that quite the opposite is true. They reported that their research "supports the view that the student's progress in this sequence of transitions is contingent upon the student's biography, social and personal adjustment, appearance and demeanor, social class, and 'social type' as well as his demonstrated ability and performance," and they concluded that "the professed ideal of equal access to educational opportunities for those of equal ability is not necessarily served by such procedures"[8]. Lavin, in a study on predicting academic performance, concluded, "some evidence suggests that implicit subjective criteria are involved in teacher grading practices. We refer here to the possibility that certain characteristics of the student, such as his sex and social class background, affect the quality of the relationship between the student and the teacher."[9]

Katz concludes, in an analytic study of teacher attitude, that "the meaning of these teacher differences is that on the average, children from low income homes, most of whom are Negro, get more than their fair share of classroom exposure to teachers who really are unqualified for their role, who basically resent teaching them, and who therefore behave in ways that foster, in the more dependent students, tendencies toward debilitating, self-criticism."[10]

While older research has attempted to attribute the lower attainment of black youth to low self-esteem, more recent studies, when controlling for economic background, have found no significant race differences in general or area-specific (school, peer, and home) self-esteem. Nevertheless, consistent with the hypothesis of differential treatment, achievement differences remain even when economic background is controlled.[11]

As previously noted, the school plays a unique role in allocating people to different positions in the division of labor through routing and grading practices. Relative success in school is, in fact, the major avenue through which discrimination in the job market is justified. Given racism as well as sexism and classism in a stratified America, it has been posited that the disproportional allocation of black Americans, women, and people of lower-class origin to the lowest labor slots is functional, and that their relative academic failure is essential to getting the job done. For example, such procedures as differentially allocating girls to home economics and sewing courses, lower-class youngsters to slower tracts, and black children to compensatory programs are common school practices with long-term educational and occupational implications. Thus, it is argued that structured educational failure legitimizes job discrimination while eliminating legal recourse— one cannot successfully sue an employer for failing to give a desired job if one arrives relatively unqualified.

It should be noted that such a process does not require a conscious conspiracy to operate, rather it is posited that Newton's law of inertia regarding material objects is also applicable to notions. Begging the issue of origins, continuing educational discriminatory practices merely require that school personnel, like other people, act on socialized unconscious beliefs in established stereotypes, which then have the capacity to become self-fulfilling prophecies. Such a process requires a conspiracy to stop, not to continue.[12] There is little reason to assume that if such processes and attitudes exist in the general culture, they would not be operative in the schools. The fact that the schools simultaneously homogenize attitudes while differentiating skills increases the probability that the youngsters themselves will accept their outcomes as the consequence of their own attributes or deficiencies.

This discussion, while not denying the existence of achievement gaps, has attempted to offer a structural alternative to conventional victim-blame type explanations. Such a notion appears not at all inconsistent with reported findings of gross race differences in academic achievement.

## The Role of Peers

As early as pre-adolescence, black children show a trend toward higher peer self-esteem than white children, and higher ratings of the importance of such social abilities as being popular and good at sports and games. The fact that they do not differ from white children in general self-esteem or home self-esteem, but tend toward lower school self-esteem, as well as significantly lower standardized reading and mathematics performance, suggests that a shift from school to peers may already be beginning to take place.[13]

It may be theorized that as black children age and progressively lose in school evaluations, they may shift toward peer evaluations in search of higher possibilities of success and ego enhancement. As stated by Castenell in a study of area-specific achievement motivation, if an adolescent is "discouraged by significant others, or through repeated failure, to perceive achievement (as possible) within the school environment, then that adolescent may choose to achieve in another arena."[14] Cummings and others have reported evidence that as black children grow older, their values are more influenced by peers than by other groups, and that the maintenance of ego and self-respect increasingly requires peer solidarity.[15] These authors further support the possible existence of a progressive shift in motivation and attachment from the school to the peers among black youth, and particularly poor black youth. What is more important, they suggest that such a shift is a logical pursuit of "achievement" and positive strokes, and a flight from failure and ego-damaging experiences. Since the benefits are short-term, in that they are unlikely to pay off in the adult occupational structure, the black adolescent peer culture may also be viewed as a long-term "wash-out" arena although a short-term achievement arena.

Consistent with Castenell's area-specific achievement motivation notion, Maehr and Lysy question traditional restricted cultural and academic notions of achievement motivation.[16] They posit that contextual conditions are important in expressions of achievement motivations, and that the particular form in which achievement is expressed is determined by the definition that culture gives to it. They further indicate that their definition suggests that motivation is manifest in a broad range of activities, and that motivational questions are ultimately about the ways in which, rather than whether, people are motivated. In some communities, such abilities as mastering street-wiseness, playground sports, sexuality, domestic and childrearing chores, supplementing family income, and taking on other aspects of adult roles at an early age provide youths opportunities to demonstrate competence. It should be noted that although the larger culture views these patterns as maladaptive and strange, they are, within the cultural milieu, perfectly realistic, adaptive, and respected responses to reality.

The black youth peer culture may be regarded as a long-term failure arena because even though it succeeds in providing alternative outlets for achievement through the demonstration of competence, as through street, athletic, and social activities, it offers little hope of long-term legitimate success. It carries the real dangers of drafting young people into the self-destructive worlds of drugs, crime, and sexual promiscuity. The notion of "peer solidarity," with its oppositional flavor, also suggests an anti-intellectual strain between the peers and the schooling experience. It should be emphasized, however, that it is more likely that the collectively negative schooling experiences of black youth produce this anti-school sentiment than the reverse, and that to whatever degree such a sentiment does exist within the culture, it is dependent upon the schools to produce the negative experiences that feed it new recruits.

In summary, given the presence of negative schooling experiences, the availability of positive peer experiences, and the inability of youth to perceive the long-term consequences of adolescent decisions, many of these youth can be said to be making what appears to them to be a logical decision in shifting from the school to the peers. In the long run, of course, they are disproportionately excluded from legitimate occupational success possibilities. They are also subsequently blamed, as adults, for the consequences of school-system-induced self-protection decisions made during adolescence. In this context, the rising crime, drug, and out-of-wedlock pregnancy rates among black youth may be seen as a consequence of the interplay of negative schooling experiences as provided by incompetent outsiders, a decline of parental control, and a significant rise in the independence of an attractive peer culture which offers positive strokes and ego-enhancement to a vulnerable population.

*The Political Context*

The political context in which these youth are found is quite different from what it was twenty years ago. The era of "black nationalism" and "civil rights" is not a conscious part of their experience and they are consequently deprived of the kinds of political socialization that was available to those of us who grew up prior to and during the era of Martin Luther King, Jr., and Malcolm X. They are more likely to blame themselves for their condition in the absence of political mentors, and less likely to understand the workings of the American social system. This knowledge void is further enhanced by youth attendance in schools we do not control in which they will more likely be taught "his-story" rather than "our-story." Since we provide no alternative structured ways for them to come to know, they are also likely to believe what they are taught. The absence of movements has also served to deny these youth the opportunity to develop the sense of community and "collective consciousness" that provided ego-protection enhancement and a sense of mission to many of us who were aware in the sixties. Such movements not only provided a shift from self-blame to system-blame, but also encouraged doing something about the group condition.

The consequences of the absence of such leadership and movements cannot be overestimated, since such spokespersons and actions provide a "redefinition of the situation" to the population, along with increased racial pride, discipline, and willingness to work collectively toward problem resolution. Not only was this true in the political arena proper, but was true of other community-effecting institutions as well.

Black music, for example, which used to give our youth such collective political messages as, "Say it loud, I'm Black and I'm proud," now instead provides such individualistic messages as "I'm bad, I'm bad, you know it." The black church, which has historically been a fertile source of child socialization, leadership, and moral development appears to have slipped in its ability to generate community solidarity and progressive leadership. Black business remains largely what E. Franklin Frazier[17] described as an economic myth, as regards its ability to employ a significant number of black people, and willingness to play a philanthropic role in the community. The black press appears less willing to fill the information void regarding the true state of the community than it is in forwarding gossip and sensationalism. If the black church can be accused of deferring gratification more than raising indignation, the black press can be accused of providing vicarious living experiences through the presentation of the lifestyles of selected "successful" blacks, most of whom are either athletes or entertainers.

This assessment is not intended to romanticize the sixties, but merely to describe the probable declines in community activism and responsibility and their likely effect on this coming generation.

*On Mass Media Intrusion*

There is an undeniable symbolic truth to George Orwell's prediction in *1984*. His error simply resided in direction when he predicted that "big brother" is watching you. The truth is that you are watching "big brother"! The average eighteen-year-old today has watched approximately 22,000 hours of television and 350,000 commercials. Aside from the exploitation of youthful insecurities by commercials, creating diseases to sell cures, such as perpetuating the need to "relax" one's hair, prevent chapped lips, and wear designer jeans, the tube serves to condition the population. Television tells youth what to want, whom to like, how to be, and what to think. It romanticizes greed, crime, infidelity, materialism, and individualism. Furthermore, it not only provides white America with distorted images of black people and black communities, but creates gross misconceptions of the world for black America as well. While comic treatment of whites on the tube is counterbalanced by serious treatment, it is hard for a viewer to conclude that the black family, for example, is anything other than a joke. It creates people who confuse reality and illusion, desensitizes people to violence, and programs all populations to a pro-male, white, and upper-class imitation pattern.

To be sure the occasional presentations of serious black programs and sporadic appearances of uniquely talented black personalities do occur, but the dominant message to black youth remains illusionary possibilities of star status as through athletics or entertainment. For example, the futility of such programmed aspirations as star status in the NBA (National Basketball Association) or NFL (National Football League) was aptly indicated by sociologist Harry Edwards, when he noted that black youth were twice as likely to be hit by a star (a falling meteorite) as they were to become one in professional sports. For the less athletic and talented, even more bizarre possibilities, such as adoption by a nice rich white man are offered. One might wonder what such program exposure does to condition young black children toward obedience to white men. Most importantly, however, one might simply wonder what else might have been done to, or for, a mind, had it not spent this amount of time (22,000 hours) sitting in front of the tube.

The point here is that, however subtle, the television is the most massive programming and socializing instrument ever created, and cannot be expected to do anything more than deactivate our youth.

While it is probably true that television previously served to bring the news of marches, protests, and rallies, etc., into the home and the American conscience, it appears that the lesson has been learned and such events are intentionally being played down, if covered at all. The management of news has become more sophisticated and a shift from straight news to sensationalistic entertainment is evident. The danger of television raising consciousness is declining.

The American population generally, and the black population specifically, have yet to measure or understand the degree to which this new television generation has been affected. People have only begun to investigate, for example, the connection between television crime and street crime, and even less has been done to assess the long-term consequences of television addiction for interaction skills or moral development. It is clear, however, that we do not control the tube and thus are surely giving strangers access to our children's minds when we fail to police their watching habits.

## On Street Models

To the extent that role models are significant, poor black youth run a high probability of exposure to successful participants in what has been called "the underground economy." While short on doctors, lawyers, engineers, and other legitimized professionals to emulate, they are differentially exposed to numbers runners, drug dealers, pimps, prostitutes, and other assortments of creative and innovative characters with apparent money, cars, and fine clothes. To the extent that models of legitimate success become unavailable, and legitimate opportunities become scarce, these youth also become vulnerable to and recruitable to such activities. This becomes even more likely when one further considers that the professionals working in their communities such as teachers, police, fire fighters, etc., are not likely to live there, and that their local religious and political leaders are also less likely to have meaningful contact with them.

Thus black youth can be said to be in a community context that is simultaneously less effective in protecting, organizing, and socializing them, while more vulnerable to negative influences. The combined facts of mass media intrusion, an absence of control over local schools, and exposure to alternative lifestyles, provide increased opportunity for our youth to be programmed contrary to our, or their, interests.

## The Psychology of Social Control

As pointed out long ago by Carter G. Woodson[18], when you control a man's thinking you do not have to worry about his actions. One does not have to accept the Grier and Cobbs[19] or Kardiner and Ovesey[20] arguments of self-hatred to acknowledge that *living under constant psychological and material abuse does have its price.* For example, some black people are successfully socialized into internalizing negative messages about themselves. Others are brought to believe what is said about the group is true, while viewing themselves as the exception.

Still others, in over-zealous defense of the group, deny that there is any effect on any group members. Just as it would be unwise to claim nothing wrong with the lower-class black family, and thereby remove the system from any responsibility for the economic strains such families suffer, it would be foolish to fail to acknowledge the special pressures affecting black people. As indicated, rather than denying effects, we relocate the causes from the group to the system, while simultaneously recognizing both our responsibilities and societal responsibilities for change.

The combination of racism, an economically "deprived" and psychologically hostile environment, and negative schooling experience is bound to have profoundly negative effect on the psychological and academic adjustment of these black youth. Amazingly, however, they are also creative and talented in the development of survival skills, and in utilizing mechanisms to protect and enhance their self-imagery even if it means the reorganization of self-definition. They are therefore capable of change and can be saved. It is toward this last capability that we must direct our energies. It is in this context that the following policy recommendations are offered.

**POLICY RECOMMENDATIONS**

(1) *Inform the Black Communities* and others concerned of the true endangered status of the youth. In addition to meetings, utilization of mass media (television, press, radio, etc.) should be sought.

(2) *Work with Other Organizations, Community Groups, and Parents* to organize programs to assist the youth in developing:

- a stronger sense of self-worth and self-discipline and commitment to academic achievement.
- a stronger sense of commitment to family.
- a stronger sense of commitment to local community.
- a stronger sense of commitment to the general black community.
- a stronger sense of connectedness to all other oppressed people.

(3) *Work with Black Business Persons, Politicians, Clergy, etc.*
to provide opportunities for black youth to be exposed to mentors and role models, as well as to understand the workings of business, government, etc.

(4) *Provide Organized Collective Activities for Youth*
the black church, for example, might prove an excellent location for the recreational, educational, and political socialization of our youth.

(5) *Develop Mechanisms of Accountability* for black professional business persons, politicians, clergy, etc.

(6) *Organize and Demand of the Federal Government:*
a) Enforcement of our rights in general.
b) Services delivery, such as health care, housing, employment, and child nutrition programs.

c) Voting rights protection.

d) Civil rights protection.

(7) *Organize and Demand of Local Government:*

   a) Quality education for our youth, as distinguished from but not as opposed to desegregated education.

   b) Services delivery, such as better drug enforcement, police service, sanitation service, fire protection, housing code enforcement, etc.

(8) *Organize, Register, and Vote*

   Such an analysis and action list is not intended to be all inclusive, but does represent a possible point of departure. It acknowledges our as well as the system's responsibilities, and suggests the need to move ahead collectively for ourselves, for oppressed peoples, and, most importantly, for our youth.

## CONCLUDING REMARKS

Given the inequality-reproducing structure of the social system, there are limits to the amount of progress we can expect to make short of radical change. There are reforms, however, that can be pursued in order to decrease the probability that black youth will continue to suffer disproportionately as "class-plus" victims in a racist class system.

We must assist youth to organize, and in some cases to reorganize, in such a way as to maximize their self-image, self-discipline, and attainment. As previously indicated, it would seem that the black church would be an ideal site for the academic and political socialization of our youth. It is through such institutions that other ethnic groups have guaranteed the moral and political socialization of their youth necessary to the integrity and continuance of the community. This task becomes increasingly important for groups who are not in charge of the schools their youngsters attend. We must be aware, however, that to raise the expectations and efforts of black youth without also placing additional pressures on the institutions, agencies, and individuals (particularly teachers) who serve them would be grossly unfair. We must, in fact, seek better control of the environment in which our youth are located. If we do not, we may well not only have wasted human resources but also created an increasing population of embittered and dangerous adults.

# Crime In The Black Community

Lee P. Brown, Ph.D.

## INTRODUCTION

Over two decades ago, the President's Commission on Law Enforcement and Administration of Justice sounded the warning that "There is much crime in America, more than ever is reported, far more than is ever solved, far too much for the health of the nation."[1] In 1987, crime continues to be a pervasive problem for American society. In one way or another, crime touches every American.

Although crime affects the lives of all Americans, there is no question that black Americans suffer disproportionately from it. Even so, it has only been recently that crime in the black community has reached the level of national debate and concern. Illustrative of this is the fact that in 1976, the National Urban League devoted a major session at its annual conference to the issue of crime in the black community. The following year, it began an in-depth analysis and evaluation of the criminal justice system nationwide. In 1980 the issue of crime received separate coverage in the League's *The State of Black America,* an annual publication. Today, the problem of crime has far-reaching implications for black communities. It is for that reason crime is currently viewed as one of the most pressing problems confronting black Americans.

Historically, Americans have adjusted their lives around crime. A visit to any urban community will show the various degrees to which security-minded people will enslave themselves in their search for safety. Their homes resemble fortresses. Apartment complexes now install television cameras and intercom systems. Public buses and delivery trucks display signs warning "Driver Does Not Carry Cash." Taxicabs have thick glass or caging wire installed to separate the driver from the passenger. The clothing industry has even advanced the idea of adopting the application of bulletproof vests to everyday wear. Clearly, the quality of life in America, and particularly its black communities, has diminished because of the problem of crime and the fear it generates.

Traditionally, Americans have relied on the criminal justice system as its primary response to the crime problem. Locally, jurisdictions have added more resources to their police departments. This is followed by the allocation of more resources to the office of the prosecutor and the courts. States, in turn, have significantly increased their prison capacity. Despite the annual infusion of billions of dollars into the system for the administration of justice, crime continues to be a major problem.

The purpose of this article is to place into proper perspective the problem of crime as it impacts the black community and suggest a more effective way of addressing it. Inherent in this article is the understanding that the system for the administration of justice alone cannot effectively address the crime problem. Rather, as steps are taken, as they must be, to address the problem of crime in the black community, it is essential to recognize that the other issues of economic, political, educational, and social concerns as discussed in other chapters in this publication, have a direct bearing on the problem of crime.

## BACKGROUND

Long before the emergence of modern society, crime plagued the peoples of the world. The first American settlers faced crime as did their countrymen who remained behind in the Old World. As long as there have been human beings on this planet, there have been murder, rape, assault, and theft; only the volume and types of crime committed and the degree to which the public views crime as a threat to its well-being have changed over the years.

The crime rate in the United States — especially the rate of violent crime — remains at an alarming level. Compared with other Western nations, U.S. citizens are three times more likely to be raped and six times more likely to be robbed than are West German citizens.[2] In 1981, the robbery rate for Great Britain was about 20 offenses for every 10,000 persons. For the United States, the rate was nearly four times as high.[3] In 1980, the number of homicides per 100,000 people was 9.2 in the United States as compared with 1.4 for West Germany, 1.3 for Denmark, 1.2 for Sweden, 0.8 for the United Kingdom and 0.8 for the Netherlands.[4]

In terms of the severity of crime, America is said to resemble some of the most volatile Third World countries rather than other developed Western societies. From 1969 through 1983, for example, the rate for violent crimes rose 61 percent nationwide. Rape went up 82 percent, robbery 44 percent, and homicide 14 percent.[5] In 1985, a crime-risk index developed by the federal Bureau of Justice Statistics showed that about three percent of Americans each year are the victims of violent crime. This percentage represents about six million victims.[6]

In calculating personal victimization rates, the Bureau of Justice Statistics estimates that five out of six Americans will be the victims of rape, robbery, or assault, either attempted or completed, at least once during their lifetimes.[7] Equally disturbing was their finding that almost half of the American population will be the victims of violent crime more than once.[8]

With respect to property crimes, the study showed that nearly every American will be the victim of personal theft at least once during their lifetime and seven out of eight persons will become victims three or more times.[9] The same study showed that over a 20-year period almost three out of four households in America will be burglarized and nine out of ten will be the victims of larceny.[10]

Crime is now one of the major problems confronting both large cities and small towns throughout the country. Crime results in fear, despair, and hardship among many Americans. However, crime, similar to many other social ills, is not evenly distributed and has a disproportional impact on the nation's black communities. Unless steps are taken to address this problem, it will only get worse. The steps that must be taken, as will be pointed out in this article, must represent a clear commitment on the part of this nation to address the ills that create the deplorable conditions that result in the factors that produce the "haves" and the "have nots". Otherwise, 10, 15, or 20 years from now we will still be addressing the problem of crime in the black community as one of the most pressing problems facing America.

Today, we find that many Americans share the common misconception that black communities across the country—especially those populated by the poor—are plagued by crime and violence and, therefore, "out of control." The media and various social institutions often reinforce this idea, as do the personal experiences of people who live or work in black neighborhoods. But in reality, all too often, the residents and businesses in America's black communities have been the prey of a handful of criminals whose actions debilitate neighborhoods. As a result, outsiders and residents alike view many black neighborhoods as crime turfs and many of the people who live there as criminals. However, such is not the case. The vast majority of persons who live in predominantly black neighborhoods are law-abiding citizens who take pride in their neighborhoods. They are citizens who want to enjoy a high quality of life. They are citizens who want peace and security in the community. Yet, their aspirations are hindered by those few who prey on the innocent. This is evidenced by crime figures prepared by the Bureau of Justice Statistics regarding crime in central cities and the persons who commit crime. These crime figures show that black neighborhoods are disproportionately affected by the problem of crime as indicated by the following.[11]

- The victimization rates for violent crime and theft are highest for residents of central cities;
- Urban households are more likely than suburban or rural households to be the victims of forcible entries;
- Victims of crime are more likely to be black than white, or a member of some other racial group;
- The violent crime rate is highest for young black males; and
- Blacks are overrepresented as victims as well as offenders.

Taken together, the above information provides a clear summary of the problem of crime in the black community. What follows is a more detailed analysis of just how crime impacts the black community.

**THE CRIME PROBLEM**

Resolution of the problem of crime in the black community must begin with an understanding of crime as it relates to blacks in the United States. At the core of this understanding is the extent of crime and its effects on black Americans.

The three basic measures of crime in the United States are the Uniform

Crime Reports (UCR) published by the Federal Bureau of Investigation (FBI), the inmate surveys conducted by the Justice Department's Bureau of Justice Statistics, and the criminal victimization survey conducted by the U.S. Department of Justice in conjunction with the U.S. Census Bureau. These sources provide nationwide data on arrests, imprisonment, and victimization.

*Arrests*

In 1986, blacks comprised approximately 12 percent of the United States population. Yet, during that year blacks accounted for 27 percent of all arrests reported to the FBI, 33.7 percent of all index crime arrests as defined by the Uniform Crime Reports,[12] 46.5 percent of all arrests for violent crimes, and 30.2 percent of all arrests for property crimes. Of the persons arrested for murder in 1986, blacks accounted for 48 percent of the total. That same year, blacks accounted for 46.6 percent of all arrests for rape, 62 percent of all arrests for robbery, 39.8 percent for assault, 29.5 percent for burglary, 30.1 percent for theft, and 34.7 percent for auto theft.[13]

The FBI also calculates all arrests that are made in cities throughout the nation. In respect to city arrests, blacks accounted for 30.8 percent of the total arrests made in 1986. Of the number of city arrests made for violent crimes (murder, forcible rape, robbery, and aggravated assault) that year, blacks accounted for almost half (49.5 percent), and 34.3 percent for property offenses (burglary, larceny, theft, motor theft, and arson).[14]

With respect to persons under 18 years of age who were arrested, blacks made up 25.1 percent of the total arrests made in 1986. In addition, blacks accounted for 54.9 percent of those under 18 who were arrested for violent crimes, 27.1 percent for property offenses, and 30.3 percent of all index crimes during 1986.[15]

*Incarceration*

The number of blacks in prisons, as compared to the number of blacks in the population, is a second method of assessing crime and its relationship to Afro-Americans. The latest prisoner survey, which was conducted on December 31, 1984, showed that there was a total of 462,422 prisoners in state and federal institutions. Of that number, 209,673, or 45 percent, were black.[16] With respect to federal institutions, 10,786 out of a total population of 34,263 were black, constituting 31 percent.[17] Out of the 428,179 prisoners in state institutions, 198,887 or 46 percent were black.[18] As of June 30, 1984, 40 percent of all jail inmates throughout the nation were black.[19] A similar situation exists for black youth. On February 1, 1985, 18,269 (61 percent) out of a total of 29,969 juveniles held in public facilities were black.[20]

On March 1, 1987, there was a total of 1,874 prisoners under sentence of death. Of that number, 777 or 42 percent were black.[21]

*Victimization*

A third way of assessing crime in the black community is to look at victimization rate surveys. Those surveys reveal the following:

- While whites are more vulnerable to personal theft, blacks are more vulnerable than whites to violent crime.[22]
- A higher percentage of black households than white or other minority households are touched by crime.[23]
- Blacks have the highest victimization rates for rape, robbery, and assault.[24]
- Blacks are more likely to be victims of violent crime than whites or members of other racial groups.[25]
- Young black males have the highest violent crime rates.[26]
- Based on the number of vehicles owned, black heads of households were victims of motor vehicle theft at a higher rate than whites or members of other minority groups.[27]
- Most violent crimes against blacks were committed by black offenders (84 percent).[28]
- Of all black households in 1985, 27 percent had been touched by crime. Two years later, black households continue to be more vulnerable than whites for violent crime (5.4 percent vs. 4.6 percent), burglary (7.6 percent vs. 5 percent), and theft in and around the home (9.1 percent vs. 7.9 percent).[29]

The chances of a person, black or white, being the victim of crime is directly related to family income: The lower the income, the greater the chances of victimization. As for specific types of crime, the typical American has a 1-in-133 chance of being murdered. However, for black males the chances are 1 in 21.[30]

The leading cause of death among black males between the ages of 15 and 24 years of age is homicide. Approximately 42 per 100,000 blacks between the ages of 15-24 die from homicide. This compares with about eight per 100,000 whites in the same age group. The victimization rate for blacks aged 25 to 44 also is especially high. For nearly all age groups, however, homicide victimization rates do not differ significantly even though there are considerably fewer blacks than whites nationwide.[31]

As can be readily seen from the preceding statistics, crime is indeed a serious problem for black Americans, and poses one of the greatest threats to the well-being of the black community. There are no simplistic answers to this complex problem. In fact, the problem of crime in the black community is complicated by many other problems. Currently, one of the most severe of those other problems is drugs.

### The Drug Problem

There is very little reliable information on the exact extent of drug use in the black community. Anyone who lives or works in the black community, however, can attest to the presence and magnitude of the problem. In the minds of many, the problem of drug abuse in the black community represents the number-one problem confronting that community. The problem is viewed in some black communities as being so pervasive that some social analysts have suggested that a large part of an entire generation will be lost to the drug cancer. Clearly, drug abuse is at epidemic levels in many segments of the black community.

Combatting the drug problem is complicated because drugs are big business in America. It has been estimated that illegal drugs constitute an estimated $110 billion-a-year industry. Thus, for many there is a strong economic incentive to see drugs consumed in the community.

Because drugs constitute such a major and serious problem in the black community, it deserves separate treatment as was the case in last year's edition of *The State of Black America.*[32] For purposes of this article, it is being succinctly discussed because it is so closely tied to the crime problem in the black community. Clearly, illegal drug use is either directly or indirectly related to much of the crime that plagues the black community.

According to a 1986 National Institute on Drug Abuse study of drug-related deaths in 27 metropolitan areas across the country, blacks accounted for 25 percent of the victims.[33] Also, according to the League's report on *The State of Black America,* blacks are disproportionately represented among person's estimated to be abusers of alcohol or drugs relative to their numbers in the U.S. population.[34] That report also noted the following:[35]

- Blacks and Hispanics are more likely to be intravenous drug users, leading to a higher incidence of AIDS in some minority communities.
- Of black drug users 25 years of age and younger, 8.2 percent prefer heroin, 68.5 percent prefer marijuana, 47.4 percent prefer PCP, and 31 percent prefer cocaine. Blacks over the age of 25, in contrast, rank heroin as the drug of choice (91.8 percent). Sixty-nine percent prefer cocaine, 52.6 percent prefer PCP, and 31.5 percent prefer marijuana.
- Of black clients who said at the time of admission to a treatment facility in 1983 that heroin abuse was their problem, 31 percent reported a secondary problem with cocaine. This percentage is three times greater than the percentage of white clients who reported the same primary and secondary drug problems.
- Twenty-seven percent of the black clients admitted for drug treatment listed freebasing, or the inhalation of cocaine, as the mode of choice for ingesting the drug. This compares with five percent of the white clients who chose freebasing as the preferred way to use cocaine. Freebasing is considered the most detrimental method of ingesting cocaine because of the method's ability to facilitate addiction.

The current epidemic of drugs in the black community, particularly teenage drug use, has added a new dimension to the crime problem. Not only is there a variety of longstanding factors that are believed to be the cause of criminal behavior, the community is now confronted with the problem of drug abuse and the knowledge that it is a major contributing factor to the high incidence of crime.

## EFFECTS OF CRIME ON THE BLACK COMMUNITY

All available criteria result in the same conclusion: crime is a serious and prevalent problem in the black community and cannot be rationalized nor minimized by denying it exists. Neither can the full extent of the problem be captured in statistics alone. As bleak as the statistical data are, they paint only one part of the crime picture. Another part of the crime tragedy in the black community is what it does to black neighborhoods and the people who live or work there. In addition to the human suffering inflicted by crimes of violence and monetary losses from theft of property, the fear of crime is an equally menacing problem. This element of the crime tragedy does not result from isolated incidents perpetrated against a few vulnerable individuals or businesses. Rather, the fear of crime stems from the fact that it is widespread and is unraveling the very fabric of life in the black community.

*Fear of Crime*

We know from *The Figgie Report on Fear of Crime* that four out of 10 Americans reported a major fear of certain crimes. Also, four out of 10 did not feel safe in their own environment.[36] In many black neighborhoods, fear already has taken its toll. Businesses, restaurants, and home owners have retreated to the suburbs; their departure has accelerated the economic isolation of urban black neighborhoods. Left behind are closed businesses, abandoned properties, and vacant houses—an environment that attracts criminal elements. The results of such a situation can be seen in the following:
- A senior citizen is afraid to walk to the store during the daytime, afraid that a black youth, who grew up in the neighborhood, will rob him.
- An elderly black woman is afraid to go to church on Sunday because she fears someone will break into her home and *again* steal her possessions.
- Mothers are worried about their young children who must walk past a "dope" house on their way to and from school.

Clearly, crime and the fear of crime are having a major psychological impact on the black community. The fear of crime saps the strength of that community and weakens its social fabric. The fear of crime is destroying some of the basic elements that make up a society: the freedom to walk the streets, the freedom to feel secure in the home, and the freedom to have peace of mind.

*Economic Impact*

It is difficult if not impossible to determine precisely the economic impact crime has on the black community. In addressing this concern, however, it must be recognized that crime is generally intra-racial in nature. This can be seen in crimes of violence, where 84 percent of such crimes against blacks are committed by blacks.[37] This is also the case in many property offenses and, as a result, households headed by blacks have a higher rate of victimization than whites or other minorities.[38] The economic impact of crime on the black community can be seen in the following observations:

- Businesses close and leave the neighborhood because of crime.
- Residents of the black neighborhoods have to pay more for the items they purchase because the cost of thefts is passed on to the consumer.
- Black-owned businesses operating in the black community make less money because of crime.
- Many black-owned businesses must close because they cannot afford to pay high insurance rates.
- Black-owned businesses that do remain in the community earn less money because they must pay higher insurance premiums.
- As businesses leave the black community because of crime, blacks lose jobs.

The above observations do not address the full extent of the economic impact crime has on the black community. They do not consider the economic impact the high rate of incarceration has on the family. They do not address the loss to the community in terms of jobs when businesses refuse to locate in the black community. Similarly, they do not address the economic impact crime has on other institutions that serve the black community.

If these types of situations are allowed to continue or to deteriorate because of crime, the progress that has been made toward economic development in the black community, as well as the efforts to improve living conditions for poor blacks, will have been for naught. The gains made over the past 25 years, many the result of the Civil Rights Movement in the 1960s, will begin and continue to unravel unless steps are taken to arrest the pervasive problem of crime in the black community. If left unchecked, the results will be unfettered crime, human suffering, and a deterioration in the quality of life in the black community.

The task at hand is to arrest the tide before it devastates the black community. In terms of significance, the battle is as fundamental as the black community's past struggle for equality and freedom. The freedom being sought today, however, is of a different sort. It is the freedom, for example, to live without bars on home windows and doors and to walk neighborhood streets without the fear of victimization.

The current and predicted increase in the incidence of crime is unacceptable. What makes the situation so troubling is that the increase has resisted the most extraordinary measures (such as tougher imprisonment policies) to reduce it. Clearly, such an approach is not the answer. It has been estimated that a 10-percent reduction in crime may require the inmate population of the nation's prisons to more than double.[39] Even the imposition of severe sentences has not had a measurable effect on reducing the level of crime. The national crime rate, for example, was at its peak when the incarceration rate was rising the fastest. Consider, for example, that in 1970, there were fewer than 200,000 persons incarcerated in the nation's state and federal penal institutions. Before the end of 1984, that number had increased to 450,000. In 1970, the imprisonment rate for state and federal prisons was 96 for every 100,000 Americans; in 1984, the imprisonment rate had grown to 195 out of every 100,000. Today, if jails are included, the imprisonment rate is 250 for every 100,000 people. This means that the United States imprisons more of its citizens than any other industrialized nation with the exception of the Soviet Union and South Africa, while at the same time having one of the highest crime rates.[40]

Based on the evidence available, it is clear that crime is a complex problem and that the criminal justice system alone cannot control it. What is needed is a comprehensive plan that addresses the causes of crime.

*What Causes Crime*

There are many theories on what are the causative factors of criminal behavior. But today, two prominent perspectives dominate the debate on what causes crime and, consequently, what should be done about it.

The most popular view that has dominated the debate for the past decade is held by the neo-conservatives. They maintain that people commit crimes after a rational consideration of the relative risks of doing so. This school of thought puts forth the notion that if the costs of committing a crime — for example, swift, sure, and severe punishment — are increased, there will be a corresponding decrease in the crime rate. This school of thought rejects the notion of "root causes" of criminal behavior as being "lenient on crime." Their approach to addressing the crime problem relies on the use of the criminal justice system. Their solution, therefore, is to "get tough" on criminals. This translates into stepping up law enforcement efforts to apprehend the criminal, imposing longer prison sentences, and increasing the capacity of imprisonment by building more prisons. Inherent in this position is the belief that a small number of individuals are responsible for the majority of the crimes. Consequently, the crime rate can be reduced by removing this small number of "career criminals" from society and imprisoning them indefinitely.[41]

The second school of thought puts forth the position that crime has its roots in the economic and social deprivations that exist in society. Included in this definition of causation are also the problems of family and community instability. The leading proponent of this position is sociologist Elliot Currie. He has conducted an exhaustive review of the comparative literature that revealed that the United States differs from other industrialized Western countries in a number of significant ways. These differences, concluded Currie, account for this country's higher crime rate.[42] Such differences focus on, among other things, a wider gap between the "haves" and "have nots", policies to deal with unemployment and underemployment, disruption of family and community ties, and support systems for the family.[43]

Many of these differences, while still apparent in 1987, were first cited in 1968 in the *Report of the National Advisory Commission on Civil Disorders* as the cause of the violence that erupted in the nation's inner cities during the 1960s. The report recommended the "enactment of programs in housing, education, employment, and welfare to eliminate discrimination and to provide greatly expanded opportunities for ghetto residents."[44] Similarly, the President's

Commission on the Causes and Prevention of Violence espoused this same philosophy and focused on individual and family violence as well as collective violence.[45]

## CRIME REMEDIES

The key to addressing crime effectively in the black community is a clear understanding of the factors that produce criminal behavior. The concluding section of this article sets forth what must be done if America is to address its crime problem effectively and successfully, particularly crime in the black community. Inherent in these recommendations is the recognition that what is being put forth is not new. The solutions are not new because they have been discussed and advocated for years by many, including this writer.[46]

Today, as in the past, crime in the black community is directly related to the relative degree of deprivation of black Americans. Thus, any sincere effort to deal with the crime problem must address the problems of unemployment, underemployment, substandard housing, inadequate health care, physical deterioration, teenage pregnancy, economic development, self-esteem, drugs, family deterioration, racism and discrimination, plus other social and economic ills.

The recommendations that follow recognize that no one program will provide the answer to the many ills of society that contribute to crime in the black community. What is needed is a commitment which will allow all aspects of decision-making to formulate policies with crime control in mind. America cannot afford to accept the crime problem as a way of life. Neither can America afford not to address the factors that contribute to crime. What follows, therefore, is a series of recommendations that should be considered as part of this country's plan to deal with crime as it impacts on the black community, understanding that successful implementation of the plan will benefit all Americans.

### Summit on Crime in the Black Community

In 1985, there was a clear recognition that the black family in America was being threatened. As a result, the National Urban League, in conjunction with the National Association for the Advancement of Colored People, convened a summit on the black family.[47]

In 1987, there is an equally pressing need to recognize that crime in the black community is of such a magnitude that it threatens the stability of the black community. For that reason, immediate steps should be taken to convene a summit on crime in the black community. All relevant black organizations should actively participate in the conference; for example, civil rights, professional, business, and fraternal organizations. The purpose of the summit should be the development of a crime control plan for the black community. Inherent in such a plan should be an understanding of the problem and the perspective in which it must be viewed. This would include an understanding and articulation of the fact that there is either a direct or indirect relationship between crime in the black community and the conditions under which many black Americans must live. Out of the summit should come an understanding that to deal effectively with crime in the black community, it is necessary to address the socioeconomic ills that impact the black community.

Such an understanding should point to the relationship between crime and the social and economic ills that can be affected by public policy. In effect, the summit on crime in the black community should report to the nation the fact that crime is a natural consequence of the social, economic, and political system of this country. It should point out that as long as unequal means of achievement exist, crime will also exist. In addition, coming out of the summit should be an understanding that crime in itself is not racially motivated. Rather, the high incidence of crime in the black community must be viewed in context of the relative degree of deprivation of blacks in this country. As a consequence, all aspects of public policy at the federal, state, and local levels should have some bearing on the issues that are believed to be causative factors of crime.

In addition to examining public policy issues as they affect the black community, the summit should explore what the black community itself can do to lessen the impact of crime:

### The Church

Historically, the black church has played a significant role in the black community. What can the black church do today to address the problem of crime in the black community?

### Educators

Throughout the country, there is a large number of black educators at the elementary, secondary, and college levels. Above and beyond what they do professionally, what can black educators do to assist in addressing the crime problem in the black community?

### The Business Community

There are increasingly large numbers of black businessmen and women in the country. Some own and/or run their own businesses, while others hold positions in the mainstream business world. The summit participants should develop a role for black business people to play in addressing the problem of crime in the black community.

### Fraternal Groups

A large number of Afro-Americans belong to a Greek or Masonic organization. Their combined resources represent a significant force in America. What role can they play in reducing crime in the black community?

### Professional Organizations

Most, if not all black professionals have professional associations that are predominantly black; e.g., the National Bar Association, National Medical

Association, National Organization of Black Law Enforcement Executives. The summit should determine a role for black professionals to play in the battle against crime in the black community.

## Youth

Much is said about the negative aspect of young black people. The vast majority of black youth are not using drugs and are not caught up in the world of crime. Youth should be represented at the summit and it should be determined what they should do to play an active part in the anti-crime plan.

There is much the black community itself can do to lessen the impact of crime. The segments of the black community mentioned above, as well as those not mentioned, are undoubtedly involved in many meaningful activities presently. It is not being suggested here that they are not. What is being suggested, however, is that the magnitude of the crime problem in the black community is of such a nature that there is a need for a unified approach—one that focuses the efforts of the entire community toward a common goal. This may involve a continuation of the same activities in some cases, new roles in other cases, and a consolidation of gains in all instances. For this to happen, there must be a plan. It is being suggested here that such a plan, one that lays out a common agenda for the control of crime in the black community, would be the product of the proposed summit on crime in the black community.

The need to develop a plan to control crime in the black community recognizes that even this country does not have a national crime control plan. Rather, the policy of the nation today, as in the past, is to view crime as a local problem and thereby rely on the agencies that comprise the system for the administration of justice (police, prosecutors, courts, and corrections) to deal with the crime problem. Inherent in what is being stated here is a recognition that the criminal justice system, by its very nature, cannot alone control crime. This does not, however, suggest that the criminal justice system does not have a role to play, because it does. It will continue to be a very important element of any effort to control crime in the black community. There is, however, reason to explore a redirection of the criminal justice system as part of an overall plan to reduce crime in the black community.

## Redirection of the Criminal Justice System

During the past decade, police agencies around the country have tested a variety of strategies designed to improve arrest rates and thereby reduce the overall level of crime. A reinvolvement of the police with the community has been the cornerstone of much of the agencies' experimentation.

Strategies that call for interaction between the police and the community are proving to have an impact on crime. Programs such as the Houston Police Department's Community Storefront Program and the reconfiguration of police beats to coincide with neighborhood boundaries bring police services directly to the community's residents. The success of such efforts have led the

Houston Police Department to initiate a process of moving from the traditional way of policing by implementing a new style of policing called Neighborhood Oriented Policing (NOP). This new style of policing is defined as an interactive process between the police and the people who live or work in a neighborhood, designed to identify jointly neighborhood problems, determine what strategies are most appropriate for addressing the problems, and then work together to use the resources of the community to solve the problems. Under NOP, the mission of the police department is to use its resources to improve the quality of life at the neighborhood level. Such a philosophy of policing is viewed as a better and smarter way of policing a community for at least two reasons. First, it involves the community as a partner in the policing effort. Second, it enables the police to focus on problems that are unique to the different neighborhoods that comprise a city. Thus, the black community would receive police services that are unique to its needs.

Other innovative policing strategies being tried throughout the nation include a return to the use of foot patrols, the "civilianization" of certain law enforcement functions so more sworn officers are available for the investigation of crimes and the apprehension of suspects, and the direct involvement of community residents in crime prevention programs such as citizen patrols, block watch groups, and victimization awareness education. Community-oriented policing clearly represents the best approach to policing in the black community.

The application of intervention strategies can reduce the level of domestic violence seen in today's society. Studies show that intervention by the police through the arrest of the domestic abuser has a positive effect on repeated violence. The provision of shelters for battered women and harsher sentencing of abusers also have a positive effect on the rate of domestic violence.

The efforts to reduce the caseload of the nation's courts have found some success through the implementation of dispute-resolution programs. These programs are designed to handle cases involving minor disputes between individuals, making it unnecessary for the courts to arbitrate such cases. Dispute resolution programs also serve a preventive function by resolving conflict before it reaches a violent level.

The emphasis on harsh sentencing has resulted in prison overcrowding, which in turn subjects prisoners to inhuman conditions that do nothing but exacerbate the problems that foster crime. A de-emphasis on incarceration as punishment for nonviolent offenders should be explored. Creation of detention centers that offer full-time, mandatory educational programs for the illiterate as well as alcohol and drug counseling and trade-skill development should be explored. Intensive supervision during probation and the expansion of parolee community service requirements are also viable alternatives for dealing with nonviolent offenders.

Because the problem of crime is so pervasive and its causes are multifaceted, its management must involve a comprehensive approach. In addition to things the black community can do and a redirected role for the criminal justice system, there are also public policy issues that must be addressed. The summit on crime in the black community should consider those public policy issues that can only be addressed by the government. What follows are some major issues that clearly must be addressed in any serious effort to reduce crime in the black community. The issues presented here are not meant to be exhaustive; rather, they represent those issues that the research on crime suggests are important factors.

*Meaningful Employment*

The relationship between unemployment and crime has long been recognized.[48] Since it has been proven that there is a direct relationship between unemployment and crime, this factor must be addressed as a major component in a crime control agenda.

The issue of employment and crime must be examined in the context of what is occurring in American society. Specifically, it must be recognized that America has undergone a quiet social revolution, having moved from an industrial society to an information society. This means that the vast majority of American people now earn their living in a highly technological service economy. Jobs in the manufacturing industries have been lost forever. This has accounted, in part, for the high unemployment rate in the black community.

Some observers have pointed out that the "high-tech" industries have created new job opportunities. That may in fact be true, but as Currie has pointed out, at least three problems cloud this hope:[49]

- A significant number of those newly created jobs in the new service economy are low-paying and low-quality. As a result, workers are incapable of supporting a family on the income derived and have little, if any, hope for advancement.
- The "good jobs" created in "high-tech" industries; for example, electronics and computers, are few in number. Even those that are created are subject to being replaced by automation.
- Those "good jobs" that have been created are generally not filled by those who are disadvantaged and at risk to getting involved in crime.

The research that has consistently shown a direct link between unemployment and underemployment and crime in the United States has shown the same in other countries as well. These findings support a broad range of crime theories and also fit the common-sense notion of who goes to prison. At the close of the 1970s, nearly 40 percent of state prison inmates and 55 percent of the inmates in local jails had not been working fulltime in the months before they were incarcerated.[50] According to a Rand Corporation study, prison inmates cited economic reasons as the primary motive for committing crime, followed by "high times" and loss of "temper."[51]

When viewed in an economic context, the link between ethnic and racial discrimination and crime has also been established. Studies both in the United States and overseas consistently show that racial and economic inequality affect not only the rate of crime but also its seriousness and its violence. Continued racial discrimination has prevented many black Americans from rising above the underclass status usually assigned to immigrant groups. Today, young black males have the highest unemployment rate in the country and are responsible for a disproportionate amount of the violent crimes committed. They also are more likely than any other population group to be the victims of crime.

Based upon the known correlation between crime among blacks and unemployment, particularly unemployment of black teenagers who reside in the nation's cities, the top priority for the agenda to deal with the crime problem should be a national policy of full employment. Such a policy should mandate a meaningful job for every American willing, able, and seeking work.

Full employment is the surest means of reducing the crime rate. The guarantee that all Americans will be engaged in meaningful work should be a national priority. In addition to efforts to create new jobs through diversification, a duplication of the work programs implemented during the Depression era—programs that offered individuals short-term employment, built the infrastructure of the nation's cities and proved successful—should be considered.

Special emphasis should be placed on employing high-risk groups such as young blacks, including teenage parents. Intensive job-training efforts, such as the federal Job Corps programs, that help such persons acquire marketable skills and play a role in reducing the nation's illiteracy rate, should be expanded.

*Black Economic Development*

As early as 1967, the President's Crime Commission reported that "studies of the distribution of crime rates in cities and of the conditions of life most commonly associated with high crime rates have been conducted for well over a century in Europe and, for many years, in the United States. The findings have been remarkably consistent. Burglary, robbery, and serious assaults occur in areas characterized by low income, low levels of education and vocational skills, high unemployment, and high population density.[52]

The public policy of this country must be to reduce the disparities between the "haves" and the "have nots". If this issue is not effectively addressed, America will enter into the 21st century suffering from the problems of today but compounded by a poor class perpetuated by the advancement of technology. Consider the following as illustrative of present-day problems:[53]

- In 1985, blacks received only 58.6 cents for each dollar attained by whites.
- In 1985 the median income for black families was only 57.6 percent of white family income.
- In 1985, 13.5 percent of black families received less than $5,000.
- In 1985, almost one out of every three blacks (31.3 percent) had incomes that placed them below the poverty level.
- The unemployment rate for whites in 1986 was 6.1 percent and 14.7 percent for blacks. Thus, the black unemployment rate was 2.4 times higher than whites.

- The unemployment rate for black teenagers in 1986 was 43.6 percent.

The keystone to a crime control strategy must be a significant betterment of the economic condition of black Americans.

## Improving Educational Opportunity

Education is viewed as the key to success in our society. Presently, however, a substantial number of black children are leaving school unprepared, uneducated, and unskilled. Millions of youth in this country are being regulated into a subclass of their own. The subclass is characterized by an extremely high rate of unemployment, idleness, and despair. Many of the members of this subclass will enter into adulthood not only unskilled and unemployed but never having had a job. The end result of this situation should be predictable: crime will be a way of life. Public policies must be developed to reverse this deplorable situation. Such policies should allow the educational system to provide meaningful education to all students. It should be designed to stop the accumulation of millions of black youth who have either dropped out or been kicked out of school. Such a policy is important because research has shown that academic achievement is an important factor in predicting juvenile delinquency; that the poorer the academic record, the greater the likelihood of involvement in illegal activities.[54]

## Adequate And Decent Housing

Adequate and decent housing have always been an integral component of any comprehensive crime control plan. That need is still valid today. Inadequate housing and overcrowdedness is a major problem for many Americans, particularly black Americans. Not only is this longstanding problem still prevalent, but today it is compounded by the recent problem of the homeless. This, the problem of crime as it relates to living conditions, is complicated by a combination of factors. On the one hand, research has shown that areas in transition, especially dilapidated low-income neighborhoods, have higher incidences of crime, including those serving as the residence of a disproportionate number of people who commit crimes. Clearly, a relationship exists among the quality of housing, density of population, overcrowdedness, home ownership, and the social problems resulting from those conditions and crime. On the other hand, American cities are now faced with the problem of having thousands of American citizens who are without homes; over 50 percent of them are black. The problem of the homeless is a relatively new phenomenon for this country. Nevertheless, we do know that the problem of lack of affordable housing is getting worse and, in fact, has doubled within the last decade. Projections indicate the problem will get worse in the future. The status of being without a home has not been studied to determine what impact it has on crime. It is clear, however, that the homeless are placed in a position of increased vulnerability to victimization. Consequently, adequate, safe, and decent housing should be a part of any crime control plan.[55]

*Family and Community Stability*

To a significant degree, family instability contributes to the commission of crime. Families burdened by the stresses of unemployment or underemployment, poor housing, inferior education, and social alienation often cannot provide the kind of environment necessary for raising individuals capable of prospering in American society. Because of the increase in the number of teenage unwed mothers, the number of such households is growing. More than one million American teenagers each year become parents without the benefits of adequate income, parenting skills, or other supports necessary for the optimum functioning of a family unit. It is only natural that an unstable family unit would result in an unstable community. Communities experiencing the same social and economic deprivation that leads to the erosion of values that prohibit criminal behavior are less likely to provide the kind of sanctions necessary for the prevention of crime. Some studies, however, have shown that in societies where the level of poverty greatly exceeds that of the United States, the level of crime remains low. In such societies, young people are not involved in criminal activity because they are part of a network of relationships that involves a variety of obligations among kin, a subclass, and the community. These relationships are important because they provide both a sense of belonging to a larger supportive community and the setting in which informal sanctions against crime can operate effectively.

Because the family is the primary institution in society and the most important institution in the socialization of children, the crime control plan should call for public policies that are supportive of the family.[56]

*Drugs and Crime Crackdown*

The linkage between drugs and crime is evident. According to a study conducted by the U.S. Department of Justice, almost one-third of all state prisoners were under the influence of an illegal drug when they committed the crime for which they were incarcerated. More than half had taken drugs during the month just prior to the crime and more than three-fourths had used drugs at some time during their lives. Prison inmates reported marijuana to be the drug most likely to have been used just prior to the commission of their crime.[57] Any crime control plan, therefore, must include the control of drug abuse as a major component.

*Reducing Domestic Violence*

The level of violence in a society contributes to the rate of violent crime. The level of domestic violence in the United States is astonishing. Spousal and child abuse ranks as a leading cause of death among American women and children. Here again, blacks are disproportionately represented in statistics on domestic violence.[58]

The use of violence is, of course, a legacy handed down to succeeding generations. Studies show that adults who were abused as children are more prone to use violence as a means of resolving conflict, and that girls who were reared in a violent setting are more likely to be abused as adults.

Public policy on all types of violence should be designed to develop strategies that will reduce the current level of violence. Violence should be viewed not only as a problem for the criminal justice system, but also as a public health problem. A model along this line has already been developed. The University of Texas Health Science Center at Houston, in conjunction with other agencies, has created a standing committee on interpersonal violence and has begun a critical examination of the forces responsible for violence in Houston. After causes of violence have been determined, the group will propose educational and other prevention programs aimed at reducing violence in Houston. Similar efforts should be undertaken nationally.

### Handgun Control

Americans enjoy a democratic opportunity for ownership of firearms. Handguns are abundantly available to all groups who want and can pay for them. The 50 million handguns owned by American citizens are impressive evidence of the vitality of this democratic system. It is estimated that by the end of this decade private ownership of handguns will exceed 80 million.

Research tells us that homicide escalates with the rise in the number of handguns. Consistently, over 50 percent of all murders are committed with a *handgun*—and over 60 percent with some type of *firearm*. In under 20 years, the number of murders by guns has tripled.

Data compiled by the National Center for Health Statistics reveal that after motor vehicles, firearms are the second leading cause of death for those in the United States between the ages of 15 to 34. As in the case with many other issues in society, death by firearms occurs more often among blacks and the poor than the population in general. A black person is six times more likely to be murdered by a gun than a white person. People who reside in low-income areas are 10 times more likely to be accidentally killed by a gun than those who reside in high-income neighborhoods.[59]

Accidental death and injury by handguns is prevalent, and many of the victims are children. In fact, research has shown that a firearm in the home is six times more likely to result in the accidental killing of a family member than a potential intruder or burglar. To deal with the problem, a crime control plan should call for legislation to control the proliferation of handguns in the society.

### Reduction in Television Violence

The medical profession has developed ample evidence to indicate that television violence has an effect on children. Research has shown that the viewing of violence on television increases aggressive behavior in young people. Curtailing the high level of violence seen daily on television should be part of a crime control plan.[60]

In developing a comprehensive approach to the crime problem, it must be recognized that crime is not a one-dimensional phenomenon. What is generally called white-collar crime also places a heavy load on those who are poor and disadvantaged, especially blacks. Illegal price-fixing, consumer fraud, and other unlawful business practices have an economic impact on the black community that is no less serious than the injuries that result from property and personal crime.[61]

Equally significant are the highly publicized crimes that occur in the business world. Illegal insider trading and drug use on Wall Street do much to create an atmosphere that is conducive to illegal behavior. This is even more true for the high governmental officials who violate the law. Thus, any plan to deal with crime must focus on crime in its entirety, including governmental corruption and white collar criminality.

## CONCLUSION

The problem of crime in the black community, its nature, its causes, and proposed solutions have long been a matter of concern. As far back as 1898, the Hampton Negro Conference addressed this issue. In 1904, when W.E.B. DuBois and other black leaders and scholars convened the Atlanta Conference, crime was on the agenda. Yet, in 1987, almost nine decades later, there is not a coordinated, systematic, and comprehensive plan to address crime in America or crime in the black community. Rather, this country has relied almost exclusively on the system for the administration of justice as a means of addressing the problem. As a result, the response to the crime problem has been reactive, with little or no effort to relate public policy in areas of socioeconomic concerns to the problem of crime.

This article has pointed out the need to recognize that crime has a disproportionate impact on the black community. It has social, psychological, economic, and even political ramifications. It is related to the degree of social and economic deprivation of black Americans.

This country must reverse the ineffective posture on crime taken by past initiatives. This can be done by acknowledging the relationship between crime and the socioeconomic problems of the nation and deviating from a tradition of relying solely on the criminal justice system as a means of crime control.

This paper lays out a series of policy considerations which, if implemented, promise to provide a reversal in the crime trend in this country, particularly in the black community. The focus of the policy recommendations, though not new, centers on what the entire nation can do to address the problems that are systemic in nature and contributing, if not causative, factors of crime among blacks. Inherent in the recommendations is the need for all blacks, individually and collectively through their many organizations and institutions, to come together to address this problem by unifying around a common agenda.

# Blacks in the Military:
# The Victory and the Challenge

Alvin J. Schexnider, Ph.D.

July 1988 will mark the fortieth anniversary of one of the most significant civil rights victories in the United States; namely, President Harry Truman's Executive Order 9981 which mandated desegregation of the military:

"It is the declared policy of the President that there shall be equality of treatment and opportunity for all persons in the armed services, without regard to race, color, or national origin. This policy shall be put into effect as rapidly as possible, having due regard to the time required to effectuate any necessary changes without impaired efficiency or morale."[1]

President Truman's edict occurred due to encouragement from within but also as a result of pressures outside the military establishment. At the height of World War II, more than a million black men and women served in the armed forces. About half of them saw overseas duty and performed in more responsible roles than previously. Pressure from civil rights organizations and the need to meet military manpower requirements figured prominently in the Truman administration's decision.

The National Urban League, working in tandem with the NAACP, the Congress of Racial Equality (CORE), the black press, and the March on Washington movement, contributed substantially to mobilizing the black community. Truman realized that his election would require the solid support of black voters and he worked assiduously to court it.

That was forty years ago. This chapter addresses itself to what has occurred with respect to black participation in the armed services since that time. Given the fact that President Truman's Executive Order 9981 antedated the major civil rights activities of the 1950s and 1960s, it should be instructive to examine the specific impact of this decision on the armed forces and on certain aspects of civilian life as well.

Desegregation of the armed services was not popularly received. In order to counter resistance to it, President Truman established a committee under the leadership of former United States Solicitor General Charles H. Fahy to monitor the implementation of his policy. Although the Fahy Committee was making progress in beginning to integrate some military training camps, it was the Korean conflict which facilitated the integration of the Army. The urgent need for manpower requirements in the field resulted in situations where black soldiers and white soldiers fought side by side. Consequently, by 1956, as Charles Moskos points out, barely three years following the end of the conflict in Korea, "the remnants of Army Jim Crow disappeared at home and in overseas installations."[2]

## THE POST-DESEGREGATION YEARS

By the middle 1950s, the services had become almost completely integrated. Among enlisted personnel blacks comprised almost nine percent; however, they comprised less than two percent of the officer corps. The decade of 1955 to 1965 was a period of increased black participation in the armed forces; however, their proportions remained roughly the same. By 1965, for example, blacks comprised approximately 10 percent of the enlisted ranks and less than two percent of the officer corps.[3]

Although this was an era of relative calm (compared to society at large), racial discrimination, especially off-base, persisted. Black servicemen and women encountered discrimination in finding decent housing, restaurants, and schools. In response to these conditions, President John F. Kennedy appointed an Equal Opportunity Committee to monitor and advise him on racial integration in the military.

The Gesell Committee (so-called after its Chairman Gerhard A. Gesell) reviewed a number of issues related to expanding the level of participation among blacks in the armed forces. The Gesell Committee

"found an unbalanced grade distribution of blacks in the armed services, segregation (or only token integration), and exclusionary practices in the National Guard and the reserves, and racial discrimination on military installations and in surrounding communities. The Gesell Committee report was invaluable because it presented for the first time since the Truman Administration a detailed quantitative picture of the relationship between blacks and the Military."[4]

## THE VIETNAM ERA

Prior to Vietnam, a major concern of civil rights leaders and defense manpower analysts turned on efforts to expand the level of black participation in the armed services and to extend black participation into different roles and duties. Both the Fahy Committee and the Gesell Committee were instrumental in these efforts.

The Vietnam War occurred during the height of civil rights activity in the country and thereby caused much tension between domestic and foreign policy concerns. Some civil rights leaders felt strongly that the war was not only immoral but that is was draining resources that should be applied to domestic policies. Perhaps most importantly, the issue of black participation in the military now came to be viewed as a matter of disproportionate risk or exposure.

President Lyndon Johnson's decision to escalate the war in Vietnam resulted in higher manpower requirements. The Selective Service System, commonly known as the draft, ensured that black youth would satisfy the need for additional manpower. A tendency among blacks to re-enlist extended the risk factor further. In 1966 at a time when casualties in Vietnam had begun to spiral dramatically, 66 percent of blacks in the Army re-enlisted, a rate more than three times as high as white enlistees.[5]

Still, there were many individuals who, during this period of intense civil rights activity, felt that the military offered redemption for the nation's black and poor youth. Daniel P. Moynihan, in a 1965 article, offered this prescient observation:

"Civil rights as an issue is fading. The poverty program is heading for dismemberment and decline. Expectations of what can be done in America are receding. Very possibly, our best hope is seriously to use the armed forces as a socializing experience for the poor—until somehow their environment begins turning out equal citizens."[6]

This was a bold statement in 1965, especially at a time when Martin Luther King and others inveighed against the war in view of the disproportionate black casualties and declining community action funds at home. Nonetheless, Moynihan went further:

"History may record that the single most important psychological event in race relations in the nineteen sixties was the appearance of Negro fighting men on the TV screens of the nation. Acquiring a reputation for military valor is one of the oldest known routes to social equality—from the Catholic Irish in the Mexican War to the Japanese Purple Heart Division of World War II."[7]

In 1966, Secretary of Defense Robert S. McNamara instituted Project 100,000. "McNamara's 100,000", as the program was affectionately referred to, lowered induction standards to accept previous rejects drawn essentially from minority and low-income groups. Ostensibly, these men were to be given the vocational training and educational opportunities they would not otherwise have received as civilians. Regretfully, more than a third of these enlistees ended up in combat roles. When the results of Project 100,000 were measured against its stated goals, it fell short of its mark since many of those who entered the Army and Marine Corps were sent to Vietnam as combatants.

The war continued to escalate and in the process blacks sustained disproportionately high casualties in Vietnam. Meanwhile at home, other civil rights leaders were expressing increasing skepticism about the war in Vietnam.

Whitney M. Young, a respected leader of the National Urban League, noted that the war was skimming the "cream of the crop" from the black community. In short, the nation's future black leaders were being called to war in numbers that were alarming.[8]

In addition to concerns regarding disproportionate black casualties, the Vietnam era also witnessed serious racial conflicts in this nation's military history. A race riot at Long Binh Jail in Vietnam brought deep-seated racial tensions to the fore. Racial clashes aboard naval vessels and on United States military installations pointed to the need for immediate attention.

Racial polarization, particularly among black enlisted personnel, resulted from existing tensions. Black servicemen developed verbalizations, gestures, signs, and emblems to symbolize their solidarity. In an effort to accommodate, the Army modified its regulations to permit "Afro" hair cuts, power shakes and salutes, as well as other less offensive demonstrations of racial solidarity.

An investigation by the NAACP into black servicemen's complaints as well as the services' desire to eliminate divisions in its ranks led to the creation of the Defense Race Relations Institute (DRRI). Established in 1971, DRRI was created to train race relations instructors, both military and civilian, who would assist in efforts to reduce racial tensions on military installations throughout the world.

Another dimension of the racial difficulties the military was experiencing resided in the numbers of black enlisted personnel and the death of black officers. In August 1968, for example, at the time of the riot at Long Binh Jail, there were no black general officers on duty. Soon afterward, Colonel Frederick Davidson was promoted to the rank of Brigadier General. By December 1969, blacks comprised 3.2 percent of the officer corps and 10.7 percent of the enlisted ranks. Only a handful of blacks held field or general officer positions.

Gradually, racial conflict in the services began to decline. The Vietnam era ended with the abandonment of the draft. The period which followed ushered in the all-volunteer force and a new set of concerns regarding black participation.

## THE ERA OF THE ALL-VOLUNTEER FORCE

Even before its inception in 1973, critics claimed that the all-volunteer force (AVF) would be comprised of predominantly black and low-income individuals. The emergent issue for black participation was no longer "equal opportunity" but "representation."

Barely two years after the draft ended, it was apparent that the critics' worst fears were being realized. The changing socioeconomic composition of the services was manifest as fewer college-bred men were entering and lower aptitude test scores were registered. What was more bothersome to a few highly placed critics was a sharp increase in the number of blacks: over one of every four new recruits in the Army.[9]

To be sure, the abandonment of conscription caused an increase in black enlistment rates. As Kenneth Coffey pointed out,

"In 1978 blacks comprised about 20 percent of enlistments in the active forces, including 28 percent of Army accessions. The AVF 'high' was reached by 1974, when 21 percent of accessions were black, including 28 percent of Army enlistees. The percentage of black officer appointments also increased. Whereas all four services still were appointing only about 1 percent black officers in 1969, the portion rose to about 7 percent by 1978."[10]

Coffey attributes the increase in black participation during this period to three factors: a) higher numbers of unemployed blacks than whites who were receptive to military service; b) the military's reputation as an egalitarian institution; and c) an increase in the numbers of blacks eligible for military service. Also, as Moskos pointed out, in the late 1970s, the proportion of black high school graduates entering the military exceeded the proportion of whites by 60 percent to 40 percent.[11]

The issue of overrepresentation in the armed services subsided during the late 1970s as black participation levels also dropped. Black enlisted participation rates declined slightly during this period as the proportion of black officers increased moderately. Let us turn to an analysis of the present and speculations about the future of black participation in the military.

## THE PRESENT

### Enlisted Ranks

The modern military, forty years after the Truman edict of 1948, is a remarkable example of social change. Approximately 400,000 black men and women currently serve in all branches of an active duty force numbering 2.1 million. This constitutes a notable increase in the level of black participation during the last four decades. The proportion of blacks in the military has risen from seven percent during World War II to 19 percent at present. As has been indicated previously, the most dramatic increase in black participation has occurred since the onset of the all-volunteer force in 1973. Historically, the vast majority of blacks have served in the Army; however, since World War II, more blacks have seen duty in the other branches as well. Currently, the distribution of blacks by service areas is illustrated in Table 1.

---

**Table 1. Percent of Blacks by Military Service**

| | |
|---|---|
| Army | 27 percent |
| Marine Corps | 19 percent |
| Air Force | 15 percent |
| Navy | 13 percent |

Source: Moskos and Butler, 1987.

---

To some extent, blacks find the military more attractive than other occupations because of limited options in the civilian marketplace. For many youth, military service is a rite of passage and an opportunity toward self-improvement. There are other factors operating which also may render a tour of duty palatable:

- a more positive image of military life as the memory of Vietnam fades;
- a vastly improved recruiting command;
- the availability (since 1982) of GI Bill-style educational benefits, and
- the generous pay earned by new recruits.[12]

What is perhaps most interesting about black participation in the military is the fact that since the end of conscription, "the proportion of high school graduates has exceeded that of whites." As Moskos points out, "in 1985, 95.4 percent of black men joining the Army had high school diplomas, in comparison with 87.6 percent of whites."[13] Although new black Army recruits do not score as high as whites on aptitude tests, they tend to have a lower attrition rate (i.e., a tendency to complete their tour of duty).

The fact that the proportion of black high school graduates is higher than that of whites is significant because military leaders, sergeants as well as generals, maintain that a high school diploma is the best predictor of adaptation and success in the military. In the words of one observer, "high school graduates make better soldiers than do drop-outs. Young people with diplomas have shown they can learn, are perseverant, and can absorb discipline. Thus, they are easier to train."[14]

These current observations compare favorably with the early years of the all-volunteer force when less than 20 percent of new entrants possessed a high school diploma. Needless to say, the Department of Defense is extremely pleased with results that show that more than 90 percent of last year's recruits were high school graduates.

It is probable that the military's desire for high school graduates will not wane. Their success is wholly dependent on an available pool of high school graduates given an expanding proportion of technical jobs in all service branches. According to one observer

"With a growing emphasis on computerized command, control communications, and intelligence functions, new systems are invariably more complicated than their predecessors and serve to increase the number of specialists in the military services. It is estimated, for example, that the Air Force's need for people with high aptitudes for electronic skills will increase by about one-third by the year 2000. Similar effects will be felt by the other services."[15]

Albeit true that the armed services are recruiting more high school graduates and more black youth among them, the future does not necessarily bode well for sustaining this trend. The number of black high school graduates appears to have peaked and may decline in future years, thereby reducing the pool of blacks eligible for military service. This will also reduce the pool of blacks eligible to attend college.

Minorities tend to drop out of high school at a rate higher than that of whites. The black high school dropout rate (27 to 29 percent) is about two-thirds higher than the white high school dropout rate (15 to 18 percent). Although there was a 29 percent increase in the number of blacks completing high school between 1975 and 1982, it may be attributed in part to the fact that our public schools are increasingly black and Hispanic. In recent years, the black high school graduation rate has remained at around 50 percent.[16]

This has resulted in the military's skimming of the best black high school graduates. In 1982, it was conservatively estimated that 42 percent of all potentially qualified black men enlisted compared to 14 percent of the potentially qualified white males.[17] If this trend persists it could result not only in fewer blacks going to college, but greater competition for black high school graduates among the armed services, the private sector, and higher education.

The College Board in a major study published in 1985 pointed out that while high school graduation rates had improved among blacks during the last two decades, their college attendance and completion rates have declined since the mid-1970s. If black youth are to be eligible to serve in the armed forces, attend college, or both, attention must be paid to their high school completion rates.

Survey results of new recruits have also pointed out that one of ten blacks and one of fourteen whites enlist in order to obtain money for a college education.[18] The desire of service men and women to acquire money to pursue a college education can be satisfied during their enlistment. For example, the Army College Fund, combined with the G.I. Bill, makes it possible for enlisted persons to accumulate as much as $17,000 to $25,000 for college study upon conclusion of their service obligation.[19]

It is likely that black youth will continue to consider military duty as a means of acquiring funds to obtain an education. The results will be modest at best, however, if the number of black high school graduates does not expand. Additionally, the services must consider the need to recruit high school graduates into technical fields. According to recent figures, blacks in the Army tend to be overrepresented in support activities (supply and service, administration, transportation, etc.) and "greatly underrepresented in technical fields."[20]

Before turning to a discussion of blacks in the officer corps, a brief comment on female enlistees is in order. Although women soldiers comprise 10 percent of the enlisted ranks, black women serve at a proportionately higher rate in each branch. In 1986, black females were distributed widely among the services. This is illustrated in Table 2.

**Table 2**
**Distribution of Black Females by Branch of Service**

| | |
|---|---|
| Army | 32 percent |
| Marine Corps | 25 percent |
| Air Force | 22 percent |
| Navy | 20 percent |

Source: Moskos and Butler, 1987.

Black female soldiers tend to have a higher entrance rate than black males. They are also more likely to complete their enlistments and exhibit fewer disciplinary problems than white females. If recent trends are a good indicator, we can safely predict that the participation rate of black women in the military will continue to expand.

*Black Officers*

As recently as 1940, there were only 5,000 blacks serving in the enlisted ranks; only five were officers. Two of the five were in combat arms (Benjamin O. Davis, Sr. and Jr.); the other three were chaplains. This was, of course, during the era of a segregated military. It was also during a time when a quota had been established to limit black enlistments to their proportion in the civilian population.

President Truman's desegregation order of 1948 signaled vast new opportunities for blacks in the officer corps. The proportion of blacks in the officer corps has increased from less than one percent in 1945 to six percent in 1986. In the Army where most blacks serve, seven percent of the generals are black.[21] The distribution of blacks in the officer corps is illustrated in Table 3:

**Table 3**
**Distribution of Black Officers by Branch of Service**

| | |
|---|---|
| Army | 10 percent |
| Marine Corps | 5 percent |
| Air Force | 5 percent |
| Navy | 5 percent |

Source: Moskos and Butler, 1987.

While the proportion of black officers has increased in all services since desegregation, it is questionable whether this trend can be sustained. For the most part, today's senior level black officers entered the military during an era when civilian occupational structures were quite narrow. A black college graduate in the 1950s or 1960s was more likely to find equal employment opportunities in the armed services than at one of the nation's industrial giants such as General Motors, Xerox, IBM, or even the federal government.

Additionally, many if not most of the military's top-ranking black officers earned their degree and received their commission through Reserve Officer Training Corps (ROTC) programs at historically black colleges and universities (HBCs) . In the not too distant past, it was a heady experience for a young black man to receive a commission and embark on a tour of duty which ultimately could lead to an extended career. Besides, the life of an officer afforded options, career status, and travel opportunities that were hard to match. With rare exception the private sector was no competition. Although the bulk of the top-ranking black officers received their commission at black institutions, this is less so today than at any time since the Truman order of 1948. Two conditions have negatively affected the black college campus as the preeminent source of officer accession in recent years: a) the tendency of black youth to matriculate at white colleges and universities, and b) perceptions regarding the quality of relatively new ROTC programs at black colleges and universities.

By current accounts, approximately two-thirds to three-fourths of all blacks enrolled in colleges and universities attend predominantly white institutions. This comes as a direct result of college desegregation efforts throughout the country. Prior to 1950, 90 percent of black students attended predominantly black institutions. Notwithstanding this fact, black colleges and universities continue to produce about one-third of all black college graduates and approximately half of the ROTC commissions awarded to blacks.[22]

The increase in black officer production at historically black institutions is due in part to an increase in the number of ROTC programs established there during the late 1960s. As Moskos and Butler point out:

"At a time when many prestigious white institutions were disestablishing ROTC units, new ROTC programs were being inaugurated at black colleges. In 1986, twenty-seven of the HBCs had ROTC programs (up from sixteen during the late 1960s) and this expansion accounts for much of the growth in the commissioning of new black second lieutenants."[23]

Although the proportion of blacks earning their commission at the service academies will likely continue to expand (it is currently eight percent at West Point), there is also a strong probability that ROTC programs on black college campuses will continue to be the major source of black officer accessions into the foreseeable future.

There is a perception among senior black officers that their ranks may not be filled in future years. Let us closely examine this concern.

If a high school diploma is the credential for gaining entry into the military's enlisted ranks, a college degree is similarly essential for membership in the officer corps. The chief impediment to maintaining if not expanding black officer production in the corps is the decline in the number of blacks who go to college. According to the American Council on Education, the proportion of blacks entering college dropped from 33.5 percent in 1976 to 26.1 percent in 1985.[24]

As has been noted, fewer blacks in the education pipeline; that is, completing high school, will adversely affect their college-going rate. This is illustrated below.

**Table 4**
**High School Completion Rates Among Blacks: Selected Years**
**(Numbers in Thousands)**

| Year | 18- and 19-Year-Olds | Number Completing High School | Percent Completing High School |
|------|----------------------|-------------------------------|--------------------------------|
| 1975 | 1,003 | 476 | 47.5 |
| 1977 | 1,057 | 463 | 43.8 |
| 1979 | 1,073 | 497 | 46.3 |
| 1981 | 1,129 | 560 | 49.6 |
| 1983 | 1,136 | 550 | 48.4 |
| 1985 | 1,092 | 556 | 50.9 |

Source: Adapted from the American Council on Education's *Fifth Annual Status Report on Minorities in Higher Education*, 1986, p. 46.

Fewer blacks attending college will also result in fewer being eligible to serve in the armed forces as officers. This is an incontrovertible fact. We can avoid this prospect only be expanding the college attendance rate among blacks.

In addition to the problem of high school graduation rates, the economics of higher education also affect the college attendance and retention rates of blacks and other minorities. According to the American Council on Education,

"The federal government's shift away from awarding scholarships and grants to providing loans has reduced the level of assistance to black students and increased the amount to whites and Hispanics. The lowest income groups who have been most dependent on grants have been hardest hit by this shift. The changes have favored middle-income students. With the lowest income of all three groups, blacks have been affected the most. Given these factors, it is not surprising that the number of blacks enrolling in college is rapidly decreasing."[25]

It is also possible that black youth may have lowered their expectations of the economic benefit of a college education. Clifton R. Wharton, a leading black educator, raised this possibility in a major address to the 1986 annual meeting of the National Urban League.[26]

Clearly, for the reasons cited above, the future does not augur well for expanding black participation in the officer corps, particularly at the most senior levels. Somewhat related and equally disturbing is the fact that for those blacks who do enter the services and attain senior position, they will probably be unable to turn their military backgrounds to their advantage in the civilian marketplace. This, despite the fact that "Blacks occupy more management positions in the military than they do in business, education, journalism, government, or any other significant sector of American society."[27]

A reversal of the downward trend in college participation rates among blacks is essential to ensuring their representation in senior positions in the officer corps. Currently, blacks comprise more than seven percent of all Army generals but only a handful in the other branches. Table 5 describes their distribution.

Excessive attention to the distribution of blacks in senior positions may mask problems of recruitment and retention of black junior officers. Identifying potential black officer talent will continue to be a challenge. Simply put, as we grapple with the desire to recruit blacks to the professions in general, so must we also seek to ensure the recruitment of blacks to the officer corps of all four branches of the armed services.

**Table 5**
**Black Generals and Admirals in Active Duty in the U.S. Armed Services**

| Branch | General/Flag Officers Number of Blacks | Percent of Total |
|---|---|---|
| Army | 30 | 7.3 |
| Navy | 5 | 1.5 |
| Marine Corps | 1 | 1.3 |
| Air Force | 4 | 1.2 |

Source: *The Wall Street Journal* citing Defense Department Statistics, September 28, 1987.

## SUMMARY OBSERVATIONS

In a recent address to a meeting of undergraduate students interested in advanced study in law, medicine, business, and academia, the author asked the mainly black attendees this question: Who is Colin Luther Powell? One lad confidently proffered that this was the son of Adam Clayton Powell. The three black cadets from the Commonwealth's Virginia Military Institute were as silent as their peers from public colleges and universities across the state. No one knew the answer.

This query of the students came one day following President Ronald Reagan's promotion of Lieutenant General Colin L. Powell to the post of National Security Adviser. Admittedly, their lack of knowledge of who General Powell was may be explained simply by the freshness of the event and the fact that they may not have read the newspapers or seen the news on television. For me, it is easier to accept the fact that black youth may be unaware of who Roy Wilkins or Whitney Young were than to accept the fact that they do not know who General Powell or General Gorden are.

Apropos of the military, Black America forty years after Executive Order 9981 can take pride in the fact of two signal appointments: that of Lieutenant General Powell as head of the National Security Council, and that of Brigadier General Fred A. Gorden as Commandant at the United States Military Academy (West Point).

Both General Powell and General Gorden have had distinguished military careers. General Powell was commissioned a second lieutenant when he completed a bachelor's degree at the City College of New York in 1958. He has had extensive field experience having won a Purple Heart for injuries sustained in Vietnam in 1963. General Powell has also garnered invaluable staff experience in the Pentagon and as an aide to former Secretary of Defense Caspar Weinberger and as deputy to former National Security Adviser Frank Carlucci. Although the Reagan administration will end in another year, General Powell will face formidable challenges to the final hour. Described as a "soldier's soldier," and a man of "peerless judgment," there is every reason to be assured that General Powell is equal to the tasks ahead.

General Gorden is a graduate of West Point, which he entered after attending a community college. The only black in his class, he graduated in 1962 and later saw duty in Vietnam, where he earned a Bronze Star. Like General Powell, he too has had both field and staff experience in addition to having taught at West Point.

As Commandant, General Gorden supervises the cadets' military training and their extracurricular activities. This appointment symbolizes the vast changes which have occurred at West Point since the first black to graduate, Henry O. Flipper, was later railroaded out of the Army on flimsy charges of embezzlement. West Point's efforts to recruit more blacks, Hispanics, and other minorities will not be hurt by General Gorden's appointment as Commandant.

## RECOMMENDATIONS

A major challenge for the nation and for black leadership is to ensure that there will be an ample supply of black talent in the future to replicate the successes of Generals Powell and Gorden. Toward this end, we must increase the number of blacks who complete college and who are willing to pursue a military career. An armed forces career is not only a fine calling and an honorable profession, it is a lucrative one as well.

Equally important, we must find ways to strengthen black leadership through the involvement of black officers, including those on active duty as well as retirees. Invariably, references to the "black elite" or "black leaders" omit high-ranking black officers. There is perhaps skepticism on the part of both civilian and military leaders since the former are often perceived as liberal and the latter as conservative; however, one suspects that not much in the way of dialogue has occurred.

There are hundreds of senior-level black officers whose executive and management skills could be put to good use in a variety of organizational settings. Unfortunately, some of the best-known examples of this aim occurred in cities with black mayors where civil unrest undermined good intentions.[28] We should not be shy about seeking out black officer retirees to work in either the public or the private sector or to provide leadership in non-profit or third-sector organizations as well. The continued expansion of black businesses, especially in high technology areas related to national defense, could be strengthened by the hiring of former officers who possess professional knowledge and managerial experience.

An additional area where black civilian and military leaders might be able to establish *rapprochement* relates to the need for developing more black officer talent for the future. It is clearly in the self-interest of both groups and the nation to do so.

The decline in college attendance rates is already well-documented. The importance of financial aid to black youth attending college has also been established. By increasing the numbers of blacks who attend and complete college, we increase the yield of those who may assume leadership positions in government, business, higher education, and the military.

Accordingly, I propose a major national conference on devising strategies to encourage more black youth to attend college and developing future black leadership for the military profession.

The future participation of blacks in the armed services, especially in the enlisted ranks, is a foregone conclusion. While the rate of participation has dropped slightly in recent years, there is nothing to indicate any dramatic shifts downward.

There are, however, troubling signs on the horizon with respect to black officers. Prior to the Truman order of 1948, blacks served in segregated units and often with white officers. Since then, it has been somewhat commonplace to witness black officers, particularly in the Army, in command of companies, brigades, and divisions. The possibility exists that we could return to a pre-1948 profile with heavy black enlisted participation and woefully few black officers. This is a retrogression which must be prevented. If we all pursue this aim with resolve, the next forty years will witness a more balanced distribution of black enlisted personnel *and* officers in all of the services and across all occupations—combat, support, and technical.

In closing, let me draw upon the wisdom and experience of General Bernard Randolph, the military's only active duty four-star black officer. General Randolph, commander at Andrews Air Force Base, has indicated his plan upon retirement is to work in the field of education at a predominantly black institution. This will enable him to develop future black leadership, both military and civilian. General Randolph's commitment is illustrated in the following quote:

"I've been concerned that young Blacks are missing the opportunity to take advantage of what the military has to offer . . . What caused me to stay in the Air Force has been the work, the stimulating environment, and educational opportunities. We as Black Americans need to emphasize the importance of education."[30]

*The author wishes to acknowledge the assistance of Virginia Reeves Schexnider in the preparation of this paper.*

# Economic Status of Blacks 1987

David H. Swinton, Ph.D.

## INTRODUCTION

This paper reports on the results of our review and analysis of the latest data available to describe the economic status of black Americans. Our findings echo those reported in this essay for the past several years. During 1986 and 1987, as was the case previously, black income remained low and unequal. Poverty rates continue to be extraordinarily high. Labor market difficulties persist, as reflected in high unemployment rates, low earnings, and unfavorable occupational distributions. Modest gains were observed reflecting the persistence of the economic recovery. However, it is clear that the recovery has still not raised the economic status of blacks to a satisfactory level. Moreover, abstracting from cyclical fluctuations, no progress is being made in reducing the level of racial inequality in economic life.

The data to substantiate this assessment will be presented in some detail. However, before we review these data, a few comments on the implications of the persisting economic difficulties of blacks is in order. The most obvious of these implications is that the current policies and strategies of the public and private sectors are inadequate to bring about racial equality in economic life. The experience of the past decade makes it clear that the relative economic disadvantage of blacks will not vanish or noticeably diminish without significant changes in policies and practices.

In the labor market, the adage that blacks are the last hired and the first fired still appears to be largely true. Indeed, the prima facie evidence of increasing racial gaps in unemployment rates and family income, especially for the most disadvantaged segments of the black population, suggests that the racial disadvantage in gaining employment opportunities has increased during the past few years. Income has recovered somewhat from its recession lows; however, in absolute terms, family income still lags behind the pre-recession peaks. And, as we will note, racial gaps in family income have increased during the past few years. Close to one-third of the population continues to be poor, and the poverty rate for blacks persists at almost three times the poverty rate of whites.

Reasonable people may quibble over the precise dimensions of the economic disadvantages of blacks; others will dispute the causes of the persisting disadvantages. However, the empirical data presented in this essay and those in recent editions of *The State of Black America* provide indisputable evidence that, for more than ten years, little progress has been made in attaining the national goal of ending the extensive inequality and poverty that has historically characterized the situation of the black American population as a whole.

The empirical evidence does show that some individual blacks have made impressive economic gains. In fact, there has been an increase in the proportion of blacks who can be classified as upper middle class. This limited upward mobility for the few cannot offset the stagnation and decline experienced by the larger numbers of black Americans whose economic status has deteriorated. The central tendency for the group as a whole is revealed by the trends in the averages. And these trends tell a consistent story of stagnation or decline.

The evidence provided by these recent trends makes it apparent that recent public and private policies have been a failure: They have not brought about any improvement in the overall economic status of blacks. Indeed, the recent policy emphasis on self-help, *laissez-faire,* and voluntary compliance with equal opportunity laws must bear major responsibility for ending the brief period of progress recorded from the mid-1960s to the mid-1970s and ushering in a new era of stagnation and decline in the economic position of the vast majority of average black Americans.

The evidence of the past decade makes it reasonable to conclude that reliance on current market forces or *laissez-faire* policies by themselves will not bring about significant progress for blacks in the near future. The economic status of blacks will fluctuate with the business cycle. Moreover, individual blacks with exceptional attributes will continue to find some degree of success. But, the cyclical fluctuations will be within a narrow band bracketing greater and lesser degrees of poverty and disadvantage. The continuation of current policies will result in a substantial majority of blacks being locked into a permanent state of economic inequality and disadvantage.

The economic difficulties of black Americans are closely related to the economic malaise of the American economy. America's economic difficulties as reflected in the towering budget and trade deficits, declining dollar, and nervous financial markets have complicated the problem of dealing with the economic difficulties of the black population. This has reduced both the resources and the will to solve the economic problems of blacks and removed the economic plight of blacks from the list of high-priority national problems.

Those who are interested in solving the economic problems of blacks and those who want to pursue the goal of racial equality in economic life more vigorously must return the problem of black economic disadvantages to the national agenda. This will not be an easy task in view of the persisting economic difficulties at the national level and marked decline in faith in the efficacy of governmental efforts to solve national problems.

Advocates of greater racial equality must work on two fronts. First, they must insist that high priority be given to solving the problem of racial inequality regardless of the state of the business cycle. This implies the need for a strategy to make the redistribution of resources, wealth, and power required to solve the persistent problem of racial inequality in economic life palatable, regardless of the cyclical state of the national economy. Second, they must seek and pursue a policy agenda that can turn the national economy around and build a national economic environment capable of providing a decent living standard for all Americans. This implies a policy agenda that involves more management of the economic environment and the rules of the economic game.

The main ideas presented in this introduction are spelled out in greater detail in the body of this chapter. The next section reviews trends in black economic status. This will update the presentations of previous essays with the most recent data available. Following this presentation is a brief discussion of the causes of these trends. This section is followed by our conclusions and a policy discussion.

## TRENDS IN ECONOMIC STATUS

### Income

Constant-dollar black income — whether it is measured in terms of per capita or median family income — has increased every year since 1982 (the depths of the last recession). Per person income data for selected years are provided in Table 1 (however, the text discussion is based on a review of data for all years).

During the last recession black family income dropped about ten percent between 1979 and 1982. This decline in per capita income was completely recovered by 1985. In 1986 income growth continued, and black per capita income of $7,207 was about five percent higher than 1985 income, and about six-percent higher than peak income in the 1970s. Note that the six percent growth in income per person between 1979 and 1986 compares very unfavorably with the almost 21 percent growth in per person income that occurred between 1969 and 1976. The performance of the past two years only looks good in comparison to the depths of the Reagan recession.

**Table 1**
**Per Capita Income (1986 $)**

|      | Black | White  | B/W  |
| ---- | ----- | ------ | ---- |
| 1986 | 7,207 | 12,352 | 58.3 |
| 1985 | 6,840 | 11,671 | 58.6 |
| 1982 | 6,089 | 10,822 | 56.3 |
| 1978 | 6,780 | 11,423 | 59.4 |
| 1970 | 5,278 | 9,471  | 55.7 |

Source: U.S. Dept. of Commerce, Bureau of the Census, *Money Income and Poverty Status . . .: 1986,* Table 13.

This fact becomes even clearer when we examine family income statistics. Median family income for blacks has also increased every year since the recession-low point of 1982. See Table 2 for selected data. However, even in 1986, family income was considerably lower than it was during the 1970s peak.

Thus, after four years of recovery, family income had not yet regained its pre-recession peak. Family income growth as measured by growth in median family income was slow in the 1970s as well. However, family income was considerably higher during the 1970s than it has been during the 1980s. Average median black family income for the 1980s is only $16,476 as compared to $17,765 for the 1970s. In seven out of the ten years of the 1970s, median family income for blacks was higher than it was in 1986, the peak year for the 1980s.

**Table 2**
**Median Family Income (1986 $)**

|      | Black  | White  | B/W  |
|------|--------|--------|------|
| 1986 | 17,604 | 30,809 | 57.1 |
| 1985 | 17,109 | 29,713 | 57.6 |
| 1982 | 15,447 | 27,948 | 55.2 |
| 1978 | 18,284 | 30,870 | 59.2 |
| 1970 | 17,730 | 28,904 | 61.3 |

Source: U.S. Dept. of Commerce, Bureau of the Census. *Money Income and Poverty Status . . .: 1986,* Table 3.

Equally as disturbing as the slow rate of growth is the increase in racial inequality in income observed during the 1980s. The last columns in Tables 1 and 2 exhibit the index of equality. Black and white income parity would be obtained if these numbers equaled 100. The per-person income indexes indicate that during the seventies, blacks had between 56 and 59 dollars per person for every $100 whites had. During the 1980s these numbers ranged between 56 and 58 dollars per 100 dollars of white income. Although income inequality by this measure has attenuated somewhat during the past two years, it was still higher during the past two years than it generally was during the last half of the 1970s.

Note that in 1986 aggregate black income of 208 billion dollars would have to increase by $148 billion for blacks to attain income parity with whites. The income parity gap of $148 billion in 1986 is up from $123 billion in 1979, and $97 billion in 1970 (all measured in terms of 1986 dollars). These numbers indicate the racial income gap is very large and is also growing.

Inequality in family income is also marked. The spending power of the typical black family is considerably less than it is for the typical white family. In 1986 the median black family had only $568 to spend for every $1,000 the median white family had to spend. Inequality in the spending power of black and white families is not only large but has increased since the 1970s. In 1978 the typical black family could spend $592 for every $1,000 spent by the typical white family; in 1970 the relative purchasing power of black families was even higher, amounting to $613 per $1,000 of white family purchasing power. Thus, since 1970, the gap in purchasing power between the median black and white families has increased by about $45 per thousand or 12 percent.

Translating these average figures to their aggregate counterparts will provide some perspective on the extent of income inequality experienced by black Americans. The aggregate family income for blacks in 1986 totaled about $161 billion. Thus, in 1986 the total additional income required to produce income equality between black and white families was about 97 billion dollars. The greater degree of family income inequality in 1986 as compared to 1978 cost black families about 4.5 billion dollars in 1986. The cost to blacks in 1986 of the increase in inequality which has occurred since 1970 is about $5.6 billion in 1986.

During the past couple of decades, the distribution of income in the black community has become more unequal. Developments in the economy have simultaneously produced a greater proportion of high income and a greater proportion of very low income recipients among black families. Selected data are shown in Table 3, which compares 1970, 1978, and 1986. The general pattern revealed by these data is moderate declines in the proportion of very low income recipients and more rapid increases in the proportion of high income recipients up until 1978. After 1978 the proportion of low income recipients increased fairly sharply, and the proportion of high income recipients rose modestly. In fact, the proportion of very high income recipients fell sharply between 1978 and 1982 and only recovered the 1978 level for the first time in 1986.

### Table 3
### Proportion of Families Receiving Income in Selected Ranges
### (1986 $)

|  | 1986 Black | 1986 White | 1978 Black | 1978 White | 1970 Black | 1970 White |
|---|---|---|---|---|---|---|
| Less Than $ 5,000 | 14.0 | 3.5 | 8.9 | 2.6 | 9.6 | 3.1 |
| Less Than $10,000 | 30.2 | 10.2 | 27.4 | 9.2 | 26.8 | 10.1 |
| More Than $35,000 | 21.2 | 42.6 | 20.3 | 41.7 | 15.7 | 35.6 |
| More Than $50,000 | 8.8 | 22.0 | 7.7 | 19.3 | 4.7 | 14.8 |

Source: U.S. Dept. of Commerce, Bureau of the Census. *Money Income and Poverty Status . . .: 1986,* Table 3.

The net result of these trends is that by 1986 8.8 percent of black families had family incomes of $50,000 or more. This proportion was up from only 4.7 percent in 1970 and 7.7 percent in 1978. In total more than 624-thousand black families had incomes of $50,000 or more in 1986. This amounts to 78,000 more families than would have had such incomes at the 1978 proportion, and 290-thousand families more than would have had such income at 1970 proportions. It is therefore clear that the number of black families enjoying high incomes has increased.

At the same time, the proportion of families receiving incomes under $5,000 increased from 8.9 percent in 1978 to 14.0 percent in 1986. In total 993-thousand black families had such low incomes in 1986. This is about 362-thousand families more than would have had such low incomes at 1978 proportions. Thus, between 1978 and 1986, the increase in black families with the lowest family incomes was almost five times the increase in the number of black families receiving the highest incomes.

The net result of these divergent trends has been an overall increase in income inequality accompanying the general decline in average income levels. This is illustrated by the increasing shares of income going to the richest 20 percent of the black population and the declining shares going to the poorest 20 percent. For example, between 1970 and 1986 the share of total black family income received by the richest 20 percent of black families increased from 43.4 percent to 46.9 percent. During the same period, the share of income received by the poorest 20 percent of the non-white population declined from 4.5 to 3.5 percent of aggregate income.

As Table 3 indicates, the trend towards greater inequality in the income distribution also occurred among white families. However, the change was not nearly as pronounced as it was for blacks. While the proportion of blacks receiving incomes under $5,000 increased by 5.1 percentage points between 1978 and 1986, the proportion of whites with such low income only increased by nine-tenths of one percentage point. Thus the absolute percentage point increase for blacks was more than five times the absolute increase in the proportion of very poor among white families. Similarly, while the absolute increase in the proportion of white families with income greater than $50,000 was 2.7 percentage points between 1978 and 1986, the absolute percentage increase in the proportion of black families with such high income was only 1.1 percentage points. Thus, over the last decade the increase in the proportion of black families receiving very low incomes was much greater while the increase in the proportions receiving very high incomes was much smaller.

Black families at every part of the black family income distribution are worse off than comparable white families (see Table 4). In other words, the poorest black families tend to be substantially poorer than the poorest white families, while the richest white families tend to be substantially richer than the richest black families. In 1986 the highest income received by a family among the 20 percent of black families with the lowest family incomes was $6,792. In comparison the upper limit of income for the lowest-income 20 percent of white families was $15,200. Thus, the lowest-income blacks had incomes that were only 45 percent as high as the incomes of the lowest-income whites.

**Table 4**
**Income at Selected Positions of the Income Distribution**
**1986**

|  | Black | White | B/W |
|---|---|---|---|
| Lowest Fifth | 6,792 | 15,200 | 44.7 |
| Second Fifth | 13,400 | 25,452 | 52.6 |
| Third Fifth | 22,700 | 36,300 | 62.5 |
| Fourth Fifth | 35,780 | 51,760 | 69.1 |
| Top Five Percent | 59,000 | 84,627 | 69.7 |

Source: U.S. Dept. of Commerce, Bureau of the Census. *Money Income and Poverty Status . . .: 1986,* Table 4.

As Table 4 makes clear, such differentials in black and white family income exist throughout the income distribution. However, the relative disparities are greatest for the lowest income families. While blacks in the lowest quintile only have $450 to spend for every $1,000 that whites in the lowest quintile of the white distribution have to spend, blacks in the top five percent of the black income distribution have about $697 for every $1,000 that comparably situated whites have to spend. Though there may have been very slight improvement during the last two years, inequality at all points of the income distribution is still higher in 1986 than it was in 1980.

**Table 5**
**Median Family Income for Regions: Selected Years**
**(1986 $)**

|  | Northwest | | Midwest | | South | | West | |
|---|---|---|---|---|---|---|---|---|
|  | Black | White | Black | White | Black | White | Black | White |
| 1986 | 20,902 | 33,348 | 17,360 | 30,511 | 16,236 | 29,141 | 22,149 | 31,378 |
| 1982 | 16,582 | 29,052 | 13,925 | 28,026 | 14,680 | 25,984 | 18,578 | 28,415 |
| 1978 | 19,413 | 31,205 | 22,773 | 31,669 | 16,385 | 28,518 | 17,985 | 31,361 |
| 1969 | 20,434 | 30,353 | 22,846 | 31,129 | 14,746 | 25,914 | 22,716 | 30,152 |

Source: U.S. Dept. of Commerce, Bureau of the Census. *Money Income and Poverty Status . . .: (various years).*

Black incomes are low and unequal in all regions of the country. This is shown by the data in Table 5. In 1986 black income was lowest and most unequal in the South; thus, the South regained its historical distinction of being the region where black incomes are absolutely lowest and most unequal. Since 1982 this distinction had been held by the Midwest. Note also that black income in both the Midwest and the South still had not regained the ground lost since

1978. The limited recovery is most pronounced in the Midwest, where black income was still over $5,400 less in 1986 than it was in 1978. Black income in the South was only slightly lower during 1986 than it was in 1978. The gain in median income for black families has been most impressive in the Northeast and the West, although there was a measured decline in median family income in the West between 1985 and 1986. For blacks, there has generally been little overall gain in family income in any of the non-southern regions since the late 1960s.

Racial inequality is high in each region. Outside of the South racial inequality in family income has generally progressed upwards since the early 1970s. The increases in racial inequality have been most dramatic in the Midwest. There, black families generally had over $700 per $1,000 of white family income during the 1960s and 1970s. However, in every year of the 1980s, black families in the Midwest have had less than $570 per $1,000 of white family income. Racial inequality is also up in the Northeast, but not nearly as dramatically. The measurement of racial inequality in the West is erratic. In the South as a whole there has been no significant change in inequality in family income since the late 1960s, although there may have been a slight increase in inequality for the 1980s taken as a whole.

*Poverty Trends*

The national poverty rate for black persons in 1986 was 31.1 percent, practically unchanged from the 31.3 percent level measured for 1985. An estimated 8,983,000 persons were in households with incomes below the official poverty level in 1986, compared to an estimate of 8,926,000 for 1985. Poverty was even higher for black children, with 42.7 percent of all black children under 18 officially classified as poor. About 53.8 percent of all persons and 67.1 percent of all children in black female-headed households were in units with incomes below the official poverty level. The 1986 poverty threshold for a three-person family was $8,737; for a four-person family, it was $11,203.

Like income levels, poverty rates also fluctuate with the business cycle. Data for selected years are displayed in Table 6. Poverty rates for blacks moderated slightly during the seventies and rose during the first part of the 1980s. By 1986 poverty rates had almost returned to the levels that existed in the last half of the 1970s.

Little progress has been recorded in reducing the high rates of black poverty during the last decade. In fact, for the decade as a whole the trend has been towards increasing rates of poverty. In 1986, as noted, nearly one out of every three black persons is below the poverty level. At its peak the recession of the early 1980s added over 2.2 million new black persons to the poverty rolls, compared to the numbers in poverty in 1978. In the four years since the recovery began, there are 1,358,000 more black persons in poverty than in 1978.

The lack of progress during the last decade is in sharp contrast with the major reduction in poverty rates that occurred during the 1960s. Between 1959 and 1970 the black poverty rate declined from 55.1 percent to 33.5 percent. The number of blacks in poverty fell by over 2,800,000 persons between 1959 and 1969. During the decade of the 1970s, up until 1978, the absolute number of persons in poverty held almost steady, fluctuating in a narrow band between 7.3 and 7.7 million.

Rates of poverty in the black community continue to be much higher than they are in the white community. As shown in Table 6, the White poverty rate in 1986 was 11 percent — about one-third of the black poverty rate. The poverty rate among white children of 15.3 percent was about one-third of the 42.7 percent rate of poverty among black children. In general the rate of poverty among blacks during the 1980s has been a little less than three times the white rate.

White poverty has also trended upwards during the past decade. This is also shown by the data in Table 6. In fact the relative increase in poverty among whites has been greater than the increase in poverty among blacks. And while black poverty rates have almost regained the levels of the late 1970s, white poverty rates are still at least 20 percent higher than the levels attained in the late 1970s.

Note also that while the proportion of blacks in poverty is almost three times the proportion of whites in poverty, there are many more white persons actually in poverty. In 1986, for example, the white poverty rate translated to 22,183,000 white persons, compared to 8,983,000 black persons. There are even more white children below the poverty level: in 1986 7,714,000 white children versus 4,039,000 black children. Thus, although black persons are much more likely to be poor than white persons, there are more poor whites than poor blacks because of the larger white population.

Poverty rates also vary by region (see Table 7). In 1986 the highest poverty rate for the black population was in the Midwest, where 34.5 percent were below the poverty level. The Midwest was also the region with greatest racial inequality in poverty rates during 1986: the black poverty rate was more than three times the white poverty rate of 10.6 percent. Poverty in the South was close to the Midwest rate at 33.6 percent; the South also had the second highest level of racial inequality in poverty rates. The lowest poverty rates for blacks in both absolute and relative terms existed in the West, followed by the Northeast.

### Table 6
### Percent of Persons Below the Poverty Level

|      | Black | White | B/W  |
|------|-------|-------|------|
| 1986 | 31.1  | 11.0  | 2.83 |
| 1985 | 31.3  | 11.4  | 2.75 |
| 1982 | 35.6  | 12.0  | 2.97 |
| 1978 | 30.6  | 8.7   | 3.52 |
| 1970 | 33.5  | 9.9   | 3.38 |

Source: U.S. Dept. of Commerce, Bureau of the Census. *Money Income and Poverty Status . . .: 1986,* Table 16.

## Table 7
## Poverty Rates for Regions: Selected Years

|      | NORTHEAST | | | MIDWEST | | | SOUTH | | | WEST | | |
|------|-----|------|------|------|------|------|------|------|------|------|------|------|
|      | Blk | Wht | B/W | Blk | Wht | B/W | Blk | Wht | B/W | Blk | Wht | B/W |
| 1986 | 24.0 | 8.9 | 2.7 | 34.5 | 10.6 | 3.3 | 33.6 | 11.8 | 2.8 | 21.7 | 12.3 | 1.8 |
| 1984 | 32.2 | 10.7 | 3.0 | 37.9 | 11.5 | 3.3 | 33.6 | 12.0 | 2.8 | 26.6 | 11.8 | 2.3 |
| 1978 | 29.1 | 8.2 | 3.5 | 24.8 | 7.4 | 3.4 | 34.1 | 10.2 | 3.3 | 26.1 | 8.9 | 2.9 |
| 1970 | 20.0 | 7.7 | 2.6 | 25.7 | 8.9 | 2.9 | 42.6 | 12.4 | 3.4 | 20.4 | 10.6 | 1.9 |

Source: U.S. Dept. of Commerce, Bureau of the Census, *Money Income and Poverty Status . . .: 1986* and Bureau of the Census, Current Population Reports, Series P-60, *Characteristics of the Population Below Poverty Level.* 1984, 1978, 1970.

Regional trends in poverty have been similar to regional trends in income. Since 1970 poverty has gone up for blacks in the Midwest and the Northeast. Poverty rates have fluctuated around the same range in the West and have declined in the South. The recession of the early 1980s raised poverty rates in all regions. The recovery has had its greatest impacts in the Northeast and the West. Moderate improvements have occurred in the South and the Midwest. However, the Midwest has clearly experienced the greatest increase in black poverty since the early 1970s.

White poverty rates have reflected a pattern of change similar to black poverty rates. As a result there was no increase in relative poverty rates during this period. In fact, except for the Midwest, white poverty may have increased at slightly faster rates than black poverty over the past decade. As a result, relative poverty rates may have declined somewhat since the late 1970s. However, blacks are nearly three times as likely to be in poverty in all regions outside of the West. Even in the West, blacks are generally twice as likely as whites to be in poverty.

## EXPLANATIONS FOR LOW BLACK ECONOMIC STATUS

The preceding pages confirm the economic status of the black population is low in both absolute and relative terms. Why do blacks continue to have so much lower incomes and higher rates of poverty than whites? And why has there been so little progress in reducing these gaps in the last decade?

The economic status of blacks depends on two factors. First, it depends on the overall structure and performance of the American economy. All else equal, the economic status of black Americans will be better if the overall performance and structure of the American economy is better. Second, the economic status of blacks depends on the level and character of black participation in American economic life. The more blacks participate at a meaningful level, the better off they will be, all else being equal.

We can thus look in two directions for an explanation of recent trends in black economic status. First, we can look at recent trends in the national economy. Black economic status could be negatively impacted by national economic trends if either the total size of the economic pie shrinks or if the structure changes in such a way as to disadvantage blacks more than it disadvantages whites. Second, we can look at recent trends in the level and character of black participation in the national economy. Black economic status will not improve if the level or character of black participation in the economy either worsens or does not improve.

It should be apparent, however, that the second of these two factors is the more important for understanding the extensive racial inequality in American economic life. This is because no change in the national economy can have a differential impact on blacks unless there are differences in the level or character of black and white participation in the economy.

*Recent Economic Performance and the Economic Status of Blacks*

As was pointed out in the 1986 and 1987 editions of this volume, several macroeconomic factors have had an impact on the level and structure of economic activity during the past few years that have probably been unfavorable to blacks. Note the rapid expansion of the labor force since the early 1970s. This expansion was fueled by the maturation of the baby-boom generation and female labor force participation. Because of the maturation of the baby boom, the working age population grew by over 23 percent between 1970 and 1980, compared to about 14 percent between 1960 and 1970. At the same time the rate of female participation in the labor force increased from 42.7 to 50.9 percent. Although the growth in the size of the working age population slowed, the rate of female participation continued to increase between 1980 and 1986, when it reached 55.3 percent.

These two factors resulted in a larger than usual increase in the supply of labor. Between 1970 and 1986 the civilian labor force increased by 35,063,000 workers, or about 42 percent. In the preceding 17 years, the labor force increased by only 28 percent, or about 17,779,000 workers. This rapid growth of the labor force has led to an upward drift in the rate of unemployment and a decline in male participation rates. These circumstances undoubtedly increased the competition between workers for relatively scarce employment opportunities and added to the difficulties blacks experienced in gaining employment.

Recent structural shifts have also had an impact on the economic status of blacks. Job growth has taken place in the low-wage service industries rather than in the high-wage goods-producing industries. For example, between 1979 and 1986, total private sector nonagricultural employment increased 12.8 percent. A net total of 9.5 million new jobs were added to the private nonagricultural sector. During this same period, jobs in the goods-producing sector actually declined by about 1.5 million jobs. Jobs in the manufacturing sector alone declined by over 1.8 million between 1979 and 1986. In contrast, the service-providing sectors added 11.9 million jobs. Retail trade alone added almost three-million jobs, while the service sector added nearly six-million new jobs.

The shift in the structure of employment has been dramatic. In 1970 manufacturing employment accounted for 33 percent of all private sector jobs and the retail and service sectors accounted for about 39 percent of private sector jobs. By 1986 the manufacturing share had dropped to 23 percent; the share of employment accounted for by the retail trade and service sectors had grown to over 49 percent.

These structural shifts have important impacts on the economic status of blacks. First, the rapidly growing sectors are the ones which have traditionally been heavy employers of female workers, while the slow-growing sectors have traditionally been heavy employers of males. In 1984, for example, manufacturing was the only one of the goods-producing sectors in which more than 20 percent of the workers were women. And female employment manufacturing was only 33 percent. On the other hand, more than half of the employees were women in all of the three most rapidly growing service-providing sectors. These job growth patterns undoubtedly have increased the pressure on male employment and the competition for jobs in the traditional male-employing sectors.

Again, the sectors that are growing most rapidly are also the low-wage sectors. The sectors which grew slowest between 1979 and 1986 were mining, durable manufacturing, nondurable manufacturing, transportation and public utilities, and construction, in that order. Their average weekly wages were $527, $426, $356, $459, and $466, respectively. The four fastest-growing sectors were services: finance; insurance and real estate; retail trade; and wholesale trade. Their wages were $265, $305, $176, and $359, respectively. There is obviously a growing shortage of good-paying jobs.

The earnings potential from working has not only been reduced because of the structural shift in employment to low-wage sectors but also because of the slow growth in real wages that has occurred since the early 1970s. Average weekly earnings of production or non-supervisory workers on nonagricultural payrolls have declined since the early 1970s. This indicator stood 15 percent lower in 1986 at $304.85 than it was in 1972 at $358.72. Wages by this measure have declined by 11 percent since 1978.

The decline in average earnings since the early 1970s has affected all industries except mining. Average weekly earnings in major industrial sectors declined from three percent to 27 percent. The only industry in which 1986 average earnings in constant dollars is higher than 1972 earnings is mining, where average earnings have increased by six percent. Some of the largest declines in average earnings since 1972 have occurred in the trade and service sectors. These sectors, which already had the lowest relative wages in 1972, have fallen further behind since the early 1970s. These are also the sectors in which employment has grown fastest.

Wage stagnation and decline has continued during the 1980s. In fact for most industries the recession of the early 1980s accelerated the pace of wage decline. Although there was a brief period of recovery for constant dollar wages in 1983 and 1984, the first two years of the recovery, wage decline and stagnation resumed in 1985 for most major sectors. Average weekly earnings in the fast-growing retail trade sector have declined over ten percent since 1980 and over seven percent since 1984. The implication of these wage trends is that much of the growth in employment opportunities for ordinary Americans has been in low-wage jobs.

## Black Participation in the National Economy

The macroeconomic trends just discussed created the environment in which black participation in the American economy has evolved during the past two decades. For most workers the past 15 years have been a period characterized by increasing competition for a shrinking pool of opportunities to earn a good living. This period has witnessed unprecedented growth in the supply of labor fueled by a baby boom and rapid transformation of the role of women in our society. Simultaneously industrial transformation has altered the distribution of jobs away from the high-paying male-dominated sectors. General wage stagnation has occurred in all of the major sectors. Moreover, a major transformation in the international comparative advantage of the United States has also been underway.

It is not surprising that the character of black participation in the economy has not improved greatly during the past two decades. As we have repeatedly pointed out, low and unequal black incomes and high rates of poverty reflect the low and unequal character of black participation in the American economy. Blacks own less of America than whites and also continue to have a relatively disadvantageous labor market status. As a result they have lower earnings from property and labor. This leads directly to their lower and unequal incomes and higher rates of poverty.

## Wealth and Business Ownership

The lack of improvement in the absolute and relative economic status of blacks during the recent past reflects the lack of improvement in the relative character of black participation in the economy. The latest evidence suggests that blacks continue to own relatively little wealth and productive property. An indication of the relatively limited business ownership among blacks is reflected in the fact that in 1986 the sales of the 256th largest company on the *Fortune 500* list were equal to the combined sales of the 100 largest black-owned businesses on the *Black Enterprise* list. According to calculations based on U.S. census data for 1982, blacks owned about 17 percent as many businesses per person as whites. And all black businesses generated only about 1.4 percent as many receipts per black person as all U.S. businesses did per person. Furthermore, the total employment of all black businesses combined in 1982 was only 165,765 persons as compared to total private sector employment of over 70 million and total black employment of 9.2 million persons. Black business ownership is clearly still very limited.

More general wealth data for 1984 from a recent Census Bureau report confirms the limited participation of blacks in the ownership of wealth. The report found that black wealth holdings of all types were significantly lower than white wealth holdings. This reflected the fact that blacks were significantly less likely to own any given type of wealth, and the average size of the holdings of those blacks who did have some wealth was significantly smaller than the average holdings of whites. As a consequence the overall median wealth holdings of blacks at $3,397 was only nine percent as large as the median wealth holdings of whites (see Billy Tidwell's "Black Wealth: Fact *and* Fiction," in the Appendix).

The limited business ownership and wealth holdings of blacks have two consequences. First, blacks are likely to have limited direct influence on private economic decisions. Second, blacks are likely to receive substantially less income from property than whites.

Although there is no direct measure of influence by race, the fact that few American corporations have black top executives and CEOs or black-controlled boards of directors suggests that blacks exert limited influence over business decisions. The limited private sector investment in majority black communities and the limited access of black businesses to financial capital are two consequences of this limited influence.

Census data make it clear that the differences in wealth ownership have large income impacts. For example, in 1984, blacks received significantly less income from sources related to the ownership of businesses or wealth than whites. They received only $113 per person from self-employment compared to $599 per person received from self-employment by whites. The disparity of income from productive wealth ownership was even larger. Income receipts from sources such as dividends, interest, rental income, and profits was only $119 per person for blacks versus $944 for whites.

Lower receipts from income sources related to wealth and property ownership are a major source of the overall income gap between blacks and whites. In 1984, for example, per-person black receipts from these sources was $1311 less than per-person white receipts. This difference accounted for about 28 percent of the overall income gap.

*Labor Market Characteristics and Black Economic Status*

The disparity in labor market participation accounts for a much larger proportion of the disparities in black and white income and poverty levels. In 1984, for example, black earnings from labor market participation were only $4,990 per person compared to $7,943 for whites. This $2,953 gap produced an 83.1-billion dollar aggregate income gap. Thus, earnings differences accounted for about 63 percent of the overall income gap.

*Demographic Characteristics*

The earnings differential arises from three factors. A demographic factor, an employment factor, and a wage rate factor. Two demographic considerations influence the relative earnings of blacks. The first is the proportion of the population that is of working age. Blacks generally have a smaller proportion of their population that is of working age. Thus, there are fewer blacks to earn.

In 1986, for example, only 72.3 percent of the black population versus 79.1 percent of the white population was of working age. Second, blacks have proportionally fewer males in their population than do whites. Indeed these "missing" males are a major cause of the relatively smaller proportion of working age persons. In 1986, for example, the black population had only 827 males for every thousand women of working age, whereas the white population had about 930 males for every thousand females. This difference amounts to a total of 1,176,000 missing black males of working age.

The two demographic factors have a significant impact on black income. A rough calculation, assuming that the income and earnings of the missing males would be equal to the average income of existing black males, suggests that the 1986 black income loss due to the missing males is about 14.3 billion dollars. This implies that 9.6 percent of the overall income gap and 12.1 percent of the wage and salary gap are results of this one demographic factor.

A similar calculation suggests that the result of the relatively smaller proportion of working age individuals excluding the missing males reduces black income by another 8.0 billion dollars. This adds another 5.3 percent to the overall income gap and 18.9 percent to the wage and salary gap. Thus the two demographic factors are jointly responsible for about 14.9 percent of the overall income gap and 18.9 percent of the wage and salary gap. The total 1986 reduction in black income due to these demographic factors is around 22.2 billion dollars, and the reduction in black wage and salary earnings is estimated at about 17.7 billion dollars.

*Employment Status*

Working-age black males and females have lower employment rates. Blacks have not always had lower employment rates than whites. Until about 1960 blacks generally had higher overall employment rates than whites. Since then, the gap between the overall rate of employment of blacks and whites has widened.

In the first seven months of 1987, on the average 54.9 percent of the black and 62.2 percent of the white working age population were employed. Thus, at the present time, working age blacks are about 88 percent as likely to be employed as working age whites.

The employment rate gaps are highest for men and teenagers. Black males over 20 are currently about 88.6 percent as likely to be employed as white males over 20, while black teenagers are only about 51.1 percent as likely to be employed as white teenagers. On the other hand, black women are about 98.8 percent as likely to be employed as white women.

All three black groups have been losing ground in employment terms for the past two decades. For adult males and teenagers this has been reflected in gradually widening gaps. For black women this was reflected in gradually declining black female advantages in employment rates until about 1980. The proportion of white adult females employed surpassed the proportion of black females employed for the first time after 1980.

Racial differences in employment rates arise from racial differences in labor force participation rates and racial differences in unemployment rates. At present both adult black males and black teenagers have slightly lower participation rates than corresponding whites. This is offset somewhat by the slightly higher participation rates among adult black females. For example, in 1987, the average participation rate for adult black males was 74.9 percent versus 78.5 percent for adult white males; for teenagers, 57.5 percent for whites versus 39.8 percent for blacks; and for adult black females, 59.5 percent versus 55.5 percent for adult white women. The overall average black participation rate in the first seven months of 1987 of 63.5 percent was 96.7 percent of the 65.7 percent white participation rate.

Only about thirty percent of the overall gap in employment rates arise from participation rate differences. The rest arises from differences in unemployment. During the past ten years, unemployment rates for blacks have been high and have drifted upwards relative to white unemployment rates. This experience has been true for black adults of both sexes as well as for teenagers.

For example, the average annual unemployment rate for blacks in 1986 was 14.5 percent versus 6.0 percent for whites, while black teenagers had a 39.3 percent unemployment rate compared to only 15.6 percent for white teenagers. Since 1975 overall unemployment has averaged 15.2 percent for blacks and 6.7 percent for whites. The ratio of black-to-white unemployment rates throughout this period has averaged well over the traditional two-to-one historical ratio. Unemployment rate gaps have grown most between black and white women.

Unemployment has declined somewhat in the past few years with recovery from the recession. For the first seven months of 1987, however — after five years of recovery, black unemployment rates remained high both absolutely and relative to white unemployment rates. Overall black unemployment averaged 13.5 percent of the labor force during this period. In contrast the white unemployment rate was only 5.5 percent. Thus, blacks were still about two and one-half times as likely to be unemployed as whites.

Even black adults continued to experience high unemployment rates during 1987. Adult male unemployment averaged 11.7 percent and adult female unemployment averaged 12.0 percent during the first seven months of the year. In contrast, white adult men and women had average unemployment rates of 5.0 and 4.7 percent, respectively. Adult black males were somewhat less than two and one-half times as likely to be unemployed as adult white males, while black female adults were slightly more than two and one-half times as likely to be unemployed as white female adults.

As one might expect from the regional variation in income and poverty rates, there is also marked variation in labor market status of blacks among the regions. The greatest absolute and relative labor market difficulties for blacks currently and for the past few years have occurred in the Midwest. During 1986 the unemployment rate for blacks in the Midwest was 19.8 percent; the employment rate was only 48.8 percent. The average unemployment rate for blacks for the last six years in the Midwest was over 23 percent. In contrast, the unemployment rates though high in the other three regions were still considerably less than in the Midwest. The average in the other regions for the past six years has ranged from 15.0 to 15.6 percent. The unemployment rate in 1986 was 11.3 percent in the Northeast, and 13.9 percent in both the South and West. Employment rates in the other three regions were 52.8 percent in the Northeast, 56 percent in the South, and 56.8 percent in the West.

Racial inequality is also substantial in all regions. The unemployment rates for blacks are much higher and the employment rates significantly lower than they are for whites in all regions. In the Midwest, white unemployment in 1986 was only 6.2 percent, which was less than one-third of the black rate. Whereas only 48.8 percent of the black population was employed, 61.3 percent of the white population in the Midwest was employed. Although the gaps were somewhat lower in the other regions, the black unemployment rate was still more than twice as high as the white unemployment rate in all the other regions, and black employment rates were significantly lower.

The widespread disparities that exist between the labor market status of black and white workers throughout the country are even more apparent when data for individual metropolitan areas are examined. Table 8 displays a summary of the level of unemployment for black and white workers in 38 large metropolitan areas with data for blacks. As can be seen there is very little overlap between the level of unemployment experienced by blacks and that experienced by whites. The highest unemployment rate recorded for whites in any area during 1986 was 9.0 percent, while blacks had unemployment rates worse than this in 35 of 38 places. In general black unemployment within each metropolitan area was at least twice the white level and in some cases up to four times the white level.

While whites had no areas where unemployment exceeded nine percent, blacks had six areas where unemployment was greater than 20 percent. In each of these metropolitan areas — Buffalo, Chicago, Cleveland, Detroit, Milwaukee, and Pittsburgh, unemployment has been over 20 percent for four years. Moreover, racial inequality is glaring in all of these places. The ratio of the black-to-white unemployment rate is over three-to-one in five of the six areas, and over four-to-one in half of the areas.

The impact of unemployment rate differentials on the economic status of blacks is substantial. Simple estimates suggest that the black employment level averaged about 1,640,000 fewer jobs in 1986 than it would have if employment parity existed. Assuming that unemployed blacks would earn on the average about as much as currently employed blacks if they had jobs, this implies a loss of about 25.6 billion dollars in black earnings. This leads us to estimate that the high employment gaps could explain as much as 30.8 percent of the overall earnings gap.

*Wage Rate Differences*

The second factor which generates differences in black and white aggregate and per-person labor market earnings is differences in wage rates. On the

**Table 8**
**Number of Large Metropolitan Areas with**
**Unemployment Rates within Specified Range by Race, 1986**

| Rate | | Black | White |
|---|---|---|---|
| 2.0 - 3.9% | | 1 | 8 |
| 4.0 - 4.9% | | 0 | 9 |
| 5.0 - 5.9% | | 2 | 12 |
| 6.0 - 8.9% | | 3 | 8 |
| 9.0 - 10.9% | | 9 | 1 |
| 11.0 - 13.9% | | 7 | 0 |
| 14.0 - 16.9% | | 6 | 0 |
| 17.0 - 19.9% | | 4 | 0 |
| 20.0% + | | 6 | 0 |
| All Ranges | | 38 | 38 |

Source: U.S. Dept. of Labor, Bureau of Labor Statistics. *Geographic Profile of Employment and Unemployment 1986,* Table 23.

average the wage rates of employed blacks are lower than the wage rates of employed whites. These lower wage rates arise from two factors: differences in the types of jobs held by black and white workers, and differences in the wages blacks receive for each type of job.

*Characteristics of Black Jobs and Their Impact on Average Wages*

Black jobs differ from white jobs in many ways. Blacks are less likely to hold part-time jobs. In 1986, for example, 17.9 percent of black jobs and 19.2 percent of white jobs were part-time. Since the average part-time job pays less than the average full-time job, this characteristic is advantageous to blacks. However, even though the total proportion of blacks working part-time is lower, the proportion of black part-timers who would like to work full-time but can't find jobs is much higher than the white proportion. In 1986, 8.4 percent of black workers were *involuntary* part-timers, compared to 4.7 percent of white workers.

In 1986 blacks earned $93 per week on the average part-time job, while the average full-time job paid blacks $291 per week. A rough calculation suggests that median black earnings would be 1.6 percent lower if blacks had the white distribution of full-time and part-time status. Since the actual estimated ratio of black-to-white median earnings was 80.5 percent, this suggests that the earnings gap is reduced by about 8.2 percent because of the lower proportions of blacks who work part-time.

Another factor that influences the earnings gap is the sex composition of the work force. A larger proportion of black than white workers is female — 49.8 percent for blacks versus 43.8 percent for whites. Since the median earnings of female workers are generally lower than the median earnings of male workers, the higher proportion of females in the black work force contributes to lower median earnings. For example, in 1986 the median earnings of black females working full-time for wages and salaries was only $263, while the median earnings for corresponding male workers ws $318. A rough calculation shows that this factor by itself accounted for about 5.1 percent of the black-white gap in median earnings for full-time wage and salary workers.

Blacks and whites are also likely to be employed as different classes of workers. Blacks are generally more likely to be employed as wage and salary workers and whites are more likely to be self-employed workers. Since self-employed workers as a class make more than wage and salary workers, the lower proportion of self-employed blacks increases the earnings gaps for blacks.

On the other hand, blacks are more likely to be employed as government wage and salary workers while white wage and salary workers are more likely to be employed in the private nonagricultural and agricultural sectors. For example, in 1986 23.7 percent of black wage and salary workers worked for the government versus 15.4 percent of corresponding white workers. Since the median earning of government workers of $409 is higher than the median wages of private wage and salary workers in both the agricultural ($216) and nonagricultural sectors ($347), this factor favors black earnings. A rough calculation suggests that the earnings of black wage and salary workers may be 1.7 percent higher because of the higher proportion of blacks who work for the government. This factor is estimated to lower the black-white earnings gap by about eight percent, but the impact is not large.

Black and white workers also have different industry distributions. Since wages and salaries vary across industries, this factor could also have impact on the observed differences in black and white earnings. Higher percentages of blacks than whites are employed in four industry sectors — government (6.8 vs. 4.4 percent), services (36.5 vs. 30.7 percent), transportation, communications, and public utilities (9.3 vs. 6.8 percent), and non-durable goods manufacturing (9.5 vs. 7.4 percent). Blacks are less likely to be employed in all the other sectors — agriculture, forestry, and fishing (1.4 vs. 3.1); mining (0.3 vs. 0.9); construction (4.6 vs. 7.0); durable manufacturing (10.0 vs. 11.6); wholesale trade (2.5 vs. 4.2); retail trade (13.9 vs. 17.0); and finance, insurance, and real estate (5.3 vs. 6.9). However, given that the pattern of wage differences is not consistently against blacks, the industry composition factor does not appear to be disadvantageous to blacks. In fact blacks appear to be helped slightly by this factor. Our rough estimate suggests that the racial gaps in earnings could be as much as 5.5 percent lower because of a favorable black industry distribution.

Finally we will consider the impact of differences in the occupational distribution of blacks and whites. It is well known that blacks have traditionally had less favorable occupational distributions than whites. Blacks are more likely to work in low-paying less prestigious occupations.

The occupational distributions for blacks and whites for 1986 are shown in Table 9. It is evident from this table that blacks are still less likely to work in the better occupations. For example, both black males and females are less likely than their white counterparts to be in managerial, professional, technician, or sales occupations, while they are more likely to be laborers, service workers, and operatives.

---

**Table 9**
**Distribution of Employed Population by Major**
**Occupational Categories by Race and Sex for 1986**

|  | Male | | Female | |
|---|---|---|---|---|
|  | Black | White | Black | White |
| Executives, Administrators & Managers | 6.2 | 13.9 | 6.0 | 10.0 |
| Professional Speciality | 6.6 | 11.9 | 10.7 | 14.6 |
| Technician and Related Support | 2.0 | 3.0 | 3.1 | 3.2 |
| Sales Occupations | 5.2 | 11.9 | 8.7 | 13.7 |
| Administrative Support Incl. Clerical | 8.6 | 5.4 | 26.5 | 29.8 |
| Precision, Craft & Repair | 16.0 | 20.7 | 2.6 | 2.3 |
| Operatives, Assemblers & Inspectors | 11.0 | 7.4 | 10.6 | 5.9 |
| Transport Operatives & Matrl. Movers | 10.8 | 6.5 | 0.1 | 0.8 |
| Handlers, Cleaners, Helpers, Laborers | 12.2 | 5.9 | 2.1 | 1.5 |
| Private Household Workers | 0.1 | 0.1 | 4.3 | 1.6 |
| Protective Service Workers | 4.2 | 2.4 | 0.8 | 0.4 |
| All Other Service Workers | 13.4 | 6.0 | 23.2 | 14.9 |
| Farming, Forestry, & Fishing | 3.7 | 4.9 | 0.4 | 1.2 |

Source: U.S. Dept. of Labor, Bureau of Labor Statistics. *Employment and Earnings, January 1987,* Table 21.

---

Rough calculations suggest that the occupational distributions of both sexes lower their earnings. The occupational factor by itself reduces black male wages relative to whites by 12.2 percent. This accounts for 45.9 percent of the wage gap between full-time black and white male workers. The occupational dissimilarity between black and white females reduces the wages of black females by 8.6 percent. This accounts for 82 percent of the gap in the median earnings of full-time female workers. Thus, the occupational differences account for a major portion of the lower-average wage rates of black males and females.

*Wage Rates within Occupational Categories*

As noted, the second major category of influences on the earnings gap is differences in wage rates for the same type of job. However, available data will not permit a detailed analysis of the contribution of this factor. At best we can examine the contribution of wage differences within broad occupational categories. However, there is substantial variation in jobs within broad occupational categories. Thus, much of the wage differences within broad occupational categories may reflect differences in the distribution of black and white workers across the subcategories which make up the broad occupation.

The latest available data suggest that there is fairly significant variation in the usual wages of black and white males within broad occupational categories. In 1982, for example, while the overall ratio of black-to-white median earnings for full-time workers was about 76 percent, the ratio ranged between 80 and 89 percent in every broad occupational category except sales, which had a ratio of 70 percent. However, there was no broad occupational category in which black male workers had usual earnings as high as the usual earnings of white males.

We performed a very rough calculation to determine the proportion of the earnings gap due to these wage differences within the same broad occupational category. The calculation based on 1981 data suggests that the ratio of black-to-white male usual earnings would be around 90 percent instead of 76 percent if black wages were equal within broad occupational categories. This implies that roughly 57 percent of the gap in usual wages of full-time black and white male workers is due to wage rate differences within broad occupations. However, a good part of the wage differences within the broad occupational categories reflects the different distribution of black males across the suboccupations which make up each broad category. Within each broad category black males tend to be distributed to the lower-wage, less prestigious suboccupations.

A similar calculation was performed for females. The differences are much smaller between black and white wages within broad occupational categories. For the seven occupational categories for which wage data were available in 1981, blacks had higher wages in one category, wages were equal in three categories, and whites had higher wages in the other three categories. However, in two of these latter three, black wages were about 95 percent of white wages, and in the other, black wages were about 88 percent of white wages.

Given the much greater wage equality among female workers, it is no surprise that wage differences within occupational categories account for a much smaller share of the smaller black-white wage gap. The calculation shows that if black females had the same wage rates as white females, there would be at most about an eight-percent reduction in the wage gap. Thus, almost all of the small wage gap between black females and white females was due to differences in job distributions. However, there has been some indication of slowly increasing wage inequality between black and white females; this may be due to gradually increasing wage rate differences within broad occupational groupings.

In summary, the black-white gap in labor market earnings arises from a number of factors. First, we discussed the demographic factors. Black labor market status is lowered because of the "missing males" and the relatively small proportions of the black population of working age. Second, we noted that blacks are disadvantaged because of lower labor-force participation rates among black males and black teenagers. Blacks receive an advantage from the higher participation rate of black females above 25. Blacks are also disadvantaged by having higher unemployment rates. Third, we noted that blacks were disadvantaged because of lower earnings rates among working blacks. These lower rates arose from differences in the types of jobs held and because of different rates of pay for the same job. The combined impact of all of the factors cost the black population about $93.8 billion dollars in 1986.

## CONCLUSIONS AND POLICY DISCUSSION

Racial inequality in economic life is still with us and is also very extensive. More disturbing is the fact that the evidence suggests that society has not been making any measurable progress in the last few years to ameliorate the high rates of poverty, low incomes, low levels of wealth, limited business ownership, and disadvantaged labor market positions that continue to characterize the economic status of the black population.

To be sure, some small gains have been realized in the absolute status of blacks in the last few years, relative to the position at the depths of the last recession. These improvements are welcome. They are too limited, however; many indicators have still not recovered to their post-recession highs. In any case the goal of parity was distant even before the current period of limited progress. Thus, little satisfaction can be taken in efforts which barely maintain the status quo and do not even begin to move us close to true economic parity.

The trend that indicates an increasing proportion of the population is slipping into the very lowest income class is also very disturbing, especially since this transformation is occurring at the same time that there has been growth in the proportion of the population that is receiving very high incomes. Too few blacks are members of the higher income classes, but the increase in the percentage of blacks receiving relatively high income is welcome. However, an increase in the percentage of individuals receiving relatively high incomes while the percentage receiving low incomes is growing is not a desirable trend. Growth in income at the lower end of the spectrum of opportunities is badly needed.

It is clear that the trends are the result of complex macroeconomic forces which have been shaping the structure and performance of our economy. These forces are limiting the capacity of the economy to provide sufficient employment opportunities at decent wages for ordinary American workers. Structural changes and other forces have been putting substantial downward pressure on wage levels. General demand factors have prevented the expansion of employment at a fast enough clip to employ fully all willing workers. These two factors jointly have reduced the economic status of all ordinary Americans—black and white. However, blacks have borne a disproportionate share of the burden.

The low relative economic status of blacks and the high share of economic burdens borne by blacks have their economic origins in blacks' limited ownership of human and nonhuman capital. These limitations have two impacts. They limit the extent of ownership and control of business enterprises. This limitation forces blacks to be dependent on white-owned or -controlled businesses for jobs, income, and goods and services. This makes them vulnerable to the possibility of discrimination. The limited human capital of blacks may make them less attractive to potential employers, which would limit the quantity and quality of opportunities that business owners are willing to provide for them. These three factors — limited ability for self-employment, limited attractiveness to employers, and racial discrimination — combine to produce the high level of racial disparities discussed above.

The experience of the last couple of decades supports several conclusions about prospects for improvement of the economic position of the black population. First it is apparent that in the absence of any significant changes in government policy or the relative ownership of businesses, wealth, and human capital, blacks will continue to bear a disproportionate share of the burdens created by economic failure. This is clearly the lesson of the recessions of the past two decades. In each recession the burdens of blacks have been disproportionately high. This conclusion is also supported by the dramatic impact that the decline in the industrial heartland has had on the economic status of blacks relative to whites. The relative burdens on blacks in comparison to whites in the Midwest region and many of our largest cities have been at unprecedented high levels during their recent economic difficulties.

The second lesson is that the relative position of blacks depends more on what is happening in the broader economy than on what is happening in the black community. The observed variation in the economic position of blacks across regions and metropolitan areas as well as across time as the economic situation changes makes this supposition apparent. Blacks fare less well in environments which are experiencing economic difficulties and fare much better in environments which experience prosperity.

It is also apparent that the economic position of blacks is generally lifted up as the economic position of the area improves. A rising tide does indeed lift all boats. However, it is equally apparent that the general prosperity of an area within the parameters that have historically characterized the American economy is not sufficient to eliminate the economic problems of blacks in either an absolute or relative sense. The economic status of blacks is generally unsatisfactory in good times as well as bad. Indeed the major share of black economic difficulties persists at all stages of the business cycle.

A slightly more complex proposition is that the position of blacks varies with the political and social traditions of their communities. Blacks still fare less well in the South as a general proposition, regardless of the level of economic activity. They also generally fare better in the West than in any other region. These regional variations do not appear to be related solely to variations in local economic conditions. Rather they appear to be connected to variations in local cultural, political, and social environments. This implies that there is room within the present structure for substantial improvement in the economic position of blacks.

It is also apparent that significant improvement in the position of blacks cannot be achieved and maintained without major reductions in the racial disparities in wealth, business ownership, and human capital. Such reductions are necessary to eliminate the income disparities that arise from returns to ownership of productive wealth and self-employment. They are also required to reduce the excessive one-way black dependency which makes them so vulnerable to racial discrimination.

The internal resources of blacks are inadequate to bring about enough increases in the ownership of businesses, human capital, and nonhuman wealth to come even close to achieving a significant reduction of racial inequality. It is apparent that significant general improvement in the position of the black community as a whole will require a significant inflow of resources from sources external to the black community.

These conclusions provide a basic framework for discussing strategies for alleviating the long-term economic subordination of the black population. First, it is apparent that significant relative improvement for blacks can only occur through three paths. Improvement can occur if there is significant improvement in the structure and or performance of the American economy. This implies that blacks will benefit from successful efforts to solve the current economic problems in a fashion which improves the structure and performance of the American economy. On the other hand solutions which look to retrenchment or squeezing the living standards and wage levels of ordinary Americans will definitely be harmful to blacks. In the absence of any significant change in policy and practice, blacks can expect to bear a greater than proportionate share of the losses from retrenchment and cost-cutting.

The second path that holds promise for ameliorating some of the economic disparities and hardships currently experienced by blacks is an effort to reduce discrimination. In the absence of significant change in the level of ownership, blacks will remain dependent on white resource owners. Discrimination by such owners has immediate and devastating impacts on the capability of blacks to prosper economically. Significant reductions in discrimination could bring immediate benefits in terms of increased opportunities to earn as well as increased opportunities to develop. Efforts to reduce the level of discrimination thus have an important role to play in the strategy for improving the relative position of blacks.

Third, improving the relative position of blacks in the overall economy is needed. This path can and should be pursued regardless of the overall performance of the economy or efforts to reduce the level of discrimination. Reductions in the disparities of ownership and power are the main pathways for achieving an improvement in the relative position of blacks. Achievement of this objective will break the cycle of excessive dependency and reduce black vulnerability to racial discrimination. Thus, this path offers the possibility of providing a permanent solution to the problem of racial inequality in economic life.

The possibility of implementing any of these strategies will depend on the ability of those in black and white communities who care about ending racial disparities in economic life to organize effective social and political coalitions to bring about change. These coalitions must get the status of blacks back on the national agenda. They must develop the social and political muscle necessary to pursue the paths presented above. Their task will be particularly difficult given the current drift towards economic retrenchment and *laissez-faire*. However, the task is not impossible and can be attained if advocates of a more equitable society are willing to put forth the required efforts.

# CONCLUSIONS AND
# RECOMMENDATIONS

# Conclusions

This thirteenth edition of *The State of Black America* continues the National Urban League commitment of presenting responsible and thoughtful analyses of key issues which confront Black America. The articles contained herein demonstrate both the magnitude, the complexity, and the entrenchment of some of the problems. To state problems is not to succumb to them, however. Underlying the analyses is a constant theme of hope, of motivation, of counting on the collective American conscience to commit to the eradication of obstacles to equality. In the spirit of the Bicentennial, we hold certain truths to be self-evident. We know that life, liberty, and the pursuit of happiness are meaningless ideals without jobs, education, housing, and other minimal requirements to live in a modern society.

Racism and poverty persist as the major obstacles isolating millions of Americans roadblocked on the way to attaining the American Dream. The number of homeless and hungry in this rich land of ours has grown. Inequities in education and job opportunities contribute to a pervasive sense of despair and helplessness. The energy of our activism has just begun to melt the indifference that has frozen this country in a veritable "ice age."

The National Urban League continues to work to bring about meaningful reforms in education, job training, social welfare, and other key areas of American life.

We continue to sound the call that America ignores at its own peril the responsibility of translating necessary and fair recommendations into realities. We call upon America to measure the success of programs not by their intent, but by the results.

We know that there are no simple solutions to complex problems, but we know, also, that we must not let despair frustrate us into complacency or lowered expectations.

We are encouraged, too, by the revival of conscience and fairness in the approaches to solving social problems, that reject further budget reductions for social welfare programs.

We are encouraged, too, by the revival of consciences and fairness in the call for full employment by such groups as the National Conference of Catholic Bishops. Voters have spoken in their rejection of extremist policies of the New Right.

We need more than rejection of extremist policies to fulfill the promise of justice and equality. We must revitalize our economy to provide jobs and opportunities as we integrate minorities into the mainstream.

Our advocacy must continue to deal with economic issues—because more blacks have lost jobs through industrial decline than through job discrimination.

Our agenda must include constant attention to crime, health, housing, and education because crack and heroin, poor health care, lack of housing, and inferior schools ruin black lives more effectively than the Klan.

While we are in the forefront of the self-responsibility evolution, we know that citizens must be aided by a compassionate government that creates opportunities and by a private sector that helps build partnerships that end poverty, create jobs, and usher in a new era of prosperity and brotherhood. We must eradicate the racism and poverty that stain our democracy.

Whitney Young gave us this vision of the future:

"It is a vision of an America in which children don't go hungry because their skin happens to be black—an America in which men don't go jobless because their skin happens to be black—an America in which mothers don't go homeless because their skin happens to be black. It is a vision of an America which provides its people with choices and with the means to exercise them. It is a vision of an America which glories in diversity and respects the unique contributions and traditions of all of its people.

"The Open Society," Young said, "will come about when all decent people, both blacks and whites, are galvanized to change the present society."

The challenge and responsibility rest not in one agency alone. All of us must work together to make a difference.

# Recommendations

## 1. Empowerment

**Active citizenship participation is the first step toward empowerment. Black people must use the power of the ballot in their own self-interest. Nowhere was black voting strength more evident than in the defeat of Robert Bork for appointment to the Supreme Court. Black voters, who found the views of Judge Bork repugnant, held accountable those officials they elected to represent their interests. In this election year, voting must be our primary agenda; those officials we elect or allow to be elected by others shape our future.**

We therefore call upon all black institutions to join with the National Urban League, our 112 affiliates, and other voter education organizations to lead a vigorous and visible public education campaign to inform black citizens of their rights and their obligation to register to vote and to vote on election day.

Because we believe that every reasonable effort must be made to enable citizens to vote, we also urge Congress and the president to support the Universal Voter Registration Act of 1987, which would establish mail-in registration and election day registration for federal elections.

## 2. Education

**Education is survival not only for individuals but also for the future viability of this country. America must increase the achievement level of black and other minority students in the public schools.**

The National Urban League's National Education Initiative is seeking to prepare black youngsters to function and prosper in today's economy. Likewise, all communities must demand the expectations of and the support for excellence in education for our children.

We call upon the Black Leadership Forum to adopt education as our continuing number-one priority until every black child is assured of the opportunity to get a quality public education. The Forum must join with the National Urban League in calling on all community services and advocacy agencies to demand that schools are funded at the levels necessary to accomplish the vital task of educating our young. We must demand a standard of excellence not only from our students but also from the institutions which are entrusted with their care.

Enrollment and success in institutions of higher learning should be a normal expectation for black youth. We must restore immediately cuts in college aid. In addition to the allocation of the necessary federal, state, and local resources, colleges and universities must make every reasonable effort to recruit, retain, and *graduate* black students.

3. **Health**

Inadequate health care is the imminent danger for many Americans, especially black Americans. It threatens a sense of security by its potential for physical and financial ruin.

We urge enactment of comprehensive health insurance legislation, including catastrophic health insurance legislation, so that the poor, the elderly, and the disadvantaged receive maximum parity in health coverage.

The devastation of AIDS requires that every sector in the community join in a commitment to stop this epidemic. While we must continue to search for a cure, our treatment of the victims of this disease must be humane and responsible. The AIDS issue must not be used as an excuse for further victimization of blacks, homosexuals, and other groups.

We call on the federal government to devote the funds necessary to combat AIDS and other sexually transmitted diseases.

4. **Family, Individual, and Child Services**

Too often programs that seek to solve some family and child problems create other problems instead, by establishing burdensome rules and inadequate support systems.

The multitude of problems requires that there be comprehensive programs for addressing them. Among the approaches is the enactment of the Youth Employment Services (YES) Act, which would offer job training to the growing number of unskilled, unemployed, young people who are in danger of becoming part of a permanent unemployable underclass.

The National Urban League recognizes that the American family is an institution in transition. We urge that programs that seek to stabilize family life consider different family structures—nuclear families, extended families, female-headed families—and the income and wealth differences between black and white families. Support efforts should be realistic and address these different structures.

Child care is an issue of importance to *all* families. We urge the federal government to provide leadership to assist states in increasing the number and quality of and the coordination among child care programs.

We encourage the U.S. Senate to support and the president to sign the legislation recently passed by the U.S. House of Representatives, the Family Welfare Reform Act of 1987 (H.R. 1720). This legislation incorporates the key principles of the National Urban League relative to welfare reform: education, training, and employment.

Black communities also have a role: to strengthen their collective moral fiber by building on the rich heritage of their past.

5. **Employment**

Joblessness tears at the fabric of American society. Lack of jobs destroys incentive and self-esteem, and undermines family life and individual stability.

Black unemployment is at official levels of 12 percent overall and approximately 35 percent for young people. Unofficial estimates are much higher.

We advocate a national goal of full employment, coupled with training and retraining to provide job opportunities, so that those who want to work can. Congress should take the initiative in establishing a full employment policy that would have a multitude of elements, including macroeconomic policies and tax reforms that stimulate expanded economic activity and encourage maximum use of the less skilled and educated workers. The policy would require aggressive affirmative action programs to ensure that blacks are included in employment gains; it should also include assistance to black businesses as well as meet the needs of displaced workers, older workers, new entrants into the work force, and female-headed households.

6. **Economic Development**
   **There is a need to develop a viable self-sustaining economic base in black communities.**

   While full employment will ultimately help in closing the wage gap, we also urge a national program of black economic development supported by the government and the private sector that assists in creating jobs in the black community and developing institutional wealth. Such an effort would not only strengthen black communities but our overall economy as well.

   Black businesses now represent only *two percent* of all businesses. That figure must be increased. The black community bears a responsibility to support all black businesses wherever and whenever possible. Government bears the responsibility of fostering minority small businesses through loan guarantees, technical assistance, and the continuation and further development of minority set-aside programs. The public/private sectors bear the responsibility of fostering black businesses by utilizing more of their services and products.

7. **Criminal Justice**
   **While crime is an American problem, it is disproportionately prevalent in black communities.**

   We urge black communities across the nation to take action now to save our communities from elements that are destroying them from within. At the same time, we urge compassionate approaches to helping to rehabilitate offenders, particularly juvenile offenders. We know that most crime has its roots outside the black community, but we also know that black people must bear their share of the responsibility to put a stop to crime and its insidious effects.

   The National Urban League's "Crime is Not a Part of Our Black Heritage" program is an effort to motivate community institutions such as churches, schools, and civic and social organizations to create a sense of culture, an appreciation of history, and a rededication to the values that have meant black survival.

   We also advocate that those who are convicted of crimes are sentenced fairly and equitably, irrespective of race or ethnic origin.

   We call on law enforcement officers to be responsible in their use of force to apprehend those suspected of committing crimes, in an effort to eliminate the stigma and stereotype that police brutality is the rule, not the exception, in black communities. We believe excessive force increases distrust of police and heightens racial tensions.

8. **Housing**

**The housing crisis is a national problem requiring a national solution. This crisis is clear evidence of the unraveling of the social safety net. Dramatically demonstrated by the increasing numbers of the homeless—including families with children, the crisis is also evident in the shrinking supply of affordable housing and in the mounting number of foreclosures against families who have lost their tenuous grip on the American Dream.**

We urge immediate intervention to help the homeless and to develop housing in the black community. There must be a national commitment to build affordable housing for low- and middle-income families.

We call upon the federal government to commit the necessary financial and human resources to solve their complex problem. We also call upon local governments to recognize and give financial support to the work of community-based groups that have created effective model housing development programs.

Where a regional solution is needed, we urge jurisdictions to develop cooperative regional approaches that prevent "dumping" the homeless problem on their neighbors.

9. **Civil Rights**

**The concept of civil rights is an enduring hallmark of American society.**

We remind Congress and the president to work toward eliminating those remaining barriers that continue to deprive individuals of those civil rights so eloquently espoused in our nation's Constitution. Passage of the Civil Rights Restoration Act and the Fair Housing Amendments are essential to ensuring continued protection of civil liberties. Also essential to these important measures is the appointment of a Supreme Court Justice who will interpret the law in fairness to all.

10. **Racism**

**Racism is a moral outrage. Failure to confront it and rid this nation of its vestiges eats at the core of our daily existence, and has economic, spiritual, and social costs.**

A great American, W.E.B. DuBois, predicted that the problem of the 20th century would be the problem of the color line. Failure to solve this problem now will carry into the 21st century a nearly 400-year-old burden that needs to be eliminated.

We must not only condemn racism, but we must commit to making America such that we can be judged "not only by the color of our skin, but by the content of our character," as Dr. Martin Luther King, Jr. said.

Our legacy to our children—black and white—must be to create a world of freedom and opportunity for them that leads to an open, pluralistic society unblemished by the terrible stain of racism.

# Chronology of Events 1987*

## Politics

Jan. 7:    New regulations are issued by the Justice Department to strengthen the Voting Rights Act. The federal government is given broader authority to reject local election changes which led to discriminatory voting results. The regulations allow civil rights lawyers to reject proposed election changes simply on the basis of discriminatory results, rather than having to prove that local officials intended to discriminate against blacks or other minority groups.

Jan. 13:   U.S. District Court Judge Harold Parker rules that black residents of Springfield, Illinois have been denied their voting rights and that they suffer the effects of 75 years of segregation. The ruling was the result of a class-action voting rights lawsuit brought against five city council members in Springfield. Blacks had won no seats on the council after the city adopted an at-large election in 1911 following a race riot.

Feb. 4:    Former Congressman Parren J. Mitchell (D–Md.) is subpoenaed in connection with the Wedtech bribery investigation which was under state and federal probe for its payments to politically connected law firms and consultants, both Democrat and Republican, while picking up millions of dollars worth of "no-bid" military contracts. Rep. Mitchell was not a suspect of the investigation.

Feb. 15:   Atlanta city councilman Hosea Williams joins black Alabama leaders and 2,000 marchers in Montgomery to protest the diminished political clout in the Alabama statehouse and an "antiblack attitude" in the White House. The march attracted a handful of white supporters as protesters followed the route taken at the end of the 1965 Selma-to-Montgomery march led by Dr. Martin Luther King, Jr.

Feb. 16:   Chicago Mayor Harold Washington is reported doing better among white voters than he did four years prior in his first bid for

*This chronology is based on news reports. In some instances, the event may have occurred a day before the news item was reported.*

office. One of Washington's opponents in the race was former Chicago mayor Jane M. Byrne.

Feb. 17: Philadelphia Mayor W. Wilson Goode declares his candidacy for a second term despite a controversial first term.

Feb. 25: Early election returns show Chicago Mayor Harold Washington winning the Democratic mayoral primary. A poll by *The New York Times*/WBBM-TV shows Washington defeating former mayor Jane M. Byrne by a margin of about six percentage points. Washington was also reported doing better among white voters than Byrne was doing among blacks.

March 12: A paper entitled "Black Initiative and Governmental Responsibility" published by the Joint Center for Political Studies urges a new vision of an old partnership for the black community. The report was written by the Committee on Policy for Racial Justice, led by historian John Hope Franklin and Eleanor Holmes Norton, a law professor at Georgetown University.

March 23: Convicted murderer Warren McCleskey awaits appeal, the first to be heard by the United States Supreme Court based on the contention that Georgia's death-sentencing process was unconstitutionally infected by racial discrimination. McCleskey's death sentence, which was handed down by a jury of 11 whites and one black, was viewed by opponents of the death penalty as perhaps the last broad-based challenge to the way the death penalty is imposed in many states; it was also seen as the last opportunity to save many of the 1,874 convicts on death row.

April 8: Mayor Harold Washington wins reelection to a second term in Chicago, defeating Alderman Edward R. Vrdolyak. With 74 percent of the precincts reporting, Washington had 398,943 votes or 48 percent, to 383,856 or 47 percent for Vrdolyak. Washington had overwhelming support among black voters.

April 16: The widow of slain civil rights leader Medgar Evers loses her bid for a seat on the Los Angeles City Council. Myrlie Evers was a candidate for the open 10th District seat.

April 27: Mayor W. Wilson Goode of Philadelphia is favored to win renomination and to be reelected in the fall. His opponents had attacked him for deterioration in public service.

| April 27: | Democratic presidential hopefuls vie for the black vote with one candidate, Gary Hart, receiving some encouragement in an Atlanta church. The candidates face the task of building black support and competing for the black vote against the Rev. Jesse Jackson. |
|---|---|
| May 7: | The newly elected mayor of Gary, Indiana, Thomas V. Barnes who defeated Richard G. Hatcher promises to cut crime and foster better relations with businesses in that city. Hatcher, the longest-serving black mayor of a major city, had seen his support eroding over the years as unemployment in Gary exceeded 20 percent and promises of a better future were left unfulfilled. |
| May 17: | A poll by *The New York Times*/CBS News shows the Rev. Jesse Jackson having more support than any other Democrat seeking the party's 1988 presidential nomination. Jackson gained strength following the withdrawal of former Senator Gary Hart of Colorado from the race. |
| May 18: | Mayor Andrew Young of Atlanta is target of a federal grand jury inquiry into whether he sought to hinder a police investigation into charges of drug use involving him and former State Senator Julian Bond which were leveled by Mrs. Bond. |
| May 20: | Philadelphia Mayor W. Wilson Goode wins the Democratic mayoral primary; former Mayor Frank L. Rizzo wins the Republican nomination, thereby putting the two in a rematch in the November election. Goode became Mayor of Philadelphia in 1983 by defeating Rizzo in the Democratic primary. |
| May 28: | Congressional Black Caucus members pledge to raise $250,000 to help pay legal expenses for Congressman Harold E. Ford, a Tennessee Democrat. Ford had been indicted by a federal grand jury on charges of conspiring with two former bankers to commit mail, bank, and tax fraud. |
| June 6: | Former Mayor of Gary, Ind., Richard G. Hatcher is named as director of a group to explore whether the Rev. Jesse Jackson should run for the presidency. Jackson also rejects suggestions that he had become the Democratic front runner "by default." |
| July 8: | Five national black political groups file legal papers in U.S. District Court in Washington as a "friend of the court" brief in which the organizations charged that D.C. Mayor Marion Barry, officials |

in his administration and black city contractors are the victims of a "white power structure" that is employing "the longstanding and enormously successful tactic of utilizing powerful law enforcement agencies to discredit black leadership."

July 17:  Lt. Gov. L. Douglas Wilder of Virginia, in a banquet speech honoring the *Norfolk Journal and Guide,* the nation's third oldest black newspaper, admonishes black leaders to grant no special favors to prominent black figures around the state who face legal or political difficulties. "You must refuse to serve as a patsy for any public official who finds that they are in trouble with the legal authorities," said Wilder, one of the country's most visible black politicians and a likely candidate to seek the governor's office when Gov. Gerald L. Baliles leaves, as required by law, in 1989.

July 26:  Rep. Harold E. Ford (D–Tenn.) introduces legislation to bolster the rights of individuals who are the subject of grand jury investigations.

July 29:  Seventy-one-year-old Ed Moss is sworn in for the Selma, Alabama City council, giving the body its first black voting majority. Moss replaces a white councilman who resigned. Moss was a participant in the 1965 demonstration in which voting rights marchers coming across the Edmund Pettus Bridge were attacked by mounted, club-swinging troops.

August 6:  A federal judge throws out claims that Attorney General Edwin Meese's involvement in the Wedtech Corp. justified dismissing charges against former Maryland senator Clarence M. Mitchell III of attempting to block a congressional investigation of Wedtech. Both Clarence Mitchell III and his brother, State Senator Michael B. Mitchell (D–Baltimore) were indicted April 2, 1987 on charges of conspiring in 1984 to block an investigation of Wedtech by the House Small Business Committee headed by their uncle, former Representative Parren J. Mitchell (D–Md.).

Sept. 6:  New Hampshire state Sen. John Chandler Jr. is removed as an honorary county chairman for the presidential campaign of Rep. Jack Kemp (R–N.Y.) after he refused to repudiate or apologize for what he said was a joke he told about the Rev. Jesse Jackson. Chandler said at various public events that "Jesse Jackson had stopped running for president because it was found out that his grandmother had posed for the centerfold of *National Geographic.*"

Sept. 8:     The Rev. Jesse Jackson announces in Pittsburgh, Pa. that he will be a candidate for the Democratic presidential nomination in 1988. Jackson also announces that he has raised about one million dollars for the campaign. October 10 is picked as the date to make a formal announcement of his candidacy. The date coincides with the National Rainbow Coalition convention in Raleigh, North Carolina.

Sept. 9:     Chicago Mayor Harold Washington endorses the presidential candidacy of the Rev. Jesse Jackson. Washington pledges to help Jackson raise money for his campaign, noting that Jackson over the past 20 years has persevered "and he has done it as a quasi-public servant."

Sept. 14:    Two blacks, Kurt L. Schmoke, a 37-year-old Rhodes scholar and prosecutor for the City of Baltimore, and Mayor Clarence H. Burns, a 68-year-old veteran of neighborhood politics, lead in that city's mayoral race. Burns, who had been president of the city council, became mayor through succession when the previous mayor, William Donald Schaefer, was elected governor of Maryland.

Sept. 22:    The number of black elected officials increased in 1986 by four percent, according to a report released by the Joint Center for Political Studies in Washington, D.C. The report noted that the number of officials rose from 6,424 to 6,681.

Sept. 27:    Three Democratic presidential candidates, along with Rep. Patricia Schroeder (D–Colo.), endorse the Congressional Black Caucus agenda on education, employment, and defense issues. The endorsements were made during the annual Congressional Black Caucus weekend in Washington, D.C.

Oct. 4:      A poll of voters in the South conducted by the Atlanta *Journal and Constitution* shows that the Rev. Jesse Jackson has taken the lead over his five rivals in the presidential race. The poll also shows Vice President George Bush with a big lead in the Republican race.

Oct. 7:      A voter registration report by the Census Bureau substantiated other analyses indicating that black voters played a pivotal role in Democrats' recapturing control of the Senate, particularly in Alabama, Georgia, Florida, North Carolina and Louisiana, where four incumbent Republicans and a fifth GOP hopeful championed by President Reagan suffered an upset. Young black voters turned out in higher proportions than young whites in the previous November's Senate and House elections.

Oct. 11: A new federal complaint is filed against Federal Judge Alcee Hastings, accusing him of approving a wiretap against a friend of Mayor Steve Clark of Dade County, Florida and then advising the mayor about it.

Oct. 12: Joanne Chesimard, who escaped in 1979 from a New Jersey prison where she had been serving a life sentence for the murder of a state trooper, is reported to be living in Cuba with her 13-year-old daughter. Chesimard, a leader of the black radical movement of the 1970s, grants an interview to *Newsday* newspaper from Cuba and says that she is living there as a "political refugee."

Oct. 16: A magazine interview that presidential candidate Jesse Jackson gave to the Jewish bimonthly, *Tikkun,* appears to have done more to irritate Jews than to heal relations. In the interview, Jackson took Israel to task for trading with South Africa and said that many Jewish groups opposed affirmative action to aid minorities.

Nov. 3: The Rev. Jesse Jackson's 1984 national presidential campaign committee is fined $13,000 by the Federal Election Commission for underreporting fundraising and spending and filing incomplete accounts of financial activities.

Nov. 4: Philadelphia Mayor W. Wilson Goode claims victory in his reelection bid over former Mayor Frank L. Rizzo. In an unofficial tally, Good received 51 percent of the votes with a total of 332,396 to Rizzo's 318,527, or 49 percent of the votes.

Nov. 7: Former Maryland State Senator Clarence M. Mitchell III and his brother, Sate Senator Michael B. Mitchell are convicted of accepting a $50,000 bribe to halt a congressional investigation of the Wedtech Corp. The two brothers are acquitted of conspiracy charges but are convicted of additional charges of wire fraud. Attorneys say the jury's verdicts are "confused" and vow to appeal the case.

Nov. 25: Presidential candidate Jesse Jackson gets backing of Rep. Charles Rangel (D-N.Y.) and Manhattan Borough President David Dinkins. The endorsements by the two leading black officials in New York City will, according to Jackson, "give breadth and depth and meaning to the campaign."

Nov. 25:     Harold Washington, the first black Mayor of Chicago, dies in his office of a heart attack. Washington, called a street-smart politician, was one of the most visible symbols of urban black political power and was in his second term as mayor. Washington was 65 years old.

Nov. 29:     Chicagoans brave a cold drizzle to mourn Mayor Harold Washington as his body lay in state in City Hall. As mourners filed past the casket, his former allies continued to battle over his successor.

Dec. 1:     A poll by *The New York Times*/CBS News indicates that large majorities of white and black Americans believe that the Rev. Jesse Jackson empathizes with them. However, the poll indicates that white Americans are uneasy about Jackson's ability to deal with international crises; they see him as lacking the experience to be a good president.

Dec. 3:     Eugene Sawyer, a black alderman, is chosen after a raucous predawn vote and 12 hours of street demonstrations to become the new Acting Mayor of Chicago. The 54-year-old Sawyer was elected by a vote of 29 to 19 with most of his support coming from white aldermen who were hostile to the late Mayor Harold Washington.

Dec. 18:     New Acting Mayor of Chicago, Eugene Sawyer faces open hostility among blacks but gets wide measure of acceptance among whites. In an effort to soothe the bitterness among blacks, Sawyer began scheduling a series of private "unity prayer meetings" with black ministers and politicians.

Dec. 19:     The predominantly black political organization in the state of Alabama, the Alabama Democratic Conference, gives its endorsement to Jesse Jackson but backs Sen. Albert Gore Jr. (D–Tenn.) as an alternate.

**Civil Rights**

Jan. 7:     Coretta Scott King, the widow of Dr. Martin Luther King, Jr., urges Americans to celebrate her late husband in a "meaningful manner."

Jan. 17:     Newly elected Gov. Evan Mecham of Arizona formally rescinds a state holiday in honor of Dr. Martin Luther King, Jr. The Republican official takes the action by voiding an executive order signed by his Democratic predecessor, Bruce Babbitt.

Feb. 3: It is reported that the Justice Department has authorized filing a lawsuit against the city of Jacksonville, N.C. for maintaining segregated sleeping accommodations for fire department employees. At the city's fire station headquarters, blacks were relegated to a back room commonly referred to as "the ghetto," a second station had one "black bed," and no blacks were assigned to a third city fire station. The Equal Employment Opportunity Commission discovered earlier that the city maintained a strict racial quota that limited blacks to only six of the 70 department slots.

Feb. 4: Sen. Edward M. Kennedy (D–Mass.) assails the Reagan administration as "the most anti-civil rights administration I have ever seen."

April 15: A study released by the United Church of Christ's Commission for Racial Justice finds that toxic waste disposal sites have been concentrated in areas with large minority populations. The report labeled such actions "environmental racism."

April 16: A House subcommittee releases a report that accuses the Department of Health and Human Service's Office for Civil Rights (OCR) of doing an extremely poor job of enforcing federal anti-discrimination laws. The report, by the Human Resources and Intergovernmental Relations subcommittee of the House Government Operations Committee, concludes that the OCR "routinely conducts superficial and inadequate investigations."

May 18: The U.S. Supreme Court, in a significant expansion of civil rights protections, rules that Arabs, Jews, and other ethnic groups may sue under the 1866 Civil Rights Act, one of the nation's strongest anti-bias measures.

June 13: Civil rights activist Julian Bond blasts the media for its willingness to "treat public figures and private citizens any way they can and any way they want to" with "gross invasions of privacy" and "pop psychoanalytic portraits of prominent figures." Bond's comments in a speech before black journalists at Howard University in Washington were in response to published reports that his estranged wife had allegedly told police that he had used cocaine.

**July 3:**  According to published reports, the Justice Department is dealt two legal setbacks in its controversial decision to prosecute black civil rights activists in Alabama on voter fraud charges. In one case, the 11th Circuit Court of Appeals in Atlanta overturned the conviction of only one of the eight defendants found guilty of voting fraud. In a second case, the Appeals Court reinstated a lawsuit by black plaintiffs who challenged the prosecutions as racially and politically motivated.

**Aug. 17:**  The AFL-CIO, joining major civil rights organizations, votes to oppose President Reagan's nomination of Robert H. Bork.

**Aug. 24:**  Long-time civil rights activist Bayard Rustin dies after suffering a heart attack. He was 77 years old. In 1941, Rustin helped organize a planned march on Washington that never came about because President Franklin D. Roosevelt issued an executive order banning racial discrimination in all industries with government contracts. In 1947, he participated in a "freedom ride" to show the effect of segregation on public accommodation. Rustin, equally active in later civil rights protests, was considered an architect of the 1963 March on Washington.

**Sept. 16:**  In an attempt to blunt criticism from civil rights groups opposed to his nomination to the Supreme Court, Robert H. Bork backs away from some of his previous writings on free speech and women's rights, saying the articles were "speculative" at the time they were published. Sen. Howell Heflin, a conservative Democrat from Alabama, summed up the reservations of many of his colleagues when he told Bork: "You've gone through a lot of changing ideas. I wish I was a psychiatrist rather than a lawyer and member of the committee to try and figure out what you would do if you sat on the Supreme Court."

**Sept. 23:**  The Senate Appropriations Committee votes to reduce funding for the controversial U.S. Commission on Civil Rights from $7.5 million in fiscal 1987 to $5.9 million in fiscal 1988. Committee members expressed disappointment in the way the commission has functioned under the leadership of Clarence Pendleton.

**Oct. 23:**  The U.S. Senate rejects Judge Robert Bork for appointment to the Supreme Court by a vote of 58 to 42. The defeat was the result of an unusual coalition of civil rights groups and conservative southern senators, many of whom owed their margin of victory in last fall's election to black voters.

Nov. 6: The Chairman of the House Judiciary Civil and Constitutional Rights Subcommittee charges that the U.S. Department of Agriculture has not taken strong enough measures to counteract an "old boy network" that is depriving department employees of their basic civil rights and equal opportunity. Rep. Don Edwards (D–Calif.) asserts that proposed changes are "modest" in comparison to the entrenched patterns of discrimination and says that the department's efforts to change the system will be reviewed in another hearing in 1988.

Dec. 10: Coretta Scott King, widow of Dr. Martin Luther King, Jr., sues Boston University to regain letters, manuscripts, and other papers the university asserts he stipulated would become its property upon his death. In her suit, King maintains that her husband intended for the materials to be kept permanently in the South. She also charges that the university has allowed the archives to deteriorate through inadequate care.

Dec. 12: Supreme Court Justice Thurgood Marshall scores the Justice Department under Attorney General Edwin Meese for attempting "to undermine the Supreme Court itself," charging that department is unable to separate its political beliefs from sound legal argument. Justice Marshall, in an interview with syndicated columnist Carl Rowan, adds that the Regan administration's labeling of critics of Supreme Court nominee Robert Bork as a "lynch mob" was unfair.

Dec. 14: Senate Judiciary Committee hearings on Supreme Court nominee Judge Anthony M. Kennedy begin. Judge Kennedy, considered a "moderate conservative," is expected to be confirmed with little trouble in February.

## Federal Budget

Jan. 8: Critics of proposed cuts in student aid in the Reagan administration's fiscal year 1988 budget contend the action will have the greatest impact on low-income minority students and contribute significantly to a continuing decline in minority college enrollment. Charles B. Saunders Jr., Vice President for Governmental Relations at the American Council on Education, says that the proposal calls for cuts of $2.5 billion, nearly a 50-percent reduction in funding for student aid. In addition, the budget proposal calls for the disqualification of one million students from the Pell grant program that assists economically disadvantaged students.

Jan. 14: The Center on Budget and Policy Priorities reveals that President Reagan's fiscal year 1988 budget proposals would reduce funding for programs serving the poor such as medicaid, food stamps, and child nutrition by $12.4 billion dollars from the amount needed to provide the same level of service delivered as in 1987. According to Robert Greenstein, the center's head, $115.8 billion in new budget authority is required; however, the president's budget request is $103.4 billion.

Jan. 21: The Congressional Budget Office (CBO) claims President Reagan's new budget proposal underestimates the size of the federal deficit by $27- to $32-billion, which it projects could reach as high as $135- to $140-billion. When the budget was submitted to Congress, the President claimed it included a $107.8-billion deficit, within the range targeted by the Gramm-Rudman-Hollings balanced budget law. House Budget Committee Chairman William H. Gray III (D–Pa.) says the CBO's findings prove his earlier contention that "there are three problems with the budget: (the lack of) realism, revenues, and fairness."

Feb. 23: The National Governor's Association's executive committee endorses a proposal to target $1 billion a year in federal and state funds into basic education, job training, and placement programs designed to help welfare recipients obtain jobs in the private sector. The proposal, drafted by a special welfare prevention task force, calls for start-up costs of $450 million entirely from federal government in its first year, FY 1988. In FY 1989, the federal government's share would be $850 million, and the states would provide $150 million. Under the current welfare program, Aid to Families with Dependent Children, federal and state governments spend about $17.7 billion a year to support 3.7 million poor families.

Feb. 25: A resolution emphasizing job training and placement, basic education, and child care assistance for welfare recipients is approved by the National Governor's Association. The only state executive dissenting from the vote is Gov. Tommy Thompson (R) of Wisconsin. Governors from both parties consider the resolution a significant accomplishment in efforts to reach a "national consensus" or the issue. While the agreement stresses seeking work as a requirement for receiving aid, it includes an income-support provision for those unable to secure employment.

March 21: Efforts to devise a fiscal year 1988 budget resolution by the House Budget Committee are halted when Republican panel members refuse to participate, charging that voting on the spending plan is designed to embarrass them and the Reagan administration. The Budge Committee Chairman, Rep. William H. Gray III (D–Pa.) denies the charge, stating that consideration of the spending plan that would freeze outlays at fiscal 1987 levels is "the most neutral way" to proceed.

March 25: Sen. Lawton Chiles, Chairman of the Senate Budget Committee, develops a fiscal year 1988 budget that will trim $12 billion from domestic programs and only six billion dollars from defense. While the total of his proposed spending cuts and new taxes parallels those sought by budget leaders in the House, strategists there want to reduce defense spending by eight billion. Both the Senate and House proposals would include a budget deficit $27 billion higher than the $108 billion target set by the Gramm-Rudman-Hollings balanced budget law.

April 10: By a vote of 230 to 192, the House approves a FY 1988 budget of one trillion dollars that calls for a deficit of $132.5 billion and increases taxes by $18 billion. Not one House Republican voted in favor of the proposal, which was also opposed by 19 Democrats.

April 30: In a preliminary vote, Democrats on the Senate Budget Committee narrowly win (50–49) approval of the one trillion dollars FY 1988 budget proposed by Chairman Lawton Chiles, which recommends $11.5 billion in new taxes and defense spending authority of $289 billion. The Chiles defense spending projections are $23 billion less than that sought by the Reagan administration.

May 7: After altering the spending blueprint proposed by its Budget Committee, the Senate, by a vote of 57 to 42, approves a final budget calling for a $7 billion increase in defense spending and $18.3 billion in new taxes. The new version also adds $2 billion for domestic programs in education, urban development, and veterans programs. The differences in the budgets of both houses of Congress must be resolved in conference.

May 14: The White House Budget Office claims President Reagan's fiscal year 1988 budget will produce a deficit of $135 billion, above the

$108 billion deficit target set by the Gramm-Rudman-Hollings balanced budget law. Changes in the country's economic conditions and new estimates of federal outlays are cited as reasons for the deficit's expansion by almost $27 billion.

May 28: A report by the Center for Population Options reveals that taxpayers spend $17.9 billion on assistance to families headed by teenage mothers, an increase of $1.3 billion from 1985. The expenditures covered direct and administrative costs for Aid to Families with Dependent Children, food stamps, and Medicare services made available to the young mothers.

June 19: A special House-Senate conference committee approves a $1-trillion tax and spending plan for FY 1988 that is denounced by President Reagan. The plan provides $64 billion in tax increases over three years, starting with an increase of $19.3 billion in the fiscal year beginning Oct. 1. In addition, the proposal allows an inflation-related increase in defense spending only if the tax hikes are enacted.

June 24: By a vote of 215 to 201, the House approves the trillion dollar fiscal year 1988 budget compromise crafted by the House-Senate conference committee. It projects a deficit of $134 billion. The budget sets Congress's guidelines for the appropriation of program funds and revenue-raising measures through legislation that must be approved by President Reagan. The president has said that he will veto legislation calling for tax increases. In later action, the Senate also passes the budget by a vote of 53 to 46.

July 3: President Reagan reportedly supports a proposal that would encourage Congress to assess in advance the probable impact of its new spending bills and to specify how they would be funded. The proposal is part of an "Economic Bill of Rights" being developed by the president with the intent of fostering so-called "truth in spending," according to White House officials. It seeks to alter the existing budget process through measures such as adopting two-year budgets and requiring Presidential approval of Congress's annual budget resolution.

July 10: Senate Budget Committee Chairman Lawton Chiles (D–Fla.) announces that Democratic and Republican party leaders will work to devise a new automatic budget-cutting mechanism to replace one deemed unconstitutional by the Supreme Court. The mechanism would set automatic spending cuts in motion whenever

Congress and the president were unable to agree on how to reduce the federal budget. The effort will include a measure that will establish new decifit-reduction targets of $36 billion per year instead of the stricter year-by-year targets mandated by law.

July 11: In the face of a projected $11-billion increase in the deficit for the new 1988 budget, President Regan asks federal departments and agencies to cut an additional $10 billion to $15 billion from their own budgets. According to an independent analysis by the House Budget Committee, the deficit will reach $182 billion in the fiscal year beginning Oct. 1, if current spending and tax policies remain the same.

July 17: Treasury Secretary James A. Baker III announces that the deficit for the fiscal year 1987 budget will be $20 billion less than anticipated, largely because of increased revenue attributed to revisions in the nation's tax code. Baker says the deficit will be about $155 billion instead of the $175 billion originally projected. However, the lowered deficit figure is still some $10 billion over the Gramm-Rudman-Hollings ceiling of $144 billion.

Aug. 7: House and Senate conferees are unable to agree on the details of a budget mechanism that authorizes automatic spending cuts to reduce the federal deficit when Congress and the president are unable to work out a compromise. The main points of contention are the length of the time the plan would need to remain in effect and the amount by which the deficit would be reduced over several years.

Sept. 24: In separate action, the House and Senate approve legislation revising an automatic spending-reduction mechanism designed to limit the growth of the federal deficit as required by the Gramm-Rudman-Hollings balanced budget law. Provisions in both pieces of legislation allow the deficit ceiling to rise to $2.8 trillion dollars, about $36 billion more than permitted by the 1985 law. In addition, the date for balancing the budget is extended from 1991 to 1993.

Sept. 27: Despite his opposition to provisions for a tax increase and reductions in military spending, President Regan says he will sign legislation crafted by Congress creating a new mechanism to reduce the federal deficit. The mechanism will trigger automatic spending cuts of $23 billion if Congress and the president fail to agree on a budget for fiscal year 1988.

Oct. 16: The Congressional Budget Office (CBO) reveals that cuts in military spending will have to be over 10 percent and as much as nine percent for domestic programs to achieve the $23 billion in automatic spending cuts sought to reduce the deficit for the FY 198 budget. According to the CBO, many programs would face spending reductions below their 1987 levels including food stamps, which would lose $3.55 million; Medicare, slashed by $2.39 billion; and the Guaranteed Student Loan Program, cut by $25 million.

Oct. 26: Three key Congressional budget negotiators assert that the federal deficit will have to be reduced by even more than the $23 billion originally proposed by legislators. Senate Budget Committee Chairman Lawton Chiles (D–Fla.) Senate Finance Committee Chairman Lloyd Bentsen (D–Tex.) and Senate Minority Leader Robert Dole (R–Kan.) all favor some type of multi-year plan that would yield larger cuts.

Nov. 21: After month-long negotiations, President Reagan and Congress reach agreement on a basic plan for reducing the federal deficit by $76 billion over two fiscal years. The plan broadly outlines the spending reductions and tax increases that are necessary, but provides few specifics on how to achieve them. Under the agreement, the deficit will be reduced by $30.2 billion in the fiscal year that began Oct. 1 and $45.9 billion in fiscal 1989.

Dec. 18: Congressional negotiators near agreement on a catchall spending bill of $600 billion, one of two bills required to complete the budget agreement reached with the Reagan administration in November. The bill, which would fund the government's operations through fiscal year 1988 which ends Sept. 30, calls for a $7.6 billion reduction in the federal deficit; it includes a $5 billion cut in defense. To meet the terms of the agreement, a second bill cutting the federal deficit by an additional $26 billion via a $9-billion tax increase and cuts in domestic programs must be worked out.

**Affirmative Action**

Jan. 10: Citing the underrepresentation of blacks, Hispanics, Native Americans, and Asians in its visitor and associate membership ranks, Robert McC. Adams, secretary of the Smithsonian Institution in Washington D.C., announces the formation of a citizens' "cultural education committee." It will advise the Smithsonian on how to present more culturally diverse exhibits and programs that will attract greater minority group attendance.

Jan. 21: Joseph Cooper, director of the Labor Department's Office of Federal Contract Compliance, resigns in protest, charging the Reagan administration with failing to enforce affirmative action hiring laws for federal contractors. Cooper, who is black, identifies Attorney General Edwin Meese III and William Bradford Reynolds as among administration officials seeking to circumvent rules requiring numerical hiring goals of some 20,000 companies that employ 23 million workers.

Feb. 16: In Norfolk, Va., blacks and women recognize they have been unable to increase significantly their numbers within the city's police and fire departments, in which white men predominate at 82 percent and 90 percent, respectively, in spite of a 12-year-old affirmative action plan. City officials contend that low starting salaries, rigorous testing standards, and a low turnover are at fault. However, the Rev. L. P. Watson, vice president of the local chapter of the NAACP, charges that minorities are underrepresented on the police and fire forces because of limited promotion opportunities.

Feb. 26: In a 5 to 4 ruling, the Supreme Court upholds the authority of judges to order strict racial promotion quotas to remedy long-standing, blatant, and pervasive discrimination. The high court's decision sanctions a 1983 temporary order issued by a judge requiring Alabama to hire one black state trooper for every white one hired. The Reagan administration had argued that such quotas are "excessive" and "profoundly illegal" and should be tailored instead to reflect the percentage of blacks applying for state police jobs.

Feb. 28: A U.S. Court of Appeals panel throws out the District of Columbia's affirmative action hiring plan mandating that 60 percent of all of the city's firefighters hired be black. The appeals panel asserts that it was unable to find evidence of discrimination requiring remediation.

March 11: At a special conference, the Institute for Journalism Education calls for a new strategy focusing on education and attitudinal changes of mid-level newsroom managers to help minority journalists move into management and other top decision-making positions in newspapers, magazines, and broadcasting. According to Institute officials and members, the dearth of minority group members in news organizations is more a problem of promotion and retention than of hiring. The news article states that minorities comprise three percent of all newspaper executives.

March 22: Fewer blacks are holding senior policy and managerial positions in the Reagan administration, according to data from the Office of Personnel Management (OPM). It revealed that the proportion of black presidential appointments to Senior Executive Service declined to 4.5 percent in 1986 from 9.5 percent in 1980. These positions include Cabinet officers, deputies, and assistant secretaries. In addition, the number of black political appointments declined from 59 in 1980 to 22 in 1986.

March 26: The Supreme Court, in a 6 to 3 ruling, says that private employers' voluntary affirmative action programs may promote minorities and women over white males, without evidence of prior racial discrimination. Justice William Brennan wrote the opinion for the majority. Citing Title VII of the 1964 Civil Rights Act, he said employers are allowed to take race and gender into account in hiring and promotion decisions intended to correct "a conspicuous imbalance in traditionally segregated job categories."

April 1: The Justice Department petitions the U.S. Court of Appeals to block the hiring of black District of Columbia firefighters under a voluntary affirmative action plan, despite a recent Supreme Court ruling upholding the legality of such plans without prior evidence of racial discrimination. In a previous ruling, the appeals court upheld the contention of the Assistant Attorney General for Civil Rights, William Bradford Reynolds, that the plan was unconstitutional because it violated 14th Amendment guarantees of "equal protection of the laws."

April 16: The *New York Daily News* is found guilty of discriminating against four of its black editorial reporters in promotions, salaries, and assignments by a federal jury after a nine-week trial. The jurors found that *The News* had discriminated against the employees in 12 out of 23 separate cases as a result of testimony by more than 40 witnesses. The jury is to reconvene to set an award for the plaintiffs — David Hardy, Causewell Vaughn, Steven Duncan, and Joan Shepard. *The News* says it will appeal the decision.

May 13: In an 86-page report, the Senate Committee on Small Business reveals that more than 70 percent of the companies participating in the federal government's program to encourage minority and female-owned businesses remain in business after graduating. Citing the results of a national survey of 461 companies leaving the program after 1980, the report said of 177 respondents, only 18 indicated they had gone out of business. Furthermore, 100 were in the top quarter of such businesses nationally. The report included 23 recommendations issued by the committee for improving the program.

May 21: The Senate Labor and Human Resources Committee votes 12 to 4 to approve the Civil Rights Restoration Act with bipartisan support strengthening the federal government's power to enforce anti-discrimination laws by withholding federal funds. Passage of the measure is intended to reverse a 1984 Supreme Court ruling that funds could be withheld only from specific discriminatory programs and not the whole institution housing them.

June 6: Federal District Judge Henry Bramwell of the Eastern District of New York urges President Reagan to name another black to replace him, in a letter announcing his retirement. Judge Bramwell also scores Republican senators for not doing more to facilitate the appointment of blacks, declaring that they have to "initiate the process." According to news reports, in the Reagan administration's first six years, only five blacks and 12 Hispanics have been named to fill almost 300 openings on federal district and appeals courts nationwide.

June 11: In an out-of-court settlement with four black editorial employees that charged they were victims of racial discrimination, the *New York Daily News* agrees to pay the plaintiffs $3.1 million and to develop an affirmative action plan to increase black representation in its newsroom. The *Daily News* agrees to report the progress of its affirmative action effort to the Equal Employment Opportunity Commission each year for two years.

July 28: The Alabama State Police Department agrees to a tentative settlement in a 15-year-old federal lawsuit that will substantially increase the number of blacks at various ranks on the force to as high as 25 percent over a three-year period. Under the terms of the agreement, the department will promote 15 blacks to the rank of corporal in a month, and ultimately have blacks comprise 20 percent of its sergeants, 15 percent of its lieutenants, and 10 percent of its captains. The settlement must be approved by Federal District Judge Myron Thompson who originally ordered the police department to hire one black officer for every white officer hired.

August 7: Citing an increase in the number of employment discrimination complaints filed by black federal employees, officials of the 20,000-member organization, Blacks in Government, urge President Reagan to establish an investigative agency independent of other federal agencies. The officials contend that timely resolution of the cases is hampered by backlogs, poor staffing, and a conflict of interest inherent in the equal employment opportunity offices' link to the government agencies. In addition, they recommend that the Equal Employment Opportunity Commission's jurisdiction extend only to private sector complaints.

August 15: Refusing to reconsider its original decision, a U.S. Court of Appeals panel maintains that a Supreme Court ruling sanctioning race-conscious affirmative action plans does not apply to a District of Columbia Fire Department hiring plan it ruled illegal. Writing for the majority, Judge Kenneth Starr says that while the panel does not "condemn" the plan's intent, "we find impermissible only the means — a rigid quota based strictly on race . . ." The details of a revised hiring and promotion plan will be reviewed by the full court.

Sept. 6: The Port Authority of New York and New Jersey is sued for $24 million by black baggage handlers and a white supervisor who allege that blacks have been routinely denied promotions at Kennedy International Airport. The federal discrimination suits by the black workers seek back pay and punitive damages. Damages are also being sought by the supervisor, who said he received anonymous death threats and poor job performance ratings in retaliation for his joining a 1985 complaint with the federal Equal Employment Opportunity Commission.

Sept. 17: Alan Keyes, the highest ranking black official in the State Department, resigns during an angry and public dispute that had racial overtones. Keyes had been at odds with Deputy Secretary John C. Whitehead over the allocation of U.S. funds to various groups within the United Nations.

Sept. 20: According to a Census Bureau study, "Characteristics of Business Owners," companies owned by women and white men are most likely to have no minority employees. The study reveals that of the 311,662 businesses owned by women, 48.3 percent had no minority employees, and for firms owned by white men, 52.1 percent of 1,268,869 were without such employees. Comparatively, minority-owned companies had work forces that were more than 75 percent minorities.

Nov. 20:  Federal District Judge Leonard B. Sand bars the city of Yonkers (N.Y.) from assisting commercial and residential development there until it develops a viable plan for building 201,000 low- and middle-income housing units in compliance with his order to desegregate area housing. In a landmark 1985 case, Judge Sand found the city guilty of intentional discrimination in the quality of education afforded minority students because of housing patterns in Yonkers established over four decades.

Nov. 24:  The full U.S. Court of Appeals for the District of Columbia votes to rehear two controversial affirmative action hiring and promotion cases involving the city's police and fire departments. Separate three-judge panels previously upheld the police department's hiring and promotion plan, but rejected the fire department plan on the grounds that evidence of prior discrimination had not been proven. At issue in the new hearings is whether a Supreme Court ruling sanctioning the right of private employers to implement voluntary affirmative action plans without evidence of past discrimination extends to the public sector as well.

## Education/Desegregation

Jan. 24:  Officials in the white community of Englewood Cliffs, N.J., petition the State Education Commissioner to allow them to send their children to the predominantly white Tenafly High School. Since Englewood Cliffs does not have its own high school, students from that town are enrolled at Englewood's Dwight Morrow High School which has an 88-percent black student population.

Feb. 12:  A Wellesley College trustee, Henrietta Holsman, resigns from the board after her remark that "blacks preferred pushing drugs to working in a factory" touches off an emotional debate.

Feb. 16:  The appointees to California's Bicentennial Commission come under fire by state legislators for including an essay on slavery that refers to black children as "pickaninnies" and states that the "constant fear of slave rebellion" made life for southern whites "a nightmare."

Feb. 26:      The Rev. Jesse Jackson appeals to President Reagan to restore five billion dollars in education budget cuts and to increase pressure on South Africa during a 45-minute meeting with the president to present a black agenda. Meeting with Jackson and the president were District Mayor Marion Barry and educator Samuel Myers.

March 18:     Conservative political economist Glenn Loury is mentioned as the nominee for Undersecretary of Education. The 38-year-old Harvard professor has opposed quotas and other preferential treatment for minorities, arguing that disadvantaged blacks in America must help themselves rather than rely on government assistance to improve their economic and social situation.

March 30:     Officials of the Education Department acknowledge repeated backdating of key documents to make it appear that they complied with a court order for quick reviews of civil rights. The practice enabled them to certify falsely to a federal judge that the U.S. government was obeying strict court-ordered deadlines for the civil rights reviews.

April 1:      A study released by the United Negro College Fund and the National Institute of Independent Colleges and Universities discloses that students attending the nation's 57 historically black private colleges are bearing the brunt of federal grant cutbacks and are going into debt to finance their education.

April 9:      Donald Stewart, President of the College Board, criticizes the Reagan administration for its efforts to cut federal aid to college students; at the same time he praises Education Secretary William Bennett for seeking to increase the rigor and coherence of a college education.

April 27:     Johnetta Cole is named president of Spelman College in Atlanta, Ga. A Hunter College anthropologist prior to her appointment, she succeeded Donald Stewart, the new president of the College Board.

April 29:     John Kluge, one of the nation's richest men with a fortune estimated at more than $3.5 billion, donates $25 million to Columbia University in New York City to create a new aid program for minority students. The gift will help Columbia recruit minority students and provide financial aid for 60 to 75 students each year as Kluge Presidential Scholars to be chosen by the university provost.

**May 20:** A report released by the U.S. Commission on Civil Rights concludes that desegregation plans significantly improved the racial balance in public schools. However, the report states that some of the progress has been offset by declines in white enrollment during the same period.

**May 22:** A sweeping education bill that renews and expands programs affecting most of the nation's elementary and secondary school children is approved by the House of Representatives. The bill, the School Improvement Act, consolidates 14 programs and renews them until 1993 at a potential cost of up to $780 million above current levels.

**June 6:** Glenn Loury, leading contender for Undersecretary of Education and a prominent political economist, withdraws his name from consideration after pleading not guilty to assault charges in Boston Municipal Court.

**June 7:** Despite a bid by Boston's public schools to block the grants, $75 million in desegregation grants are awarded to 38 school districts by the Department of Education. Boston had been one of 88 districts seeking funds but was not selected for a grant. Winning districts receive grants ranging from $291,407 to $4 million in order to support schools offering special programs to attract students from different racial, social, economic, and ethnic backgrounds.

**July 10:** Mark Whitaker of Portsmouth, Va., became the first basketball player recruited by Virginia Tech in the last six years to graduate; he tells a story of becoming disillusioned by the "superficial" emphasis placed on academics at the institution.

**July 28:** Marva Collins, who has made national headlines because of her preparatory school, announces plans to open a second school in California with the help of a local fundraising committee. The Marva Collins Preparatory School Campaign, a private committee, offers to build an $800,000 school for 220 students in Compton, Calif.

**Aug. 7:** The NAACP Legal Defense and Educational Fund reports that five southern states failed to obey court orders to desegregate the higher education systems. The rights group said that the Department of Education had refused to begin enforcement proceedings against the states — Arkansas, Florida, Georgia, Oklahoma, and Virginia.

Aug. 31: An elementary school in Little Rock, Ark., is named for Daisy Bates. The former NAACP official helped students known as the "Little Rock Nine" to desegregate the school system.

Aug. 31: A uniform dress code is instituted at the first of four Baltimore (Md.) public schools to build self-pride and to counter the increasing high cost of regular clothing.

Sept. 2: Charles Harris Wesley, a pioneer in the study of blacks and one of the nation's most eminent black scholars, dies at the age of 95 at Howard University Hospital in Washington, D.C. Wesley wrote a number of books that broke ground in the writing of black history. He was a former professor and dean at Howard University.

Sept. 17: In a move to wipe out the vestiges of racial discrimination in the Kansas City, Missouri school system, Federal District Judge Russell Clark orders sharp increases in property and income taxes to pay for sweeping improvements. The ruling grew out of a long series of litigation over school desegregation with the primary outcome being Judge Clark's order for improvements in the system, including magnet schools designed to attract students from suburban and private schools in the city.

Sept. 23: Substantial gains continue to be made by black students across the country on the Scholastic Aptitude Test. But the College Board reports in its assessment that overall average school scores remained unchanged for the third straight year.

Sept. 25: Howard University in Washington, D.C. observes its 120th anniversary. Howard was created by a congressional act in 1867 and opened with a single building and four students.

Oct. 4: A study by the House Committee on Government Operations reports that Virginia and nine other southern and border states failed to eliminate racial discrimination in their colleges and universities. The report also cites disparities between black and white student enrollment and retention rates, shortages of black faculty, and low black enrollment in graduate and professional schools.

Oct. 26: David Kearns, Chairman of the Xerox Corporation and immediate past chairman of the National Urban League Board of Trustees, calls for restructuring schools in a speech to the Detroit Economic Club. Kearns said, "America's public schools have put the United

States at a terrible competitive disadvantage by turning out workers with a 50-percent defect rate."

Dec. 3: The Census Bureau releases a report that whites are twice as likely as blacks to complete college. The report notes that there is a far smaller gap between the races in finishing high school. The report is disputed by some educators who say the figures tend to be exaggerated slightly because of people's reluctance to tell an interviewer they did not graduate from high school or college.

**Race Relations**

Jan. 21: The Federal Bureau of Investigation investigates assaults on civil rights demonstrators in Forsyth County, Ga. In a brief statement, the FBI said it will "focus on the perpetrators of the assaults" to determine whether they have violated federal criminal civil-rights laws on conspiracy and interference with federally protected activities.

Jan. 25: Twenty-thousand people, most of them white, are met by a crowd of white supremacists shouting taunts and racial slurs as they march to the courthouse in Cummings, Ga., in a "march for brotherhood" in the all-white county.

Feb. 7: About 100 members and supporters of the Ku Klux Klan marched through College Park, Ga., chanting "white power." With raised fists, the white supremacists were met by a small group of counterdemonstrators and some 300 state and local police officers.

Feb. 10: A Queens, New York grand jury votes criminal indictments against 12 youths in the racial attack in Howard Beach which resulted in the death of 23-year-old Michael Griffith, who was struck and killed as he fled onto a parkway.

Feb. 11: Murder charges are lodged against three white teenagers who participated in the Howard Beach racial attack. Racial tensions in New York City were heightened as a result of the attack and put some black leaders at odds with others. Governor Mario Cuomo appointed a special prosecutor to take over the inquiry from the Queens District Attorney after the attorney for the two surviving victims of the attack charged that the case was being mishandled.

Feb. 12:     Witnesses in a $10-million lawsuit against the Ku Klux Klan testify in Mobile, Ala., that a Klan leader called the sight of a black teenager's hanged body a "pretty sight." Seventy-year-old Bennie Jack Hays, who held the title of Titan and also controlled Klan activity in southern Alabama, denied making the statement and, acting as his own attorney, called the witnesses liars.

Feb. 21:     Violence breaks out in Tampa, Fla., following the death of a young black man subdued by a white police officer using a chokehold, the subject of protest in many major cities. Isolated groups of roaming youths broke windows with stones and bottles in the predominantly black neighborhood.

Feb. 24:     Law enforcement officials in two parishes in New Orleans pledge to work together to combat robberies and drug traffic. The agreement came after wood and steel barricades were constructed on two streets in Jefferson Parish leading to a predominantly black neighborhood in New Orleans. Some blacks on the New Orleans side had dubbed the barriers "The Berlin Wall" which, according to the head of the Jefferson Parish Council, Robert Evans, Jr., were erected to cut off an escape route for criminals who had victimized the neighborhood.

Feb. 27:     In New York City, white police officer Stephen Sullivan is acquitted of manslaughter in the 1984 death of Eleanor Bumpers, the 66-year-old, 300-pound woman who resisted eviction with a knife from her city-owned apartment.

March 3:     Despite highly publicized racial attacks in New York and Georgia, Assistant Attorney General William Bradford Reynolds calls the incidents isolated events best explained by a breakdown of public education and family values. Reynolds, speaking to a conference of the Florida Bar Association in Orlando, Fla., said there was no evidence of growing tension.

March 14:    Freddie Hickmon, one-time mayor of High Springs, Fla., an elected city councilman, and pastor of a large church in that city, files a detailed complaint with Agriculture Secretary Richard Lyng, charging that the department's Agricultural Stabilization and Conservation Service discriminated against him and other blacks in its Florida operations.

April 5:     Rep. Charles Rangel (D-N.Y.) introduces two measures in Congress to have the late Marcus Garvey exonerated of mail fraud charges. The move by Rangel came on the heels of new evidence which indicates that Garvey's conviction may have been politically motivated. That evidence was discovered by Robert Hill, editor of the Marcus Garvey papers project at the University of California at Los Angeles.

April 18: Al Campanis, Los Angeles Dodgers vice president in charge of player personnel, resigns from his job after remarking that blacks might not be qualified to be managers or hold executive positions in baseball. The remarks were made by Campanis on the ABC News program "Nightline." The program focused on Jackie Robinson, who in 1947 became the first black player in the major leagues.

April 23: The Supreme Court rejects arguments that a state's capital punishment system must be struck down because of statistics that suggest it is racially discriminatory. Justice Lewis Powell, in a 5 to 4 opinion, wrote that statistical discrepancies in sentencing are an inevitable part of the criminal justice system and that without stronger proof of discrimination, the court will not strike down laws or invalidate sentences.

April 23: Columbia College in New York City finds a white male student guilty of verbal abuse following a month-long investigation into a campus fight between black and white students. The disciplinary action was termed "severe" by Robert Pollack, dean of the college.

April 25: Ten white supremacists are indicted by a Fort Smith, Ark., federal grand jury on charges of conspiring to assassinate federal officials, including a judge, and to kill members of ethnic groups through bombings. The leader of the Aryan Nations Church, Richard Girnt Butler, was named in the indictment, along with nine others affiliated with the church and other white supremacist groups such as The Order and the Ku Klux Klan.

May 3: Japanese Prime Minister Yasuhiro Nakasone meets with the Congressional Black Caucus and other black leaders after he triggered charges of racism against him because of a speech which angered blacks and other ethnic groups. Following the meeting Nakasone agreed to pursue Japanese investments in minority-owned American banks, exchange programs between Japanese colleges and black American colleges, and the location of Japanese companies in predominantly black areas.

May 3:      An affirmative action manual used to train 100 New York state employees is recalled because it characterized all white Americans as racist. The booklet was compiled by the agency's affirmative action officer, a black woman, and was distributed to employees of the State Insurance Fund during three training sessions.

May 19:     A 67-year-old black woman from Alabama gets keys to the door and the deed to the headquarters of one of the nation's largest Ku Klux Klan organizations. Mrs. Beulah Mae Donald of Mobile, Ala., was given the property deed to a building and 6.5 acres of wooded land near Tuscaloosa. Two weeks prior to her acquisition, the property was the national headquarters of the United Klans of America. The murder of Mrs. Donald's son was linked to the Klan; the building was part of the judgment in a $7-million civil lawsuit she brought against the KKK.

May 23:     The president of a Boston rowing club apologizes for asking a New York club to leave its black members home during an Irish rowing event. The president of the Boston club had told officers of the St. Brendan Project Rowing club of Manhattan that he could not guarantee the safety of black members in south Boston.

May 26:     Racial discord is abated in Boston during an Irish rowing event. The discord was touched off when an all-white Boston team said black rowers on a New York City club would not be welcome. The settlement included an invitation to the rowing event for the black members.

June 7:     Six-hundred protesters march through the downtown area of Greensboro, North Carolina a day before the first Ku Klux Klan rally in that city since 1979. Police surrounded the marchers as they protested the Klan's return and shouted slogans such as "Klan no, unity yes" and "Go back to the woods."

June 8:     Taunts and cheers greet about 150 Ku Klux Klan members dressed in hoods and robes as they march through downtown Greensboro, N.C. waving Confederate flags and surrounded by police. The Klan called the rally a "freedom and recruitment drive."

June 17:    Bernhard Goetz, on trial for shooting four teenagers on a New York City subway train, is acquitted of attempted murder, but is convicted of illegal weapons possession for the gun used in the shootings.

July 1:     Brooklyn, N.Y. District Attorney Elizabeth Holtzman files a civil suit aimed at preventing defense attorneys from excluding prospective jurors because of their race. Named in the suit as defendants were the State Supreme Court and Criminal Court in Brooklyn and the judges assigned to criminal cases.

July 13:     Arizona citizens' groups begin efforts to recall the governor, Evan Mecham. The governor became the object of controversy when he canceled plans to observe the birthday of Dr. Martin Luther King, Jr. as a state holiday.

July 15:     Radio talk show host Ed Tyll in Atlanta is suspended after he called Representative John Lewis (D–Ga.) a "moron" on the air.

July 18:     Black citizens in Norwalk, Conn. charge that plans to improve race relations following the killing of two men by police are cosmetic and that little has been done to ease the sometimes overt hostility between police and the city's minority groups.

Aug. 7:     Dr. Harry Edwards, hired by Baseball Commissioner Peter Ueberroth to identify black and Hispanic former players who could work in baseball management, offers a consultant job to Al Campanis who came under fire when he made remarks alleging the inability of blacks to hold managerial jobs in baseball.

Aug. 7:     Reginald Lewis, head of the minority firm TLC Group L.P. (a New York investment concern), acquires international operation of the Beatrice Companies. The acquisition is the largest of its kind for a black American.

Aug. 13:     During a visit to New Orleans as part of his trip to the United States, Pope John Paul II denounces the economic deprivation suffered by American blacks while praising the nonviolent tactics of the civil rights movement as divinely inspired.

Aug. 15:     A 22-year-old black University of Georgia College of Pharmacy student is dismissed from her practical training job at a Tifton, Ga. pharmacy because one of the owners feared negative customer reaction. However, the second co-owner of the store said that he would ask the student to return.

Aug. 21:     The Nation of Islam sues operators of the Jacob K. Javits Convention Center in New York City because the Center had reneged on an oral agreement to rent space to the group for a religious rally.

Although a spokesman for the center denied the accusations, he noted that the New York Convention Development Corporation considers any gathering involving Rev. Louis Farrakhan, head of the Nation of Islam, a potential threat to public safety.

Sept. 5:     The American Civil Liberties Union opposes a plan by the police chief of Homestead, Pa. to fingerprint only black men in a search for the rapist of five elderly women. The ACLU, in its protest, said that the plan violated blacks' constitutional rights.

Sept. 8:     The Howard Beach murder trial gets under way in Queens Courthouse in Kew Gardens, Queens, N.Y., capping 8$^1/_2$ months of tension which put the national spotlight on the white working-class neighborhood.

Oct. 21:     Reports on a book written by Terrel Bell, former Secretary of Education, disclose that mid-level administration officials in the Reagan administration made racist jokes and sexist remarks in discussions on civil rights at the White House.

Oct. 27:     John Oliver Killens, writer, teacher, and a founder of the Harlem Writers Guild, dies of cancer at the Metropolitan Jewish Geriatric Center in Brooklyn, New York, at the age of 71. Killens is credited with tutoring such writers as Nikki Giovanni, Richard Perry, Arthur Flowers, Wesley Brown, and Barbara Sommers.

Nov. 2:      Nineteen children of the late Black Muslim leader, Elijah Muhammad, battle the world's largest bank, Dai Ichi Kangyo of Japan, in a legal dispute over a $5.7 million bank account.

Nov. 18:     Seven U.S. missionaries are asked to leave Kenya after it was disclosed that they were involved in a plot supported by the Ku Klux Klan to overthrow the government of President Daniel arap Moi. At the same time a letter cited as evidence of the overthrow was classified as being forged.

Nov. 18:     A 37-year-old black man, Cedric Sandiford, who was with Michael Griffith the night he was killed in Howard Beach, Queens, N.Y., takes the stand and maintains his story that he was attacked and severely beaten by a group of whites.

Dec. 3:      The workforce of mostly minority women who work as maids are ordered by Boston's luxurious Copley Plaza Hotel to put aside their mops and start scrubbing floors by hand. Complaining about the new policy was the Boston chapter of the National Organization for Women as well as Local No. 26 of the Boston Hotel and Restaurant Workers Union which represents the chambermaids. The hotel later rescinded the order.

Dec. 21:    Demonstrators snarl rush-hour traffic in New York City as a protest against racism in the city. Seventy-three people were arrested including several ministers and political leaders.

Dec. 21:    Three white teenagers are convicted of manslaughter and assault charges which stemmed from an attack leading to the death of a 23-year-old black man, Michael Griffin. Griffin was killed as he ran onto the Belt Parkway in Howard Beach, Queens, N.Y., after being chased by a mob of whites.

Dec. 21:    Lawyers for most of the seven defendants in the second trial in the Howard Beach case announce plans to move to have charges against their clients dismissed based on the verdict of the first trial.

Dec. 21:    Enough signatures are validated to force Arizona Governor Evan Mecham into a recall election. The governor came under fire in January when he refused to recognize the birthday of Dr. Martin Luther King, Jr. as a state holiday by rescinding the previous governor's executive order.

# APPENDIXES

# Black Wealth: Facts *and* Fiction

Billy J. Tidwell, Ph.D.
*Director of Research*
*National Urban League, Inc.*

## INTRODUCTION

*No hope was more compelling or more enduring to the freedmen than the hope that the government would give each freedman "forty acres and a mule." [M]any freedmen bought halters for the promised mules and colorful pegs to mark off the promised land (Bennett, 1969:37).*

Black Americans never got the 40 acres and a mule. Instead, they were relegated to the fringe of the nation's economy and systematically denied opportunities to advance themselves. One hundred years later, the economic status of blacks is, in both absolute and relative terms, much improved. Given the point from which they started, the change has been truly remarkable. Moreover, their economic progress has come about largely through the perseverance and resourcefulness of black Americans themselves, against pervasive institutional forces dedicated to their subordination.

It has become increasingly popular to emphasize the degree of black economic progress over the long-term. Recent studies, such as the Rand report (Smith and Welch, 1986) and that issued by the U.S. Commission on Civil Rights (1986), have been widely promulgated as empirical proof that blacks have reached the point of economic well-being. The findings from such studies have been seized by the current administration to justify the view that the nation's constitutional obligations have been met and that any further policy initiatives on behalf of equal economic opportunity are unnecessary. The administration's broad-based campaign to undermine affirmative action is a particularly compelling expression of this sentiment.

While there has been significant improvement in the earnings and income of blacks, the higher standard of living associated with this improvement is not secure. Indeed, the present analysis will show that in terms of the ownership of wealth and income-producing assets, the relative economic condition of black Americans remains highly precarious. Black Americans across the income spectrum lack the resources that allow one to withstand disruptions in income flow or unanticipated emergencies that require a significant expenditure of funds to alleviate.

The black wealth issue has been a neglected subject. With few exceptions, economists and other social scientists have not written about the black/white wealth gap, while they have devoted a great amount of attention to earnings differentials. Policymakers have not deliberated on the black/white wealth gap, while they have debated intensely the black/white disparity in public dependency. Similarly, journalists have not reported stories on the black/white wealth gap, while their coverage of the black/white gap in unemployment has been extensive.

In one sense, this inattention to wealth as a measure of black economic well-being may be understandable. Popular definitions of the concept emphasize "abundance of resources" and equate wealth with "affluence". In the public view, then, the term wealth seems reserved for "the rich and the super-rich," that elite class of Americans who are positioned well beyond the mainstream of the economic order. This group is perceived to be separate and apart from the rest of us, and the blacks among them are distinct oddities. This subject provides titillating fodder for movies, novels, and the society pages; therefore, we tend not to regard wealth as an issue that is germane to the life experiences of the vast majority of black *or* white Americans, and thus not an issue warranting analysis along racial lines. However, another less restrictive conceptualization makes wealth a compelling social concern. This view stresses an individual's or family's *net worth* — that is, financial assets less liabilities — the disposable resources that provide security against economic setbacks and broaden the family's life choices.

## WEALTH ACCUMULATION

Despite significant gains, wide disparities exist in the incomes of black and white families (Swinton, 1987). Thus, black Americans are significantly less able to purchase the goods and services that determine a family's well-being. They are subject to the same consumer prices as whites but still operate at a distinct income disadvantage[1]. However, economic well-being is not just a function of income. It also depends on the amount of assets one owns and one's financial liabilities at a given point in time. The difference between assets and liabilities represents net worth; "wealth," as the term is used here.

While there is a strong positive association between them, income and wealth are very different variables, which pose different concerns about the economic condition of black Americans. According to Browne (1970:60):

Income is a "flow" and refers usually to the purchasing power which accrues to an individual over a period of time either as a payment for services rendered (wages) or as a payment for the use of his assets (rent, interests, profits). *Wealth,* on the other hand, is a "stock" concept and refers to the assets themselves . . .

A more practical view is offered by O'Hare (1983:1–2):

Past income does not indicate the resources currently available . . . because it may have been spent as fast as it was received. Wealth, however, reflects savings and investments that can be drawn on in times of need.

It also reflects those resources that can be passed on from one generation to the next.

The distinction between income and wealth is made painfully clear when a family has its income seriously disrupted through the sudden unemployment of a principal breadwinner. How well the family survives such a misfortune until the income stream is restored is greatly dependent upon the amount of financial resources it has accumulated and at its disposal. The adversity might be endured with only modest changes in lifestyle; or the situation could necessitate drastic adjustments in consumption behavior and a downscaled standard of living; or the family might find itself hard-pressed to meet even basic subsistence needs without assistance. The varying possibilities connote differences in economic security that are not determined by income alone.

*Comparative Net Worth*

Based on current census data,[2] the total net worth of all U.S. households is approximately $6,830 billion. Blacks account for $192 billion, or a miniscule 2.8 percent of the total. By contrast, the aggregate net worth of white households is $6,498 billion or 95 percent of the national total. The percentage figures differ sharply from the share of the household population each group represents. Thus, the net worth estimate for black households is more than eight percent below their proportion of the population, while the net worth of white households exceeds their population share by a comparable margin. Converted into dollar terms, black households are "undervalued" by some $559 billion, relative to their proportion of the U.S. population.

On a per-household basis, whites enjoy about 12 times the net worth of blacks. The average net worth of black households is $3,400, compared to $39,000 for white households.[3] Viewed from any perspective, the position of black Americans is very marginal.

Table 1 shows the distribution of black and white households by level of net worth. It is immediately apparent that the distribution for whites is much flatter, while black households are heavily concentrated in the lower net worth categories. Thus, more than one-half of all black households have a net worth of less than $5,000, compared to less than a quarter of white households. Further, most of the black households in this subgroup either have no net worth (i.e., their liabilities match their assets) or have a negative value (i.e., their liabilities exceed their assets). Fewer than one in ten white households find themselves in this circumstance. The two distributions diverge again at the higher net worth values. About 44 percent of white households enjoy a net worth of $50,000 or more, while just 13 percent of blacks are so well situated. Almost seven percent of white households are in the enviable wealth class beginning at $250,000; the proportion of blacks at this level is negligible.

In short, the personal wealth of black Americans is not only far less than that of whites, but it is also distributed much differently. A great number of black households own little or no wealth at all, while a few are relatively well off. As is the case with income, black female-headed households account for much of the imbalance. When net worth is broken down by type of household (Table 2), we find that black married couples average about $13,000 in net worth, or nearly 20 times as much as black female-headed households. Black households maintained by a male average 4.5 times as much as female-headed households. Compared by race, the black/white ratios for married couples and male-maintained households are roughly comparable at .24 and .26, respectively. However, the ratio for female-headed households is strikingly low: For every dollar of net worth of white female heads, black female heads average a mere three cents.

**Table 1**
**Percent Distribution of Households**
**by Net Worth and Race**

| Net Worth | Blacks | Whites |
|---|---|---|
|  | 100.0 | 100.0 |
| zero or negative | 30.5 | 8.4 |
| $1 to $4,999 | 23.9 | 14.0 |
| $5,000 to $9,999 | 6.8 | 6.3 |
| $10,000 to $24,999 | 14.0 | 12.2 |
| $25,000 to $49,999 | 11.7 | 15.0 |
| $50,000 to $99,999 | 9.3 | 20.7 |
| $100,000 to $249,000 | 3.3 | 16.9 |
| $250,000 to $499,999 | 0.5 | 4.4 |
| $500,000 or over | 0.1 | 2.1 |

Source: U.S. Census Bureau, *Household Wealth and Asset Ownership: 1984,* Table 4.

*Income and Net Worth*

We mentioned earlier that there is a strong relationship between income and wealth. Of course, as O'Hare (1983:3) points out, "people can obtain wealth that is totally unrelated to their income . . . (and) income can be spent in ways that result in no wealth accumulation whatsoever." Nevertheless, wealth tends to expand with increasing income, simply because higher-income groups are better positioned to acquire wealth-producing assets. It is widely acknowledged, for example, that the rate of saving, a traditional method of asset accumulation, rises with income (Friedman, 1957; Morley, 1984).

The census data indicate that the general pattern occurs among blacks as well as whites (see Table 3). The average net worth of black households increases from $88 for households with a monthly income of less than $900 to about $58,750 for households whose monthly income is at least $4,000. Similarly, the net worth of white households rises from $8,443 to $128,237 from the one income level to the next. These results are not surprising. On the other hand, it is interesting to note that while the net worth of blacks is invariably far below that of whites, the differential becomes progressively and sharply smaller at each higher level of income. The black-to-white ratio jumps from an infinitesimal .01 for the lowest income category to .46 among households with incomes of $4,000 or more. In other words, blacks seem to close the wealth gap at an accelerated rate as they move up the income scale.

**Table 2**
**Median Net Worth by Race and Type of Household**

| Monthly Income | Net Worth | | Black/White Ratio |
| | Blacks | Whites | |
| --- | --- | --- | --- |
| All households | $ 3,397 | $39,135 | .09 |
| Married couple | 13,061 | 54,184 | .24 |
| Female householder | 671 | 22,500 | .03 |
| Male householder | 3,022 | 11,826 | .26 |

Source: U.S. Census Bureau, *Household Wealth and Asset Ownership: 1984,* Table G.

On balance, however, the data are extremely distressing. Poor blacks, in particular, are in a highly precarious net worth position, in both absolute and relative terms. Barely able to meet their basic needs, low-income black families are hard-pressed indeed to survive *any* unexpected curtailment of their income flow for *any* period of time. The wealth data presented here justify continued concern about the constant overrepresentation of blacks at the lower end of the income scale.

One other income-related comparison deserves mentioning: The black/white wealth gap is much larger than the difference in income between the two races. Based on median monthly income for 1984, black households averaged 62 percent of the income of white households, while averaging just nine percent of white net worth. Much of this huge discrepancy between wealth and income ratios is probably accounted for by differences in inheritance. We do not have the data to investigate directly this possibility. However, it is reasonable to assume that blacks have not benefited nearly as much as whites from intergenerational transfers of wealth. Stated differently, the contemporary black/white wealth gap is largely a legacy of the historical experience of blacks in America. The following assessment is instructive in this regard:

Clearly, if income were low in the past, little saving took place and hence few assets were available to pass on to descendants. Moreover, what little wealth was available for transfer, particularly land in the South, leaked from the community because of tax sales, mortgage foreclosures, partition sales and outright theft. In 1910 blacks had managed to accumulate an estimated 15 million acres of land. By 1972, the total had fallen to less than six million acres . . . (Browne, 1974:31).

**Table 3**
**Median Net Worth by Race and Monthly Household Income**

| | Net Worth | | Black/White |
| Monthly Income | Blacks | Whites | Ratio |
|---|---|---|---|
| Less than $900 | $    88 | $  8,443 | .01 |
| $900 to $1,999 | 4,218 | 30,714 | .14 |
| $2,000 to $3,999 | 15,977 | 50,529 | .32 |
| $4,000 or more | 58,758 | 128,237 | .46 |

Source: U.S. Census Bureau, *Household Wealth and Asset Ownership: 1984,* Table G.

Others have stressed the historical tribulations of blacks in land ownership and that "limited black control over land has deprived the black community of a major source of wealth in this country" (Nelson, 1978:253). The more general point, however, is that past practices of racial discrimination and exploitation severely limited the ability of black Americans to amass assets that might be passed on to the next generation.

A second reason that the wealth gap is so much larger than the income gap is that "only the portion of income not needed for immediate consumption is available for wealth-accumulating activities such as saving and investment. Because blacks have lower incomes than whites, they have much less income available for investment after immediate necessities are taken care of" (O'Hare, 1983:7).

For these and other reasons, the overwhelming wealth disadvantage of black Americans is not only much larger but also much more difficult to alleviate than the black/white income gap. Racial differences in types of asset holdings provide further insight into this problem.

**ASSET HOLDINGS**

Net worth or wealth is accumulated in the form of specific assets—savings, investments, property, etc. Some assets, such as stocks and mutual funds shares, are income-producing; others, such as real property, may be converted to income through liquidation. Property may also be rented. In either case, the assets one owns represent disposable resources that can be called upon as needed for an emergency or some exceptional expenditure. In this section, we take a more in-depth look at the net worth of black and white households by comparing the asset holdings of the two groups. Specific types of assets owned, the value of given assets, and the distribution of household net worth by type of asset are examined. The analysis will shed more light on the black/white wealth gap by disaggregating it in these ways.

*Asset Types and Dollar Values*

Table 4 shows the percentages of black and white households owning a particular type of asset.[4] We observe, first, that the frequency of asset ownership is consistently lower for blacks. For example, only 32 percent of blacks have a regular checking account, the simplest financial account to establish and access, compared to 57 percent of whites. Similarly, 65 percent of black households own a motor vehicle, the most prevalent asset type among both groups, as against 88 percent of white households. A second significant feature of these data is that blacks compare much less favorably in the ownership of financial and income-producing assets than in the ownership of durable assets. Thus, white households are four times as likely to own stocks and mutual fund shares (22 percent versus 5.4 percent) and 3.5 times as likely to own a business (14 percent versus four percent), but they are only 1.5 times as likely as black households to own a home (67.3 percent versus 43.8 percent). Aside from the paltry size of black wealth overall, the disadvantageous pattern of their wealth holdings has been the dominant finding of previous studies (Terrell, 1971; O'Hare, 1983).

**Table 4**
**Percent of Households Owning Asset Type by Race**

| Asset Type | Blacks | Whites | Black/White Ratio |
|---|---|---|---|
| Interest-earning assets at financial institutions | 43.8 | 75.4 | .58 |
| Other interest-earning assets | 2.1 | 9.4 | .22 |
| Regular checking accounts | 32.0 | 56.9 | .56 |
| Stocks and mutual fund shares | 5.4 | 22.0 | .24 |
| Own business or profession | 4.0 | 14.0 | .28 |
| Motor vehicles | 65.0 | 88.5 | .73 |
| Own home | 43.8 | 67.3 | .65 |
| Rental property | 6.6 | 10.1 | .65 |
| Other real estate | 3.3 | 10.9 | .30 |
| Mortgages | 0.1 | 3.3 | .03 |
| U.S. savings bonds | 7.4 | 16.1 | .46 |
| IRA or Keogh accounts | 5.1 | 21.4 | .24 |
| Other assets | 0.7 | 3.9 | .18 |

Source: U.S. Census Bureau, *Household Wealth and Asset Ownership, 1984,* Table 1.

Interest-earning financial assets command special attention because they have a direct and predictable impact on income and are often relied upon as a supplementary income source. Three out of four white households own interest-bearing assets at financial institutions, second only to the proportion that own motor vehicles. Although the ownership rate is far lower, this type of asset also ranks highly among blacks. On the other hand, breaking down the broad category into more discrete financial assets reveals some instructive black/white differences (see Table 5). White households are less than two times as likely to own a passbook savings account, but they are almost seven times as likely to own a money market deposit account. Likewise, they are five times as likely as black households to hold certificates of deposit (CDs). The latter assets generate higher interest rates than passbook savings and are, therefore, more attractive as income-producing investments.

### Table 5
### Percent of Households Owning Interest-Earning
### Assets by Race

| Asset | Blacks | Whites |
|---|---|---|
| Held at financial institutions | 43.8 | 75.4 |
| Passbook savings accounts | 41.6 | 65.7 |
| Money market deposit accounts | 2.6 | 17.4 |
| Certificates of deposit | 4.2 | 21.2 |
| Interest-earning checking accounts | 7.2 | 27.0 |
| Other interest-earning assets | 2.1 | 9.4 |
| Money market funds | 0.9 | 4.2 |
| U.S. Government securities | 0.1 | 1.6 |
| Municipal and corporate bonds | 0.3 | 2.9 |
| Other assets | 1.0 | 3.0 |

Source: U.S. Census Bureau, *Household Wealth and Asset Ownership: 1984,* Table 2.

Money-market accounts became popular with the deregulation of the banking industry in 1982. However, one must be prepared to meet the preset conditions associated with these financial accounts. Blacks are much less able to do so than whites. This inability is also reflected in the decidedly lower frequency of interest-earning checking accounts and other interest-earning assets (e.g., U.S. Government securities and municipal and corporate bonds) among black households.

The racial differences in rates of owning financial assets, including stocks and mutual fund shares, further underscore the relationship between income and wealth. Again, the income condition of black families is such that many of them simply cannot afford expenditures beyond those necessary to meet basic consumption needs. Generally, black Americans are both severely limited in wealth and poorly positioned to advance themselves through the acquisition of wealth-producing assets. This predicament epitomizes their collective economic situation and the narrow margin of security that distinguishes it.

Just as the percentage of blacks who own assets is consistently and substantially smaller than the percentage of whites, there are also sizeable differences in the dollar value of assets that are owned (see Table 6). The median value of assets held by black households at financial institutions, for example, is $739, just 21 percent of the average holdings of white households ($3,457). The ratio is undoubtedly smaller for the more potent money market deposits and CDs. Blacks who own stocks and mutual fund shares average $2,777 in holdings, compared to $3,908 for whites. Again, however, the ownership rate for this asset among black households is very low. Ownership of motor vehicles, a durable asset, is much more widespread, but the average value of this asset ($2,691) is some $1,600 less than the corresponding figure for whites ($4,293). Similarly, equity in a home, another widely prevalent asset, averages just $24,000 for black homeowners as opposed to $42,000 for whites.

### Table 6
### Median Value of Holdings for Asset Owners by Race

| Asset type | Blacks | Whites | Black/White Ratio |
|---|---|---|---|
| Interest-earning assets at financial institutions | $739 | 3,457 | .21 |
| Other interest-earning assets | (b)[1] | 9,826 | — |
| Regular checking accounts | 318 | 457 | .70 |
| Stocks and mutual fund shares | 2,777 | 3,908 | .71 |
| Equity in business or profession | 2,054 | 7,113 | .29 |
| Equity in own home | 24,077 | 41,999 | .57 |
| Equity in motor vehicles | 2,691 | 4,293 | .63 |
| Rental property equity | 27,291 | 34,516 | .79 |
| Other real estate equity | 10,423 | 15,488 | .67 |
| U.S. savings bonds | 200 | 305 | .66 |
| IRA or Keogh accounts | 2,450 | 4,922 | .50 |
| Other assets | (b) | 13,089 | — |

Source: U.S. Census Bureau, *Household Wealth and Asset Ownership: 1984*, Table 5.
[1]Subminimum base.

Productive wealth is heavily concentrated in business enterprise. In this area, too, black households are seriously disadvantaged by both a low frequency of ownership and low equity values. The four percent of black households that own a business average about $2,000 in equity, or less than one-third of the amount enjoyed by white business owners. The difference is largely a reflection of the kinds of businesses blacks tend to own. As Browne (1974:32) states:

> . . . because most black firms are concentrated in the retail and service sectors, which are saturated with small and marginal enterprises, there is little market for equity and there is often a massive capital loss suffered if the owner of a firm is forced to liquidate . . .

This assessment continues to characterize the general condition of black entrepreneurship (U.S. Census Bureau, 1985).

In summary, the combination of low asset ownership rates and low asset values accounts for the markedly depressed net worth of blacks relative to whites. And the *pattern* of ownership, in which income-producing assets (as contrasted with durables) are much less prevalent among the black population, does not augur well for the future of black wealth. Examining the distribution of total net worth by type of asset underscores this point.

*Distribution of Net Worth by Asset*

Reflecting the different asset ownership rates and dollar values, the total net worth of blacks differs in composition from the net worth of whites (see Table 7). In general, black wealth is much less diversified across assets. In particular, durable assets account for a much larger share of black than white wealth. Thus, about three-quarters of black wealth is in the form of home equity (65 percent) and equity in motor vehicles (11 percent). These assets make up less than half of the total wealth of white households—41 percent and six percent for home equity and vehicle equity, respectively. By contrast, financial assets constitute a relatively small proportion of black wealth. Only eight percent of black household wealth is in interest-earning assets, as against 18 percent of white wealth. Similarly, stocks and mutual fund shares barely contribute to the overall wealth of black households (about one percent), while accounting for seven percent of total white wealth.

As Table 8 shows, the racial differences in wealth composition are not significantly affected by income level. For example, black households with a monthly income in the $2,000-$3,999 range have 79 percent of their net worth in home and vehicle equity and only 10 percent in financial assets. The net worth of comparable white households consists of about 53 percent home and vehicle equity and 24 percent financial assets.

The distribution of their wealth limits the ability of black Americans to cope with economic emergencies, such as the unemployment of a family's main breadwinner. In such circumstances, having financial assets or assets that are readily convertible into cash afford the family a measure of flexibility and choice that could be vital during the crisis period. Lacking such resources, the family could find it difficult to avoid the arduous and painful ordeal of liquidating its durable assets—a car or even their home—just to get by. Having their wealth so heavily concentrated in durable goods, then, puts black Americans at a higher risk of serious hardships when their normal income stream is disrupted. On the other hand, the overall wealth status of black families is so

## Table 7

| Asset type | Blacks | Whites |
|---|---|---|
| | 100.0 | 100.0 |
| Interest-earning assets at financial institutions | 6.8 | 14.7 |
| Other interest-earning assets | 0.7 | 3.2 |
| Stocks and mutual funds shares | 0.8 | 7.1 |
| Own home | 64.7 | 40.5 |
| Motor vehicles | 11.1 | 5.9 |
| Business or profession | 6.7 | 10.5 |
| IRA or Keogh accounts | 0.9 | 2.2 |
| Other assets | 8.3 | 15.9 |

Source: U.S. Census Bureau, *Household Wealth and Asset Ownership: 1984,* Table H.

depressed that the more compelling issue may be the extent to which they have disposable resources *at all,* as opposed to the composition of these resources.

## BEYOND THE MARGIN

The wealth data paint a sobering picture of the current economic status of black Americans. The economic well-being of blacks is much more limited than is commonly recognized. The present realities represent a continuing challenge that must be faced squarely by the nation as well as by black Americans themselves. They also exist for reasons that have little to do with the motivation, industry, or capabilities of black individuals and families. Rather, they derive from historical deprivations based on racial discrimination and the interlocking discriminatory processes that continue to define racism in American society.

In this section, we comment upon the role of discrimination with respect to some of our major findings. The observations provide a context that is important for balanced interpretation. In addition, we present some concerns about current public policy and outline a key type of economic improvement strategy that blacks should pursue more vigorously on their own behalf.

### The Influence of Race

That the freedmen did not receive their "forty acres and a mule" was in itself a race-based deprivation of monumental consequence. There is little doubt but that such a measure would have facilitated the emergence of a viable black economy. Perhaps DuBois (1968:602) overstates the point in suggesting that the allotment "would have made a basis of real democracy in the United States that might easily have transformed the modern world." Nevertheless, the potential for economic development that was denied to black Americans by that unfulfilled promise is inestimable. As Thurow (1975:133) has emphasized, "any initial inequalities in the distribution of wealth . . . are apt to be magnified in the process of accumulation." The forty-acre formula, or some similar provision, would have markedly reduced the economic inequality between blacks and whites at a strategic point in the black experience.

Even without the forty-acre stake, however, the economic status of black Americans would look far different today had the group not been systematically hindered by discriminatory economic policies and practices. One analyst (Browne, 1974:30) summarizes the problem in terms of the ability of blacks to save.

Racial discrimination in the labor market has kept wage income so low as to preclude any significant savings by black laborers. Racial discrimination in credit markets has excluded blacks from the business sector, where most savings originate. Racial discrimination in the real estate market has kept the income of black landowners low, so savings from this sector also have been negligible.

Coupled with their low incidence of inheritance, this assessment goes a long way toward explaining the staggeringly low wealth position blacks occupy.

Aside from the sheer magnitude of the black/white wealth gap, the single most telling finding of our analysis is the degree to which black wealth is concentrated in durable as opposed to financial assets. To some extent, of course, the composition of a given asset portfolio reflects consumption preferences. For black families, however, it is more likely to reflect limited choice. Because of their historically depressed levels of income, blacks have been forced to apply the lion's share of their resources to consumption services such as housing and transportation (Terrell, 1971). Financial investments for all families normally fall well below basic consumption needs in order of priority. Moreover, even when blacks are in position to pursue some kind of financial investment, their opportunities may be restricted in important ways. To quote Browne (1974:32):

Certain types of high value income-earning assets are generally sold in large lots and at prices blacks cannot ordinarily afford to pay. Lack of credit further hinders blacks from participating in the market for these assets. The choice between acquiring consumption-providing assets for which credit is often available, and income-producing assets, thus is not faced by blacks. It is not at all clear that, given a choice, they would not choose income-bearing assets over consumption-providing assets, at all income levels.

The relative importance of business equity versus stocks to the wealth of blacks may also represent a problem of limited choice. As we have seen, about seven percent of total black wealth is equity in a business or profession, while only one percent is in the form of stocks and mutual fund shares. By contrast,

## Table 8
### Distribution of Net Worth, by Race, Type of Asset, and Monthly Income

| Monthly income | Interest-earning assets at financial institutions | Other interest-earning assets | Stocks and mutual fund shares | Equity in own home | Equity in motor vehicles | Equity in own business or profession | IRA or Keogh accounts | Other Assets |
|---|---|---|---|---|---|---|---|---|
| **Blacks** | | | | | | | | |
| Less than $900 | 3.2 | 0.8 | 0.4 | 78.2 | 10.1 | 6.1 | 0.4 | 0.8 |
| $900 to $1,999 | 8.1 | 0.5 | 0.7 | 62.5 | 11.4 | 11.2 | 0.6 | 5.0 |
| $2,000 to $3,999 | 8.9 | 0.7 | 0.7 | 65.9 | 12.7 | 2.2 | 1.2 | 7.7 |
| $4000 or more | 4.8 | 0.7 | 1.3 | 52.6 | 8.4 | 8.4 | 1.2 | 22.6 |
| **Whites** | | | | | | | | |
| Less than $900 | 14.4 | 1.5 | 3.2 | 53.1 | 6.3 | 10.4 | 1.0 | 10.1 |
| $900 to $1,999 | 19.0 | 2.7 | 2.7 | 47.4 | 7.1 | 8.2 | 1.7 | 11.2 |
| $2,000 to $3,999 | 16.1 | 2.6 | 5.4 | 45.2 | 7.4 | 8.5 | 2.4 | 12.4 |
| $4,000 or more | 11.8 | 4.4 | 11.7 | 29.8 | 3.8 | 13.4 | 2.7 | 22.4 |

Source: Unpublished tabulations from the Survey of Income and Program Participation.

the wealth of whites is much more evenly split between these two asset categories—11 percent and seven percent for business equity and stocks, respectively. These differences call attention to the historical segregation of black businesses. "Black businessmen have enjoyed a protective barrier of segregation within a rather limited market environment. The relatively small and predominately local markets were not large enough to support a securities market but instead were more conducive to the acquisition of business equity" (Terrell, 1971:368). In other words, blacks' inability to penetrate national business markets because of segregationist policies and practices has contributed to their marked underaccumulation of stocks.

In addition to suppressing the overall wealth position of black Americans and causing an overconcentration of black wealth in durable goods, race discrimination has also limited the returns blacks realize from their principal asset, viz., housing. Again, housing equity accounts for 65 percent of black wealth, compared to 40 percent of the wealth of white households. However, racially segregated housing markets, sustained by discriminatory real estate practices and unwritten "redlining" policies of mortgage lending institutions, deflate the market value of black-owned homes. In his rigorous analysis of racial differences in housing equity, Parcel (1982:208) reaffirmed that both "institutional and more individual sources of discrimination" militate against black wealth accumulation. Among other things:

. . . discrimination policies of the Federal Housing Administration and the real estate industry constitute institutional forces which benefit whites and hinder blacks in the accumulation of equity. At the more individual level, the accumulation of socioeconomic disadvantages throughout the life cycle contributes to the racial differences . . .

In practical terms, housing discrimination has often limited blacks to dwellings and locations that result in less equity accumulation than whites enjoy. Thus, the market value of most black-owned homes is much less likely to be driven up by buyer demand. With respect to the black/white wealth gap, O'Hare (1983:32) pointedly assesses the predicament blacks face:

Until the forces that devalue black-owned homes begin to change, there appears to be little hope that black-owned homes will appreciate as rapidly as white-owned homes. Since equity in a home is the biggest single asset category in wealth portfolios, this represents a major roadblock for wealth parity.

While other examples could be mentioned, it suffices to say that discrimination is a primary determinant of the marginal economic status of black Americans. That they have managed to progress as much as they have in spite of the constraints is a momentous achievement in itself. How much farther blacks will move beyond the margin in the years ahead largely depends upon the course of public policy as well as the actions taken by the black community itself.

## Public Policy Concerns

A basic prerequisite to enhancing the general economic well-being of black Americans is improving their employment situation. An exceedingly large proportion of the total income of black families is in the form of labor income. It is imperative therefore that much more be done to reduce the continuing high rates of black unemployment. The overall incidence of joblessness among blacks persists at more than double the rate of whites. This situation reflects both a failure of basic economic policy and the continued operation of racial discrimination in the labor market.

The so-called "economic recovery" has not produced a substantial positive effect for the black labor force (Swinton, 1987; Vaughn-Cooke, 1985). Indeed, Swinton's caustic analysis prompts him to conclude that the recent recovery "has had such weak impact on blacks that their current labor market conditions are still more depressed than they were at the bottom of all previous post-war recessions" (p. 49). Of course, some would challenge this assessment by pointing to the absolute decrease in black unemployment since 1982. They would also stress the number of new jobs the economy has generated in recent years, implying that there is not a shortage of jobs that accounts for continued high levels of black joblessness but lack of work motivation and skills. Such arguments are fundamentally unconvincing, however.

The fact is that the rate of new job creation has slowed substantially, contributing to higher average rates of unemployment in the 1980s than in prior years. Additionally, the new jobs that have been created have been concentrated at the low end of the wage scale. Some 58 percent of the net new jobs generated between 1979 and 1984 paid less than $7,000 a year. Thus, not only is job availability a major problem, but also job quality as well (Bluestone and Harrison, 1986). These conditions obviously have an acute and adverse effect on the incomes of black Americans, and call for new economic policies to rejuvenate the "great American job machine." Among other things, economic initiatives should be aimed at reversing the decline in the manufacturing sector that has spelled such hardship for the black work force. Also, the nation should commit itself to a full employment policy that effectively ensures employment for all persons who are able and willing to work (Smith, 1986; Glasgow, 1984).

Of course, many black Americans need to improve their skills to enable them to compete more effectively for the better paying jobs in all sectors of the economy. Meeting this need requires a more serious investment in human resources development programs. The recent trend has been in the opposite direction, as federal expenditures for employment training have been drastically reduced. Similarly, funding for education, the traditional means of human capital development, has been slashed sharply since 1980. These retrenchments are clearly antithetical to the economic well-being of black Americans and should be reversed (Tidwell, 1984; Simms, 1984).

Our analysis disclosed that, in general, black female family heads are especially disadvantaged. Also, they are 2.5 times more likely than their white counterparts to be dependent on public assistance. Any consideration of new employment initiatives therefore must give particular attention to the needs of this subgroup of black families. In this connection, it is disturbing that the recent "welfare reform" debate has been dominated by an attitude of retribution ("make them work, no matter what!") as opposed to a genuine concern with promoting the economic self-sufficiency of welfare-dependent female family heads. This sentiment emanates from a more general neoconservative view of black poverty that essentially treats it as a "lost cause" (Glasgow, 1987). Thus, black welfare mothers are perceived to be content to live off the public dole rather than seek the independence of gainful employment. Such stereotypes have been flatly repudiated by empirical studies (Bane and Ellwood, 1983; Goodwin, 1972). Work motivation is not the issue. What is needed is a welfare/ employment policy that provides dependent individuals real alternatives for raising their standard of living, not the punitive "workfare" mentality that effectively writes them off.

A final point we would stress is the need for vigorous enforcement of antidiscrimination statutes in all economic areas and by all levels of government. Racial discrimination remains a serious problem for black Americans, and popular arguments to the contrary simply do not stand up well against the facts. In the employment area, for example, it is impossible to account fully for the disproportionate joblessness of black Americans without acknowledging the adverse influence of race. Even at the upper levels of the occupational distribution, blacks are much more likely than whites to experience unemployment. Indeed, the black/white unemployment ratio among some types of managers and administrators is 4.5 to 1 (Tidwell, 1987).

Now is not the time to relax enforcement of antidiscrimination measures or to roll back provisions designed to ensure equal economic opportunity. The recent proposal to amend Executive Order 11246, by removing the requirement that federal contractors institute numerical goals and timetables for hiring minorities, is a prime example of misguided public policy. Existing affirmative action initiatives have not only worked but continue to be vital to the economic well-being of black Americans.

*Black Community Initiatives*

While public policy actions of the sort indicated are obviously crucial to improving the general economic status of blacks, it is also important that the black community itself move forward with collective efforts that serve its economic interests. This is not to suggest that black Americans can overturn the structured inequalities that are the effects of centuries of racial subjugation. Any such notion is frivolous and disregards the complexity of the problem and the pervasive interdependencies between blacks and the existing economic system. Within the present system, however, there is potential for self-initiated improvement that can produce tangible and significant benefits for many black individuals and families. The data in this report underscore the need to tap this potential as fully as possible.

The basic strategy being advocated here is cooperative economic enterprise by which blacks combine their individual resources and use them as leverage for both individual and group advancement. The pooled resources could be a valuable source of capital for entrepreneurial activity which, in turn, could expand employment opportunities for blacks. They could also be targeted to choice investment opportunities in financial markets that require substantial outlays of funds. Finally, they could be a vital source of assistance for black families that need emergency financial support and have no other alternatives.

# Crime Is Not A Part Of Our Black Heritage: A Theoretical Essay

Garry A. Mendez, Jr., Ph.D.
*Director of Criminal Justice Programs*
*National Urban League, Inc.*

## INTRODUCTION

In the Spring of 1984, the National Urban League and the NAACP convened a historic Black Family Summit at Fisk University in Nashville, Tennessee. Among the many problems discussed, crime in the black community loomed as an issue requiring critical attention. That this attention is well-founded is supported by Lee Brown's detailed report in this volume.

Although the problem of crime is widespread in American society, both the Uniform Crime Reports and the National Victimization Surveys indicate that the problem is disproportionately prevalent in black communities. Crime in the black community is mostly intra-racial with blacks committing crimes against other blacks. Reports inform us that blacks represent 46 percent of the individuals arrested for violent crime in America (Uniform Crime Report, 1986). Furthermore, blacks represent approximately 50 percent of the prison population (American Correctional Association, 1987), and 40 percent of the jail population (Jail Inmates, 1985).

According to Criminal Victimization in the United States (1985):

- Blacks were victims of violent crime at a higher rate than whites or any other non-white group.
- When race and sex are considered jointly black males have the highest rate of violent crime victimization.
- Rates of victimization for burglary, household larceny, and motor vehicle theft are generally higher for black households regardless of annual family income.
- Eighty-four percent of the violent crime committed against blacks was committed by other blacks.

The U.S. Department of Health and Human Services (January 1986) reports:

- The leading cause of death for young black citizens between the ages of 16-34 is homicide.

The Uniform Crime Statistics for 1986 indicate:

- Ninety-five percent of black murder victims (5,128) were slain by a black offender.

In 1974, the National Advisory Commission on Criminal Justice Standards and Goals stated that "criminal justice professionals readily and repeatedly admit that, in the absence of citizen assistance, neither more manpower, improved technology, nor additional money will enable law enforcement to shoulder the monumental burden of combating crime in America."

Given this statement, it is obvious that failure on the part of blacks to address the problem of crime in our communities will result in the continued decline of our neighborhoods.

## TRADITIONAL RESPONSES TO STREET CRIME

For the most part, the response to street crime has been focused on two levels which may sometimes overlap—government response and local community response.

Governmental response generally is centered around building prisons, increasing law enforcement personnel, re-instituting the death penalty, longer prison sentences, career criminal programs, and trying youths as adults. Many criminal justice practitioners—researchers as well as politicians—have argued that rehabilitation is totally ineffective and the idea should be abandoned in favor of "tougher punishment" policies.

All of these governmental responses mentioned have failed and failed miserably, yet few argue to abandon them. Instead they argue forcefully for more of the same.

Local or community response is an effort to join with the police in fighting crime on the theory that the police cannot do it alone; they need the help of the citizens.

If one examines the historical relationship between blacks and the police, particularly poor blacks, it is understandable that some citizens have been reluctant to join with or support the police.

Lack of understanding on the part of many criminal justice practitioners, social scientists, and politicians has led them to conclude inaccurately that blacks do not care about the problem of crime in the community; therefore, it is assumed that blacks cannot be organized to address the issue.

## AN ALTERNATIVE THEORY

The problem of crime and many of the other social problems that plague black communities are exacerbated by the lack of positive ethnic identity. In the effort to become part of the melting pot like everyone else, blacks have given up their identity. Europeans are the only groups that have not only melted into the pot, but they have also maintained their culture, history, heritage, values, and ofttimes languages. They have found strength in their ethnicity.

When segregation was legal, blacks used ethnicity as a strength and were able to address and overcome many problems; witness the Civil Rights movement. However, with the passage of civil rights and the breaking down of overt barriers, many blacks have moved away from their ethnicity—to their detriment.

For any people to survive, they must first understand who they are. They must have a base, a motherland. Every ethnic group in America identifies with both America and their motherland. They tell people proudly that they are Irish-Americans, German-Americans, Jewish-Americans, Polish-Americans, etc. The only exception to this is Americans of African descent who identify only with a color, black, rather than African-American. Black has become a culture, heritage, and a value system.

The absence of an identity with a motherland and an ethnic group has created havoc—disunity and fragmentation—in the black community.

As long as this disunity and fragmentation exist, blacks will find it difficult to unite to address the problem of crime or any other social ill.

Black citizens must assume an Afrocentric view of the world; that is, a reality that is based upon a view of the world that operates in the best interest of blacks.

## "CRIME IS NOT A PART OF OUR BLACK HERITAGE"

"Crime Is Not a Part of Our Black Heritage," a National Urban League statement on crime, builds on ethnic pride as a motivator to assist in addressing the problem of black-on-black crime.

Most crime prevention programs have focused, primarily, on what would be considered defensive measures; e.g., block watches, tenant patrols, strong locks, burglar bars, and dogs. Such efforts essentially lock up the community. "Crime is Not a Part of Our Black Heritage" is directed towards opening up the community by changing the attitudes and behavior of black citizens towards one another.

The community must be expected to take the position that crime will not be tolerated. The community must establish a code of behavior with rules and regulations and make them known to all of its members: the community taking ownership of a responsibility for itself. Changes in the community are dependent upon changes in the community members and not upon outside forces or individuals.

*Historical/Conceptual Framework*

Most crime prevention literature indicates that motivating and organizing citizens may be most difficult in areas that need crime prevention programs most. Practitioners believe that communities that lack cohesion or social integration or that are inhabited by persons with weak ties to the community (and hence less of a stake in its future) pose particular problems for crime prevention organizers.

This argument places particular emphasis on the individual family unit; however, little attention is paid to the broader family, which in this program is defined as the total community. This program argues that the total family must assume a greater role in the lives of the individual family units. It must establish rules and regulations based upon a common value system. It should be focused on the black experience both in America and Africa, to function more effectively in American society.

In the traditional black community, elders established the rules and regulations and passed them on to each new generation. The family was expected to live by and enforce the rules within the family constellation. Should the family be unable to control the family members, the elders would intervene.

Furthermore, it was the responsibility of the young males between the ages of 13 and 25 to protect and guard the community against any violations of the rules. Their community responsibility was learned behavior which is not being taught today.

## Program Goal and Objectives

### Goal

- Reduce the level of black-on-black crime and make black communities safer places to live.

### Objectives

- Develop an awareness and understanding of the problem of black-on-black crime and the need for the black community to be more involved.
- Develop an understanding in the black community of the relationship between community responsibility and crime prevention.
- Improve the self-concept of black youth, specifically, and the community in general.
- Develop an understanding in the black community of the relationship between community organization and the solving of social problems.
- Strengthen black families and communities.
- Improve the "quality of life" in black communities.
- Improve the relationship between the police and the black community.

## Program Components

### Media Community Awareness Campaign

The media campaign is designed to bring awareness to the black community as to the extent and nature of its crime problems. The campaign also promotes the position that crime will not be tolerated.

### Task Force

In conjunction with the media campaign, each participating community establishes a crime task force with the specific responsibility of examining the crime problem in the community. This includes problem-definition, analysis, and solution from an Afrocentric view of the world, which assumes responsibility for the solution to the problem.

It is a basic self-help paradigm that has been the backbone of Urban League activities in this country for many years.

### Children of the Sun

As a complement to the education provided by the public school system, each community develops an informal educational program that focuses on teaching culture, heritage, history, and values. This component is called "Children of the Sun" after the African sun god, Ra. It uses positive mythology to encourage pride and positive values—building-blocks for all of the ethnic groups in America.

In Tampa the director of the program has cultivated volunteer students and faculty from the University of South Florida who tutor young people in housing projects. Probation officers involve their probationers in the program, even working with the courts to make it a part of probation to attend the sessions.

In the same city the director is attempting to make informal education a part of the work program that is sponsored by a local company.

The California Youth Authority, the San Francisco Juvenile, and the Detroit Public Schools Alternative Programs are all exploring methods to implement educational activities on an experimental basis to see if they will affect the behavior and attitudes of the young people with whom they are working.

Values and sense of history are critical for the healthy community development of all citizens, and they are often ignored in the black community except during black history month.

*Community Councils*

The councils are designed to intervene in community disputes, misdemeanor cases, and some felonies, particularly for first offenders and juveniles. The councils represent the community's role in determining what sanctions should be attached to the violation of its rules and laws. They represent the community enforcing social control, which is often lacking in many black communities.

*Current Activities*

Cities that are currently involved in the program display a series of posters that draw attention to the problem of crime in their communities and its impact.

For example, one poster notes that the leading cause of death for young black males is homicide, and in 95 percent of the cases, the death was caused by another black male.

In addition to the posters are flyers, brochures, and buttons—all with the theme "Crime Is Not A Part Of Our Black Heritage."

The statement is also made on local television and radio shows, through the printed media, and in schools. In some cities the church has taken an active role in supporting the program and conducted "No Crime Sundays." On a designated Sunday, black ministers devote their services to the issue of crime and urge their congregations to get involved in crime prevention and eradication efforts.

In several communities in Florida, the message is carried via a theme entitled "Run Crime Out of the Black Community." The participants run a course through a high-crime neighborhood and rally the citizens to establish community watches and other activities.

In San Francisco, several thousand people were brought together by the San Francisco Religious Council to participate in a march and rally against drugs. As a result of this, a crime abatement committee was formed; citizens have begun to explore methods of changing their neighborhoods.

In Tampa Bay, the NFL Buccaneers have joined the local Urban League in promoting the message. The team members make appearances at schools and recreation areas and talk about responsibility individual and group to stop crime.

During the past two years, a process evaluation has been conducted in two cities. Although this work is not finalized, there are several preliminary findings that are of interest.

A key person pre- and post-test survey was conducted in each of the cities. The preliminary results indicate that:

- In one city the relationship between the police and the citizens changed; citizens felt that the police were beginning to listen to them and were more responsive to citizens' concerns. The police indicated that the people have become concerned.

  In the other city where there have been a series of deaths of citizens at the hands of the police, the community works on the problem but is very skeptical of the police in general.

- In both cities the citizens and police have tried to work together to establish lines of communication.

- In both cities the respondents indicated that there is a greater feeling of community and cohesiveness. They report that the citizens are more concerned about crime and crime prevention. Furthermore, they indicated that the neighborhoods feel that it is their responsibility to address the problem of crime.

- Almost unanimously they indicate that drugs are the major crime problem in the neighborhoods. However, approximately 80 percent of the respondents felt that it was also the families' responsibility to do something about the problem.

These very preliminary findings support the concept that black citizens can be organized to address the problem.

The key to the entire program is local leadership. The leadership must come from the black community and must stress the dual responsibility for self and the community.

This program represents a major undertaking that requires both time and commitment to change attitudes and behavior.

# NOTES AND
# REFERENCES

## FOOTNOTES

[1]Quoted from *The Chronicle of Higher Education,* September 2, 1987, p. 1. This highlight directs the reader to the article by Scott Jaschik, "College Outlook Grim for Blacks 25 Years After Barriers Fell," pp. A88–A91.

[2]Isabel Wilkerson, "Campus Race Incidents Disquiet U. of Michigan," *The New York Times,* March 9, 1987, p. 8.

[3]Ibid.; see also "Michigan Meets Black Students Demands"; "Columbia Rocked by Allegations of Racism," *The Chronicle of Higher Education,* April 1, 1987, pp. 27–28.

[4]Ibid.

[5]Michele N-K. Collison, "Racial Incidents Worry Campus Officials, Prompt U. of Massachusetts Study," *The Chronicle of Higher Education,* March 18, 1987, pp. 1 and 40–43; see also "White Student at U. of Mass. Faces Charges," *The Chronicle of Higher Education,* May 27, 1987, p. 26.

[6]Collison, ibid.

[7]"Columbia Rocked by Allegations of Racism," op. cit.

[8]Collison, op. cit.

[9]*Equality and Excellence: The Educational Status of Black Americans* (New York: College Entrance Examination Board, 1985), pp. 11–15; *Minorities in Higher Education: Fifth Annual Status Report, 1986* (Washington, D.C.: American Council on Education Office of Minority Concerns, 1986), pp. 8 and 24.

[10]*Minorities in Higher Education: Fourth Annual Status Report, 1985* (Washington, D.C.: American Council on Education, Office of Minority Concerns, 1985), p. 13.

[11]*Equality and Excellence,* op. cit., "The condition outlined in this report is alarming. . . ," p. vii.

[12]See, for example, *Report on Minorities, Handicappers, and Women in Michigan's Colleges and Universities,* State Superintendent's Special Advisory Committee, Niara Sudarkasa, Chair (East Lansing: Michigan Department of Education, 1986); "Strategies for Improving the Status of Blacks in Post-Secondary Education," *Journal of the Society of Ethnic and Special Studies* (Special Issue of Selected Conference Proceedings), Volume 6, Number 2, Winter/Spring 1984; "Strategies for Improving the Status of Blacks in Post-Secondary Education," Selected Proceedings, Illinois Committee on Black Concerns in Higher Education, Vol. 1, No. 1, Spring 1985; "Strategies for Improving the Status of Blacks in Post-Secondary Education," Selected Proceedings, Illinois Committee on Black Concerns in Higher Education, Vol. 2, No. 1, Spring 1986; "The Status of the Higher Education of Blacks: Historical Perspectives and Future Directions," *Planning & Changing: A Journal for School Administrators* (Special Issue), Vol. 14, No. 1, Spring 1983. See also Clewell and Ficklen, cited in fn. 33 below; and Sudarkasa and Gaborit, cited in fn. 34 below.

[13]Niara Sudarkasa, "When the Millenium Comes: The Case for Educational Equity in the 21st Century," Inaugural Address, Lincoln University, October 10, 1987, pp. 16–17 (address excerpted in *Higher Education and National Affairs,* Newsletter of the American Council on Education, November 16, 1987, pp. 7–8).

[14]Walter Allen, *Gender and Campus Race Differences in Black Student Academic Performance, Racial Attitudes and College Satisfaction* (Atlanta: Southern Education Foundation, 1986).

[15]Ibid.; Jacqueline Fleming, *Blacks in College* (San Francisco: Jossey-Bass, 1984).

[16]*Minorities in Higher Education (1986),* op. cit., p. 8, passim.

[17]*Minorities in Higher Education (1985),* op. cit., p. 7; *Minorities in Higher Education (1986),* op. cit.,

pp. 18 and 24.

[18]Edward B. Fiske, "Colleges Open New Minority Drives," *The New York Times,* November 18, 1987, p. B6 (statistics cited from Census Bureau).

[19]Alexander Astin, graph entitled "The Educational Pipeline in the United States," reproduced in *Equality and Excellence,* op. cit., p. 13, from Astin's *Minorities in American Higher Education* (San Francisco: Jossey Bass, 1982).

[20]Fiske, op. cit.

[21]Samuel Myers, "Blacks in College: NAFEO Trend Analysis," *American Visions: The Magazine of Afro-American Culture,* Volume 2, No. 5, October 1987, pp. 44–46.

[22]J.L. Preer, *Minority Access to Higher Education,* AAHE:ERIC Higher Education Research Report No. 1 (Washington, D.C.: American Association for Higher Education, 1982).

[23]For a discussion of the shifts in financial aid policy in the sixties and seventies, see Donald A. Gillespie and Nancy Carlson, *Trends in Student Aid: 1963 to 1983* (Washington, D.C.: The Washington Office of the College Board, December 1983).
The impact of the recession of the late seventies and early eighties on black families in Michigan as a factor in the enrollment of black students at the University of Michigan was discussed by the author in a number of reports, including: Niara Sudarkasa, "Undergraduate Minority Enrollment: Policy Issues and Recommendations Related to Recruitment and Financial Aid" (Ann Arbor: The University of Michigan, Office of Academic Affairs, October, 1984).

[24]"Trends in Student Aid, 1980–81 to 1986–87," *The Chronicle of Higher Education* (source: The College Board), December 2, 1987, p. A36.

[25]Ibid.

[26]"U.S. Report Adds Fuel to Heated Debate over College Attendance by Blacks," *The Chronicle of Higher Education,* April 29, 1987, pp. 21 and 26. Report cited is *College Enrollment Patterns of Black and White Students* (Washington, D.C.: U.S. Department of Education, Office of Planning, Budget, and Evaluation, 1987).

[27]*Equality and Excellence,* op. cit., p. 15.

[28]*Equality and Excellence,* op. cit., p. 14.; Susan T. Hill, *The Traditionally Black Institutions of Higher Education, 1960 to 1982,* (Washington, D.C.: National Center for Education Statistics, 1985), pp. xvi and 45.

[29]*Minorities in Higher Education: Third Annual Status Report 1984,* (Washington, D.C.: American Council on Education Office of Minority Concerns, 1984), p. 9; *The Traditionally Black Institutions,* op. cit., p. 15.

[30]*The Traditionally Black Institutions,* op. cit., p. ix, pp. xiii–xiv, and pp. 44–45.

[31]*Equality and Excellence,* op. cit., p. 14; *The Traditionally Black Institutions,* op. cit., pp. 14–15, 44–49.

[32]*The Traditionally Black Institutions,* op. cit., p. xvi; Allen, op. cit., pp. 6–7.

[33]Beatriz C. Clewell and Myra S. Ficklen, *Improving Minority Retention in Higher Education: A Search for Effective Institutional Practice* (Princeton: Educational Testing Service, 1986), p. 1.

[34]Niara Sudarkasa and Mauricio Gaborit, "Minority Undergraduate Student Retention at the University of Michigan: Creating Conditions for Success" (Ann Arbor: The University of Michigan, Office of Academic Affairs, 1987). For data on Michigan and Michigan State's black student graduation rates, see: *Report on Minorities, Handicappers, and Women,* op. cit., Appendix on "Minority Retention Rates," pp. 51–52. The author also had privileged access to data on black graduation rates from a number of Big Ten universities and other public institutions, which reported, with a promise of confidentiality, black graduation rates in the ranges cited in this essay.

[35]*Equality and Excellence,* op. cit., p. 14.

[36]Data collected by the author in the course of preparing reports on undergraduate recruitment and retention at the University of Michigan. See references above.

[37]*The Traditionally Black Institutions,* op. cit., p. xix.

[38]Allen, op. cit., passim; Fleming, op. cit., passim.; Donald Smith, "Social and Academic Environments of Black Students on White Campuses," *Journal of Negro Education,* Volume 50, No. 3, Summer 1981, pp. 299–306.

[39]Allen, op. cit., p. 38.

[40]Ibid., p. 39.

[41]Ibid., p. 45; see also D.S. Webster, et al., "Black Student Elite: Enrollment Shifts of High-Achieving, High Socio-Economic Status Black Students from Black to White Colleges During the 1970s," *College and University,* Spring 1981, pp. 283–291, cited in *Traditionally Black Institutions,* p. 15.

[42]Allen, ibid., p. 47.

[43]Kathleen J. Beauvais and Caroline A. Gould, "Nonformal Education and Strategies for Black Retention," *Journal of the Society of Ethnic and Special Studies* (Edwardsville, Ill.: Southern Illinois University), Volume 6, No. 2, Winter/Spring 1984, pp. 3–7.

[44]*The Traditionally Black Institutions,* p. xvi; Allen, op. cit., passim.; Fleming, op. cit., passim.

[45]Personal communication from Dr. Joseph Johnson, President, Grambling State University, December, 1987.

[46]*The Traditionally Black Institutions,* p. xix, p. 55.

[47]*The Traditionally Black Institutions,* p. xix, p. 55; *Equality and Excellence,* p. 18.

[48]*Minorities in Higher Education (1985),* p. 19.

[49]Niara Sudarkasa, "When the Millenium Comes: The Case for Educational Equity in the 21st Century," Inaugural Address, Lincoln University, October 10, 1987, pp. 16–17 (address excerpted in *Higher Education and National Affairs,* Newsletter of the American Council on Education, November 16, 1987, pp. 7–8).

[50]Ibid., p. 8, passim.

[51]Ibid., pp. 15–16.; Bernard Harleston also called for cooperation between predominantly black and white institutions on behalf of black students in his paper, "Access, Opportunity and Higher Education for Minority Students," presented at the Lincoln University Inaugural Conference, "Black Education into the 21st Century: Agenda & Issues," October 9, 1987.

[52]Reginald Wilson, "Recruitment & Retention of Minority Faculty and Staff," and Niara Sudarkasa, "Affirmative Action or Affirmation of the Status Quo? Black Faculty and Administrators in Higher Education," *Bulletin* (Washington, D.C.: American Association for Higher Education), Volume 39, No. 6, February 1987. See also: Brent Staples, "The Dwindling Black Presence on Campus," *The New York Times Magazine,* April 27, 1986, between pp. 46 and 62.

[53]Niara Sudarkasa, "Racial and Cultural Diversity Is a Key Part of the Pursuit of Excellence in the University," *The Chronicle of Higher Education,* February 25, 1987, p. 42.

---

**Tomorrow's Teachers: Who Will They Be, What Will They Know?**, *Bernard C. Watson, Ph.D., with Fasaha M. Traylor, M.A.*

## FOOTNOTES

[1]For a summary description of state reforms, see Chris Pipho, "States Move Reform Closer to Reality," *Kappan Special Report,* December 1986, p. K7.

Competency testing of teachers is among the more popular measures devised by states to shore up standards; however, impact studies have found that they tend to have a discriminatory impact on black and Hispanic teachers. See especially Sharon P. Robinson, "Taking Charge: An Approach to Making the Educational Problems of Blacks Comprehensible and Manageable," in *The State of Black America 1987*, Janet Dewart, ed. (New York: National Urban League, 1987), p. 33. For an especially lucid and detailed historical analysis, see G. Pritchy Smith, "The Impact of Competency Tests on Teacher Education: Ethical and Legal Issues in Selecting and Certifying Teachers," ERIC Document Reproduction Service No. ED 254493, Clearinghouse on Teacher Reeducation No. SP 019478.

[2]National Commission on Excellence in Education, *A Nation at Risk: The Imperative for Educational Reform* (Washington, D.C.: Department of Education, 1983), p. 22.

[3]The Holmes Group, *Tomorrow's Teachers* (East Lansing, Mich.: The Holmes Group, April 1986), p. 4. The Holmes Group, named after a former dean of the Harvard Graduate School of Education, consisted of deans and professors of 50 colleges and universities who worked on the report for 15 months. Three-fifths of the participants were from universities or colleges in the Northeast/Midwest, almost one-quarter (22 percent) was from western states, 10 percent were from the South, and eight percent were from the Southwest. Five of the 11 private colleges or universities represented were Harvard, Stanford, Columbia, the University of Chicago, and Vanderbilt. No traditionally black institution was represented.

The Holmes Group membership also decided to "give primary emphasis to the preparation of Professional Teachers and Career Professional Teachers," thereby opting out of what would become (if proposals are implemented) entry tiers of the teaching profession.

[4]Ibid., pp. 15–17.

[5]Ibid., p. 4.

[6]Although nearly everyone agrees that "good teachers should earn more than bad teachers," the problem of how to distinguish the good from the bad has not yet been solved—not even by merit pay. For a glimpse of how complex such determinations can be, see Thomas B. Timar and David L. Kirp, "Educational Reform and Institutional Competence," *Harvard Educational Review*, 57 (1987): 308–330.

[7]The Holmes Group, p. 4.

[8]Ibid., p. 65.

[9]Ibid., p. 4.

[10]Ibid., p. 67.

[11]Ibid., p. 4.

[12]Ibid., p. 27.

[13]The Carnegie Forum on Education and the Economy Task Force, *A Nation Prepared: Teachers for the 21st Century*, Report of the Task Force on Teaching as a Profession (New York: Carnegie Corporation, 1986), p. 55.

[14]Ibid., p. 57.

[15]The salary scale proposed by the Carnegie Forum Task Force takes into account both regional differences in education financing as well as differences in time-in-grade among teachers. The result is that entry-level salaries could range anywhere from $15,000/year for an inexperienced teacher in a poorer district to $25,000 in the wealthier district for a teacher with more experience in the entry-level grade. See the Carnegie Forum, p. 102.

[16]The Carnegie Forum Task Force, p. 55.

[17]Ibid., p. 62.

[18]Ibid., p. 64.

[19]Ibid., p. 69.

[20]As Eliot Friedson recently documented in painstaking detail, professions typically rely on "two

overlapping systems" as the cornerstone of their effort "to carve out a labor-market shelter, a social closure, or a sinecure for 'their' members." The first of these—occupational credentialing—is the activity which is currently being launched as the primary function of the standards board. The second—institutional credentialing, or accreditation—is designed to ensure that an educational program is in "conformity with approved standards," and is what enables course credits to be interchangeable and transferable from one institution to another. See Eliot Friedson, *Professional Powers: A Study of the Institutionalization of Formal Knowledge* (Chicago: University of Chicago Press, 1986), pp. 59, 64–75.

[21]Harold L. Hodgkinson, *All One System* (Washington, D.C.: Institute for Educational Leadership, 1985), p. 1.

[22]The Carnegie Forum Task Force, p. 32.

[23]The Holmes Group, p. 66.

[24]Hodgkinson, p. 3.

[25]Ibid.

[26]Ibid., pp. 3–5.

[27]Ibid., p. 7.

[28]Ibid.

[29]Ibid.

[30]Ibid., pp. 3–5.

[31]Bernard C. Watson, *Plain Talk About Education: Conversations With Myself* (Washington, D.C.: National Urban Coalition, 1987), p. 19.

[32]*Teacher Supply and Quality in the South: A Search for Strategies and Solutions,* Report on the Consultation on Teacher Supply and Quality convened by the Southern Education Foundation (Atlanta: Southern Education Foundation, 1986), pp. 8–17.

[33]Ibid., p. 8.

[34]Lynn Olson, "Certification-Panel Head Selected," *Education Week,* October 21, 1987, p. 7.

[35]Paul Starr, *The Social Transformation of American Medicine* (New York: Basic Books, 1982), p. 15.

[36]Magali Sarfitti Larson, *The Rise of Professionalism: A Sociological Analysis* (Berkeley: University of California Press, 1977), p. 164.

[37]Starr, *The Social Transformation,* p. 124.

[38]Ibid.

[39]Larson, op. cit.

[40]Starr, op. cit., p. 126.

[41]Karl Llewellyn, "The Bar Specializes—With What Results?," *Annals* of the American Academy of Policy and Social Science 167 (1933): 177 quoted in John P. Heinz and Edward O. Laumann, *Chicago Lawyers* (New York: Russell Sage and the American Bar Foundations, 1982), p. 18.

[42]Heinz and Laumann, pp. 192-193.

[43]Starr, op. cit., p. 91.

[44]Friedson, *Professional Powers,* p. 175.

[45]John E. Jacob, remarks to the Carnegie Forum on Education and the Economy, San Diego, Calif., May 17, 1986.

[46]Ibid.

**Civil Rights and the Future of the American Presidency,** *Dianne M. Pinderhughes, Ph.D.*

## FOOTNOTES

[1]See for example the large and growing historical and sociological literature on the civil rights movement, the organizations and the individuals within it published within the last decade: Carmichael and Hamilton, 1967; Carson, 1981; Garrow, 1978; Grant, 1968; King, 1958; McAdam, 1982; Morris, 1984; Meier and Rudwick, 1975; Raines, 1977; Robinson, 1987; Watters and Cleghorn, 1967; Whalen and Whalen, 1985.

[2]For research on black political participation, see Walton, 1972; Barker and Walters, forthcoming; Persons, 1987; Pinderhughes, 1983, 1985, 1987; Preston, Henderson, and Puryear, 1987; Marable, 1985; Whalen and Whalen, 1985; Foster, 1985; Davidson, 1984; Thernstrom, 1987; Cavanaugh, 1987.

[3]These issues arise out of the Voting Rights Act, enacted in 1965 and extended at irregular intervals since then. See, for example, Davidson, 1984; Foster, 1985; and Pinderhughes (forthcoming) for a discussion of the law and issues such as at-large and district electoral systems.

[4]This was the first case to reach the Supreme Court after the 1982 Voting Rights Act Extension.

[5]Jerry T. Jennings, *Voting and Registration in The Election of November 1986,* U.S., Department of Commerce, Bureau of the Census, *Current Population Reports, Population Characteristics,* Series P-20, No. 414, 1987, p. 1.

[6]Those holding primaries on March 8 include Florida, Alabama, Georgia, Texas, Kentucky, Louisiana, Massachusetts, North Carolina, Missouri, Virginia, Tennessee, Oklahoma, Massachusetts, Rhode Island, and Mississippi. Those holding party caucuses include Texas, Hawaii, Idaho, Nevada and Washington. See Rhodes Cook, *The Race For The Presidency: Winning The 1988 Nomination,* Washington, D.C.: Congressional Quarterly, 1987. See page 31 especially.

[7]Anthony Messina pointed out that presidents are highly attentive not only to their electoral constituencies, but also to their financial constituencies who would be unlikely to support affirmative action because it is too expensive. Rodolfo de la Garza also commented that there are not many areas in civil rights left on which presidents are likely to take initiatives because the basics have been dealt with. Conference on "Ethnic And Racial Minorities in Advanced Industrial Democracies," Notre Dame University, December 3-5, 1987. With apologies to my colleagues for having the last word, there is some evidence that changing demographic considerations; that is, a significant increase in the proportion of blacks and Hispanics entering the workforce, will reshape the economic and political considerations of American business, and will increase their willingness to support such policies. Civil rights therefore means voting, employment, housing, education, and health policy areas. As demographics reshape political and economic policy, then voting, employment, and education will become somewhat less controversial if nevertheless costly; housing and health issues should receive greater attention. The demographic aspects of race and ethnicity will be discussed later in this article.

[8]See Bunche, 1975; Lawson, 1976; Woodward, 1957; Hine, 1979; and Key, 1949 for information about southern voting discrimination and for the erection of a complex array of legal barriers intended to reduce and/or eliminate black *and* white voting participation in the late nineteenth and early twentieth centuries. Among those barriers: the grandfather clause, the white primary, complex registration procedures, the poll tax, and the literacy test.

[9]A supporting quotation from Wilson is still included in contemporary versions of the film.

[10]See articles by Blacksher and Menefee (1984) and Davidson and Korbel (1984) on this subject.

[11]Some of the actors in this network of civil rights attorneys—James Blacksher, Frank Parker, Armand Derfner, and Lani Guinier—describe their work; others, including Napolean Williams, Victor McTeer, and Barbara Phillips, are described in Davidson, 1984, and Foster, 1985. They are associated with the NAACP, the American Civil Liberties Union Southern Regional Office, the NAACP Legal Defense Fund, the Lawyers' Committee for Civil Rights Under Law, the Joint Center for Political Studies, and the Campaign

for Full Political Participation. The civil rights lobby is also described in a forthcoming article by the author. Also see Ball, Krane, and Lauth (1982) for a description of the complications associated with implementing the 1965 Act and of the fiscal limitations imposed on the Justice Department's Civil Rights Division.

[12]Human SERVE promotes voter registration by and within local government agencies. At the October, 1987 conference of the Campaign for Full Political Participation in San Antonio, Texas, city councilmember Martinez explained the city's programs which permit voter registration in city offices. Sandra Levine of the Harris County Hospital district explained how voter registration is conducted on-site.

[13]Combs, Hibbing, and Welch (1984). In contrast, Bullock (1985) concludes that race and urbanism are no longer important in explaining southern voting patterns. Shaffer (1982) and Campbell (1977) indicate how much of a shift has occurred recently in congressional voting and southern citizens' partisan identification patterns.

[14]See Wicker, 1987.

[15]For recent studies of Chicago politics, see Gove and Masotti, 1982; Preston, 1987; Pinderhughes, 1987; Grimshaw, 1980; and Kleppner, 1985.

[16]Compare for example Preston's 1982 and 1987 articles on black politics in Chicago; he concluded that black leadership was the biggest problem facing blacks in the city in 1982. By 1987, this was moot. One week after Washington's death, it had again become the biggest problem facing blacks in the city. City councilman Timothy Evans ("the reformer") and councilman Eugene Sawyer ("the machinist") refused to work out a political accommodation and split with what seemed to be some finality in the competition to be elected interim mayor. Sawyer was elected mayor by the city council with white "machine" support on December 1, 1987. By December 8, the *Chicago Defender* pictured Sawyer, Evans, and the Reverend Jesse Jackson at a "unity breakfast." (Strausberg, December 9, 1987, p. 1.)

[17]Civil rights organizations and the Civil Rights Division strongly disagree over whether the death of Michael Griffith at Howard Beach in New York was an incident of racially motivated violence and whether this was part of a trend. The numbers cited have been reported inconsistently in the Community Relations Service's *Annual Reports* beginning in 1965 by both Democratic and Republican administrations. They are also reported in categories that make it impossible to determine whether the "incidents" cited actually involve violence.

[18]In the past, presidents had not challenged racial subordination. Sundiata Jua-Cha argues that lynching in the earlier era

"is a form of vigilantism which not only does not challenge the State's sovereignty but functions as a reserve arm of the Repressive State Apparatus . . . a parallel structure. To paraphrase Althusser, it's unimportant whether institutions or actors are 'public' or 'private,' what's important is how they function. Lynching is a form of social control. And after 1890 it was the penultimate instrument of racial repression" (Jua-Cha, 1987, 2).

With the 1954 *Brown* decision and the Civil Rights bills passed after 1957, presidents challenged local public officials, and they responded.

[19]Presidential scholar Bert Rockman notes that "much of the literature on the American presidency unavoidably focuses on the dilemmas of generating leadership in a system not designed to endure much of it" (Rockman, 1984, xv).

## REFERENCES

Alkalimat, Abdul and Doug Gills. 1984. "Chicago Black Power vs. Racism: Harold Washington Becomes Mayor", 53–180, in Rod Bush (ed.), *The New Black Vote*. San Francisco: Synthesis Publications.

Ball, Howard, Dale Krane, and Thomas P. Lauth. 1982. *Compromised Compliance Implementation of the 1965 Voting Rights Act*. Westport, Conn.: Greenwood Press.

Barger, Harold. 1984. *The Impossible Presidency,* Glenview, Illinois: Scott, Foresman and Company.

Barker, Lucius J. 1987. "Ronald Reagan, Jesse Jackson and the 1984 Presidential Election: The Continuing American Dilemma of Race" 29–45, in Michael B. Preston, Lenneal J. Henderson, Jr., and Paul L. Puryear (eds.), *The New Black Politics*. New York: Longman.

Barker, Lucius J. and Ronald Walters. Forthcoming. *Jesse Jackson's 1984 Democratic Presidential Campaign: Its Meaning and Significance.* Urbana: University of Illinois Press.

Barnett, Marguerite Ross and Linda Faye Williams. 1986. "Affirmative Action and the Politics of the Contemporary Era," 35–92 in Marguerite Ross Barnett, Charles P. Harrington, and Philip V. White, (eds.), *Education Policy in An Era of Conservative Reform.* New York: AMS Press.

Barone, Michael and Grant Ujifusa. 1987. *The Almanac of American Politics 1988.* Washington, D.C.: The National Journal.

Binkin, Martin and Jan Eitelberg. 1982. *Blacks and the Military.* Washington, D.C.: The Brookings Institution.

Blacksher, James and Larry Menefee. 1984. "At-Large Elections and One Person, One Vote," 203–248 in Chandler Davidson (ed.), *Minority Vote Dilution.* Washington, D.C.: Joint Center for Political Studies.

Bullock, Charles S. 1985. "Congressional Roll Call Voting in a Two-Party South," *Social Science Quarterly* 66 (December 1985):789–804.

Bunche, Ralph J. 1975. *The Political Status of the Negro in the Age of FDR.* Chicago: University of Chicago Press.

Burk, Robert Frederick. 1984. *The Eisenhower Administration and Black Civil Rights.* Knoxville: University of Tennessee Press.

Campbell, Bruce A. 1977. "Patterns of Change in the Partisan Loyalties of Native Southerners: 1952–1972," *The Journal of Politics* 39 (1977):730–61.

Carmichael, Stokely and Charles V. Hamilton. 1967. *Black Power.* New York: Vintage Books.

Carson, Clayborne. 1981. *In Struggle: SNCC and the Black Awakening of the 1960s.* Cambridge: Harvard University Press.

Cavanaugh, Thomas E., ed. 1987. *Strategies for Mobilizing Black Voters Four Case Studies,* Washington, D.C.: Joint Center for Political Studies.

Combs, Michael W., John R. Hibbing, and Susan Welch. 1984. "Black Constituents and Congressional Roll Call Votes, *Western Political Quarterly, 37 (Spring 1984):* 424–34.

Community Relations Service. *Annual Report,* 1979, 1980, 1981, 1982, 1983, 1984.

Cook, Rhodes. 1987. *The Race For The Presidency: Winning the 1988 Nomination.* Washington, D.C.: Congressional Quarterly.

Cronin, Thomas E. 1975. *The State of The Presidency.* Boston: Little, Brown and Company.

Davidson, Chandler and George Korbel. 1984. "At-Large Elections and Minority Group Representation, A Reexamination of Historical and Contemporary Evidence," 65–84 in Chandler Davidson (ed.), *Minority Vote Dilution.* Washington, D.C.: Joint Center for Political Studies.

DeFranco, Joseph A. 1987. "Blacks and Affirmative Action in the U.S. Military," M.A.P.A. Paper. Urbana-Champaign: University of Illinois.

Edwards, George C. 1980. *Presidential Influence in Congress.* San Francisco: W.H. Freeman and Company.

Fleming, Harold. 1965. "The Federal Executive and Civil Rights: 1961–65." *Daedalus,* Fall 1965, 921–48.

Foster, Lorn S., ed. 1985. *The Voting Rights Act Consequences and Implications.* New York: Praeger.

French, Howard. 1987. "New York Registration Drive Aimed at Minorities." *The New York Times,* December 13, 1987a, A21.

_____. "Business Schools Cautioned on Minority Role." *The New York Times,* December 13, 1987b, A18.

Garfinkel, Herbert. 1969. *When Negroes March.* New York: Atheneum.

Garrett, Romeo B. 1982. *The Presidents and The Negro.* Peoria.

Garrow, David. 1978. *Protest at Selma: Martin Luther King, Jr., and the Voting Rights Act of 1965.* New Haven: Yale University Press.

Gove, Samuel K. and Louis H. Masotti. 1982. *After Daley Chicago Politics in Transition.* Urbana: University of Illinois Press.

Grant, Joanne. 1968. *Black Protest.* Greenwich, Conn.: Fawcett Premier Books.

Grimshaw, Williams J. 1980. *Black Politics in Chicago: The Quest for Leadership, 1939–1979.* Chicago: Center for Urban Policy, Loyola University of Chicago.

Henderson, Lenneal J. 1987. "Black Politics and the American Presidential Elections," 3–28 in Michael B. Preston, Lenneal J. Henderson, Jr., and Paul L. Puryear (eds.), *The New Black Politics.* New York: Longman.

Hine, Darlene Clark. 1979. *Black Victory.* New York: Millwood.

Holden, Jr., Mathew. 1986. "The President, Congress, and Race Relations." Ernest Patterson Memorial Lecture. Boulder: University of Colorado, April, 1986.

_____. 1987. "Tabulation of Bills and Proposed Resolutions Relative to Afro-Americans, The 57th Through the 80th Congresses (1901–1948)." Unpublished from The Mathew Holden, Jr. Archives.

Jennings, Jerry T. 1987. *Voting and Registration in the Election of November 1986.* U.S., Bureau of the Census, *Current Population Reports,* Series P-20, No. 414.

Joint Center for Political Studies. 1987. *Black Elected Officials A National Roster, 1987,* Washington, D.C.: Joint Center for Political Studies.

Jua-Cha, Sundiata. 1987. "The Lynching of Samuel J. Bush: Vigilantism As An Expression of the Repressive State Apparatus." Unpublished paper, University of Illinois, Urbana-Champaign.

Kellogg, Charles Flint. 1967. *NAACP: A History of the National Association for The Advancement of Colored People, 1909–1920,* Vol. 1. Baltimore: Johns Hopkins University Press.

Key, Jr., V.O. 1949. *Southern Politics in State and Nation.* New York: Random House.

King, Jr., Martin Luther. 1958. *Stride Toward Freedom.* New York: Ballantine Books.

Kleppner, Paul. 1985. *Chicago Divided: The Making of A Black Mayor.* De Kalb: Northern Illinois University Press.

Ladd, Jr., Everett Carll. 1969. *Negro Political Leadership in the South.* New York: Atheneum.

Laski, Harold J. 1940. *The American Presidency: An Interpretation.* New York: Harper and Brothers.

Lawson, Steven F. 1976. *Black Ballots.* New York: Columbia University Press.

Light, Paul Charles. 1982. *The President's Agenda: Domestic Policy Choice From Kennedy to Carter (With Notes on Ronald Reagan).* Baltimore: The Johns Hopkins University Press.

Litwack, Leon R. 1961. *North of Slavery.* Chicago: University of Chicago.

Marable, Manning. 1985. *Black American Politics.* London: Verso.

McAdam, Doug. 1982. *Political Process and the Development of Black Insurgency, 1930–1970.* Chicago: University of Chicago Press.

Meier, August and Elliott Rudwick. 1975. *CORE: A Study in the Civil Rights Movement, 1942–1968.* Urbana: University of Illinois Press.

Miller, Merle. 1980. *Lyndon An Oral Biography.* New York: G.P. Putnam's Sons.

Ming, Jr., William R. 1947. "The Present Legal and Social Status of the American Negro," 47–61 in W.E.B. DuBois (ed.), *An Appeal To The World*. New York: National Association for the Advancement of Colored People.

Morgan, Ruth P. 1970. *The President and Civil Rights Policy Making By Executive Order*. New York: St. Martin's Press.

Morris, Aldon. 1984. *The Origins of the Civil Rights Movement: Black Communities Organizing for Change*. New York: Free Press.

Morrow, E. Frederic. 1963. *Black Man in the White House*. New York: Coward-McCann.

Neustadt, Richard. 1960. *Presidential Power*. New York: Wiley.

Oehlsen, Nadia Anne. 1987. "Reporting and Responding to Move-In Violence Against Blacks." Student Paper, University of Illinois, Urbana.

Persons, Georgia A. 1987. "Blacks in State and Local Government: Progress and Constraints," 167–93 in Janet Dewart (ed.), *The State of Black America 1987*. New York: National Urban League.

Petrocik, John R. 1981. *Party Coalitions*. Chicago: The University of Chicago Press.

Pinderhughes, Dianne M. 1984. "The Black Vote The Sleeping Giant," 69–94, in *The State of Black America 1984*. New York: National Urban League.

_____. 1985. "Legal Strategies for Voting Rights: Political Science and the Law," *Howard University Law Journal*, 28 (1985):515–40.

_____. 1986. "Political Choices: A Realignment in Partisanship Among Black Voters?", 85–113 in *The State of Black America 1986*. New York: National Urban League.

_____. 1987. *Race and Ethnicity in Chicago Politics: A Reexamination of Pluralist Theory*. Urbana: University of Illinois Press.

_____. Forthcoming. "How the Lobby Shaped the Law, How the Law Shaped the Lobby," in Wayne Parent and Huey Perry (eds.), *Black Politics in the American Political System*. Baton Rouge: Louisiana State University Press.

Pitkin, Hanna F. 1967. *The Concept of Representation*. Berkeley: University of California Press.

Polsby, Nelson W. 1968. "The Institutionalization of the U.S. House of Representatives," *American Political Science Review*, 62 (March 1968):144–68.

_____. 1969. "The Growth of Seniority in the U.S. House of Representatives," *American Political Science Review*, 62 (September 1969):787–809.

Preston, Michael B. 1982. "Black Politics in the Post-Daley Era," 88–117 in Samuel K. Gove and Louis H. Masotti (eds.), *After Daley*. Urbana: University of Illinois Press.

_____. 1987. "The Election of Harold Washington: An Examination of the SES Model in the 1983 Chicago Mayoral Election," 139–171 in Michael B. Preston, Lenneal J. Henderson, Jr., and Paul L. Puryear (eds.), *The New Black Politics*. New York: Longman.

_____, Lenneal J. Henderson, Jr., Paul L. Puryear, eds. 1987. *The New Black Politics The Search For Political Power*. New York: Longman.

Raines, Howell. 1977. *My Soul Is Rested*. New York: Bantam Books.

Robinson, Jo Ann. 1987. *The Montgomery Bus Boycott and the Women Who Started It,* David J. Garrow (ed.). Knoxville: The University of Tennessee Press.

Robinson, Pearl T. 1982. "Whither the Future of Blacks in the Republican Party?" *Political Science Quarterly*, 97 (Summer 1982):207–31.

Rockman, Bert A. 1984. *The Leadership Question*. New York: Praeger.

Rossiter, Clinton. 1956. *The American Presidency*. New York: A Harvest Book.

228

St. James, Warren D. 1980. *NAACP Triumphs of A Pressure Group 1909-1980*. Smithtown, N.Y.: Exposition Press.

Shaffer, William R. 1982. "Party and Ideology in the U.S. House of Representatives, *Western Political Quarterly,* 35 (March 1982):92-106.

Sitkoff, Harvard. 1978. *A New Deal for Blacks*. New York: Oxford University Press.

Smith, Robert C. and Joseph P. McCormick, II. 1985. "The Challenge of A Black Presidential Candidacy (1984)," *New Directions,* April 1985, 25-31; May 1985, 22-25.

Strausberg, Chinta. 1987. "Mayor, Evans United." *Chicago Defender,* December 9, 1987, 1.

Thernstrom, Abigail M. 1987. *Whose Votes Count? Affirmative Action and Minority Voting Rights*. Cambridge: Harvard University Press.

U.S. Commission on Civil Rights. 1981. *The Voting Rights Act: Unfulfilled Goals*. Washington, D.C.

Walton, Jr., Hanes. 1972. *Black Politics: A Theoretical and Structural Analysis*. New York: J.B. Lippincott Company.

_____. 1985. *Invisible Politics Black Political Behavior*. Albany, N.Y.: State University of New York Press.

Watson, Richard A. 1987. *The Presidential Contest*. Washington, D.C.: Congressional Quarterly.

Watters, Pat and Reese Cleghorn. 1967. *Climbing Jacob's Ladder, The Arrival of Negroes in Southern Politics*. New York: Harcourt, Brace and World.

Whalen, Charles and Barbara. 1985. *The Longest Debate A Legislative History of the Civil Rights Act*. New York: New American Library.

Wicker, Tom. 1987. *The New York Times*. October 4, 1987.

Williams, Juan. 1987. *Eyes on The Prize*. New York: Viking Books.

Williams, Linda. 1986. "1986 Elections: Major Implications for Black Politics," *Focus,* 14 (November-December 1986):5-7.

_____. 1987. "Black Political Participation in the 1980s: The Electoral Arena," 97-136 in Michael B. Preston, Lenneal J. Henderson, Jr., and Paul L. Puryear (eds.), *The New Black Politics The Search For Political Power*. New York: Longman.

Woodward, C. Vann. 1957. *Reunion and Reaction: The Compromise of 1877 and the End of Reconstruction*. Boston: Little, Brown.

Zangrando, Robert L. 1980. *The NAACP Crusade Against Lynching, 1909-1950*. Philadelphia: Temple University Press.

---

**Critical Perspectives on the Psychology of Race,** *Price M. Cobbs, M.D.*

## BIBLIOGRAPHY

Cobbs, Price M. "Ethnotherapy in Groups," in *New Perspectives on Encounter Groups,* Eds. Lawrence M. Solomon and Betty Berzon. San Francisco: Jossey-Bass, 1972. Pp. 383-392.

Dancy, Vernon. "From the Editor's Desk." *The Crown Newsletter.* Vol. 3, No. 3. Los Angeles: September 1987, p. 6.

DuBois, W.E.B. *Writings: The Suppression of the African Slave-Trade, The Souls of Black Folk, Dusk of Dawn, Essays and Articles*. New York: Literary Classics of the United States, 1986.

Frazier, E. Franklin. *Black Bourgeoisie*. Glencoe, Ill.: Free Press, 1957.

Freud, Sigmund. *The Basic Writings of Sigmund Freud*. Trans. by A.A. Brill. New York: Modern Library, 1938.

Grier, William H. and Price M. Cobbs. *Black Rage*. New York: Basic Books, 1980.

_____. *The Jesus Bag*. New York: McGraw-Hill Book Company 1971.

Gwaltney, John Langston. *DryLongSo: A Self-Portrait of Black America*. New York: Vintage Books, 1980.

Jensen, Arthur R. "How Much Can We Boost I.Q. and Scholastic Achievement." *Harvard Educational Review*, Winter 1969. Pp. 115–117.

Jones, Edward W. "Black Managers: The Dream Deferred." *Harvard Business Review*. Vol. 64, No. 3, May-June 1986. Pp. 84–95.

Jung, C.G. *Contributions to Analytical Psychology*. New York: Harcourt, Brace, 1928.

Leonard, George. "A Southerner's Appeal." *Look Magazine*. August 11, 1964. Pp. 7–26.

Pear, Robert. "The Bureaucracy: Blacks and the Elitist Stereotype." *The New York Times*, September 29, 1987.

Pierce, C.M. 1968. "Manpower: the Need for Negro Psychiatrists." *Journal of the National Medical Association*. 60: 30–33.

_____. 1970. "Research and Careers for Blacks." *American Journal of Psychiatry*. 127: 817–818.

Shockley, W. "Possible transfer of metallurgical and astronomical approaches to the problem of environment versus ethnic heredity." Quoted by Birch, H.G. in Mead et al., *Science and the Concept of Race*, 1968.

Sowell, Thomas. *The Economics and Politics of Race: An International Perspective*. New York: Quill, 1983.

---

**The Black Family: Striving Toward Freedom,** *Charles V. Willie, Ph.D.*

### REFERENCES

Coleman, Richard P. and Lee Rainwater. 1978. *Social Standing in America*. New York: Basic Books.

Dobzhansky, Theodosius. 1951. *Genetics and the Origin of the Species*. New York: Columbia University Press.

Farley, Reynolds. 1984. *Blacks and Whites*. Cambridge: Harvard University Press.

Farley, Reynolds and Walter R. Allen. 1987. *The Color Line and the Quality of Life in America*. New York: Russell Sage Foundation.

Frazier, E. Franklin. 1968. "The Negro Family in America." In *Franklin Frazier on Race Relations,* edited by G. Franklin Edwards. Chicago: University of Chicago Press.

Keniston, Kenneth, 1977. *All Our Children*. New York: Harcourt Brace Jovanovich.

King, Martin Luther, Jr. 1958. *Stride Toward Freedom*. New York: Harper and Row.

Miller, Herman. 1964. *Rich Man, Poor Man*. New York: Crowell.

Morgan, D.H.J. 1975. *Social Theory and the Family*. London: Routledge and Kegan Paul.

Myers, Hector F. 1982. "Research on the Afro-American Family: A Critical Review." In Barbara Ann Bass, Gail Elizabeth Wyatt, and Gloria Johnson Powell (eds.), *The Afro-American Family*. New York: Grune and Stratton, pp. 35–68.

U.S. Bureau of the Census. 1980. *Social Indicators III*. Washington, D.C.: Government Printing Office.

U.S. Bureau of the Census. 1985. *Household Wealth and Asset Ownership: 1984*. Washington, D.C.: Government Printing Office.

U.S. Bureau of the Census. 1985. *Statistical Abstract of the United States*. Washington, D.C.: Government Printing Office.

U.S. Bureau of Labor Statistics. 1980. *Handbook of Labor Statistics*. Washington, D.C.: Government Printing Office.

Wilkerson, Isabel. 1987. "Growth of the Very Poor Is Focus on New Studies," *The New York Times* (December 20), p. 26.

Willie, Charles Vert. 1981. *A New Look at Black Families*. Dix Hills, N.Y.: General Hall.

_____. 1983. *Race, Ethnicity, and Socioeconomic Status*. Dix Hills, N.Y.: General Hall.

_____. 1985. *Black and White Families*. Dix Hills, N.Y.: General Hall.

Wilson, William Julius. 1978. *The Declining Significance of Race*. Chicago: University of Chicago Press.

_____. 1987. *The Truly Disadvantaged*. Chicago: The University of Chicago Press.

---

**Black Youth at Risk,** *Bruce R. Hare, Ph.D.*

## FOOTNOTES

[1]Samuel Bowles and Herbert Gintis, *Schooling in Capitalist America* (New York: Basic Books, 1976).

[2]*Crisis,* 93 (March 1986), entire issue on the topic, "Black Males in Jeopardy."

[3]Walter Allen, "Family Roles, Occupational Statuses, and Achievement Among Black Women in the United States," *Journal of Women in Culture and Society,* 4 (1979): 670–686.

[4]Diane I. Lewis, "The Black Family: Socialization and Sex Roles," *Phylon,* 36 (1975): 221–237.

[5]Lorraine Mayfield, "Early Parenthood Among Low-Income Adolescent Girls," in Robert Staples, ed., *The Black Family: Essays and Studies* (Belmont, Calif.: Wadsworth Publishing, 1986).

[6]*Brown V. Board of Education of Topeka,* 347 U.S. 483 (1954).

[7]Bruce R. Hare, "Black and White Child Self-Esteem in Social Science: An Overview," *Journal of Negro Education,* 46 (1977): 141–156; A. Wade Boykin, Anderson J. Franklin, and J. Frank Yates, eds., *Research Directions of Black Psychologists* (New York: Russell Sage Foundation, 1979); and Margaret Spencer, Geraldine K. Brookins, and Walter R. Allen, eds., *Beginnings: The Social and Affective Development of Black Children* (Hillsdale, N.J.: Lawrence Erlbaum Associates, 1985).

[8]Aaron Cicourel and John Kitsuse, *The Educational Decision Makers* (Indianapolis: Bobbs-Merrill, 1963), pp. 136–137.

[9]David Lavin, *The Predictions of Academic Performance* (New York: Russell Sage Foundation, 1963).

[10]Irwin Katz, "The Socialization of Academic Motivation in Minority Group Children," in D. Levine, ed., *Nebraska Symposium on Motivation* (Lincoln: University of Nebraska Press, 1967).

[11]Bruce R. Hare, "Self-Perception and Academic Achievement Variations in a Desegregated Setting," *American Journal of Psychiatry,* 137 (1980): 683–689.

[12]_____, "Development and Change among Desegregated Adolescents: A Longitudinal Study of Self-Perception and Achievement," in David E. Bartz and Martin L. Maehr, eds., *Advances in Motivation and Achievement,* Vol. 1 (Greenwich, Conn.: JAI Press, 1984).

[13]_____, "Stability and Change in Self-Perception and Achievement Among Black Adolescents: A Longitudinal Study," *Journal of Black Psychology,* 11 (1985): 29–42.

[14]Louis A. Castenell, "Achievement Motivation: An Investigation of Adolescent Achievement Patterns," *American Educational Research Journal,* 20 (1983): 503-510.

[15]Scott Cummings, "Family Socialization and Fatalism Among Black Adolescents," *Journal of Negro Education,* 46 (1977): 62-75.

[16]Martin Maehr and A. Lysy, "Motivating Students of Diverse Sociocultural Backgrounds to Achieve," *International Journal of Intercultural Relations,* 2 (1979): 38-70.

[17]E. Franklin Frazier, *Black Bourgeoisie* (Glencoe, Ill.: Free Press, 1957).

[18]Carter G. Woodson, *The Mis-Education of the Negro,* 2nd Ed. (Washington, D.C.: Associated Publishers, 1969).

[19]William Grier and Price M. Cobbs, *Black Rage* (New York: Bantam, 1968).

[20]Abram Kardiner and Lionel Ovesey, *The Mark of Oppression* (New York: Norton, 1951).

---

**Crime in the Black Community,** *Lee P. Brown, Ph.D.*

## FOOTNOTES

[1]The President's Commission on Law Enforcement and Administration of Justice, *The Challenge of Crime in a Free Society* (Washington, D.C.: Government Printing Office, 1967), p. 1.

[2]Elliot Currie, *Confronting Crime: An American Challenge* (New York: Pantheon Books, 1985), p. 5.

[3]Ibid., p. 6.

[4]Keith Melville, *Crime: What We Fear, What Can be Done* (Dayton, Ohio: Domestic Policy Association, 1986), p. 26.

[5]Currie, op. cit., pp. 6-7.

[6]Patrick A. Langan and Christopher Innes, "The Risk of Violent Crime," *Bureau of Justice Statistics Special Report"* (Washington, D.C.: Government Printing Office, 1985), p. 1.

[7]Herbert Koppel, "Lifetime Likelihood of Victimization," *Bureau of Justice Statistics Technical Report* (Washington, D.C.: Government Printing Office, 1987), p. 3.

[8]Ibid.

[9]Ibid.

[10]Ibid.

[11]See U.S., Department of Justice, Bureau of Justice Statistics, *Criminal Victimization in the United States, 1985* (Washington, D.C.: Government Printing Office, 1987).

[12]Index crimes consist of murder and non-negligent manslaughter, forcible rape, robbery, aggravated assault, burglary, larceny-theft, motor vehicle theft, and arson.

[13]U.S., Federal Bureau of Investigation, *Crime In The United States, Uniform Crime Reports* (Washington, D.C.: Government Printing Office, 1987), p. 182.

[14]Ibid.

[15]Ibid., p. 196.

[16]U.S., Department of Justice, Bureau of Justice Statistics, *Prisoners in State and Federal Institutions on December 31, 1984* (Washington, D.C.: Government Printing Office, 1986), p. 17.

[17]Ibid.

[18]Ibid.

[19]U.S., Department of Justice, Bureau of Justice Statistics, *Jail Inmates, 1985* (Washington, D.C.: Government Printing Office, 1987), p. 2.

[20]U.S., Department of Justice, Bureau of Justice Statistics, *Children in Custody* (Washington, D.C.: Government Printing Office, 1986), p. 3.

[21]U.S., Department of Justice, Bureau of Justice Statistics, *Source Book of Criminal Justice Statistics — 1986* (Washington, D.C.: Government Printing Office, 1987), p. 428.

[22]U.S., Department of Justice, Bureau of Justice Statistics, *Households Touched by Crime, 1986* (Washington, D.C.: Government Printing Office, 1987), p. 2.

[23]Ibid.

[24]U.S., Department of Justice, op. cit., at footnote 11, p. 39.

[25]Ibid., p. 3.

[26]Ibid., p. 5.

[27]Ibid., pp. 28–29.

[28]Ibid. p. 5.

[29]U.S., Department of Justice, op. cit., at footnote 22, p. 3.

[30]U.S., Department of Justice, Bureau of Justice Statistics, *Criminal Victimization in the United States, 1985, National Survey Report* (Washington, D.C.: Government Printing Office, 1987).

[31]U.S., Department of Justice, Bureau of Justice Statistics, *The Risk of Violent Crime* (Washington, D.C.: Government Printing Office, 1985).

[32]Beny J. Primm, "Drug Use: Special Implications for Black America," in Janet Dewart (ed.), *The State of Black America 1987* (New York: National Urban League, 1987), pp. 145–158.

[33]National Institute on Drug Abuse, *Annual Data 1986; Data From Abuse Warning Network* (Washington, D.C.: U.S. Department of Health and Human Services, 1987), p. 52.

[34]Primm, op. cit., p. 148.

[35]Ibid.; totals exceed 100 percent where respondents indicated more than one preference.

[36]Research and Forecasts, Inc., *The Figgie Report on Fear of Crime: America Afraid, Part I—The General Public* (Willoughby, Ohio: A-T-O, Inc., 1987), p. 28.

[37]U.S., Department of Justice, op. cit., at footnote 11, p. 5.

[38]Ibid., p. 4.

[39]Alfred Blumstein and Jacqueline Cohn, *Criminal Careers and Career Criminals* (Washington, D.C.: National Academy Press, 1986), pp. 123–143.

[40]Melville, op. cit., p. 27.

[41]See, for example, James Q. Wilson, *Thinking About Crime* (New York: Basic Books, 1983), and James Q. Wilson and Richard J. Herrnstein, *Crime and Human Nature* (New York: Simon and Schuster, 1985).

[42]Currie, op. cit.

[43]Ibid.

[44]*Report of the National Advisory Commission on Civil Disorders* (Washington, D.C.: Government Printing Office, 1968), pp. 91–93.

[45]*Report of the National Commission on the Causes and Prevention of Violence: Final Report*

(Washington, D.C.: Government Printing Office, 1969), pp. 271–282.

[46]See, for example, Lee P. Brown, "The Impact of Crime on the Black Community: An Agenda for Change," an address delivered before the Symposium on Crime Reduction in Low Income Areas, Washington, D.C., September 8, 1976, and Lee P. Brown, "Crime in the Black Community: The Federal Response," a position paper prepared for the National Urban League, February 1978.

[47]See, for example, The National Urban League and The National Association for the Advancement of Colored People, *Proceedings of the Black Family Summit* (Washington, D.C.: National Urban League, 1985).

[48]See, for example, Currie, op. cit., at footnote 2, and Harvey Brenner, "Estimating the Social Costs of National Economic Policy: Implications for Mental and Physical and Criminal Aggression," a study prepared for the Joint Economic Committee of the Congress of the United States (Washington, D.C.: Government Printing Office, October 26, 1976).

[49]Currie, *What Kind of Future? Violence and Public Safety in the Year 2000* (San Francisco: National Council on Crime and Delinquency, 1987), p. 9.

[50]Currie, op. cit., at footnote 2, p. 106.

[51]Joan Petersilia, "Racial Disparities in the Criminal Justice System: A Summary," *Crime and Delinquency,* January, 1985, p. 25.

[52]The President's Commission on Law Enforcement and Administration of Justice, op. cit., p. 35.

[53]David Swinton, "Economic Status of Blacks 1986," in Janet Dewart (ed.), *The State of Black America 1987* (New York: National Urban League, 1987), pp. 49–74.

[54]See Travis Hirschi, "Intelligence and Delinquency," *American Sociological Review,* Vol. 42, 1977; Frank Jerse and M. Ebrahim Fakouri, "Juvenile Delinquency: An Academic Deficiency," *Contemporary Education,* Vol. 49, 1978; and Kenneth Polk and Walter Schafer, *Schools and Delinquency* (Englewood Cliffs, N.J.: Prentice Hall, 1972).

[55]See, for example, Martha Fleetwood, *Avenues Out of Despair: Homeless Programs in the San Francisco Bay Area* (San Francisco: Public Advocates, Inc., 1987); Richard H. Ropers, *Blacks and Other Minorities Among the Homeless* (Chicago: Chicago Urban League, 1986), and Phillip L. Clay, *At Risk of Loss: The Endangered Future of Low-Income Rental Housing Resources* (Washington, D.C.: Neighborhood Reinvestment Corporation, 1987).

[56]See Marian Wright Edelman, *Families in Peril: An Agenda for Social Change* (Cambridge, Mass.: Harvard University Press, 1987).

[57]U.S., Department of Justice, Bureau of Justice Statistics Report, *Prisoners and Drugs* (Washington, D.C.: Government Printing Office, 1983).

[58]Lorraine Perry, Ernest Harburg, and Joan E. Crowley, "Urban Families and Assault: A Framework for Research Focused on Black Families," in Laura Otter (ed.), *Colloquium on the Correlates of Crime and the Determinants of Criminal Behavior* (McLean, Virginia: The Mitre Corporation, 1978).

[59]See Ronald Kotulak, "America Bites the Bullet," *Houston Chronicle,* June 8, 1985.

[60]D. Pearl, L. Bon Thilet, and J. Lazar (eds.), *Television and Behavior: Ten Years of Scientific Progress and Implications for the Eighties* (Rockville, Md.: National Institute of Mental Health, 1982).

[61]See Winston Williams, "White Collar Crime: Booming Again," *The New York Times,* July 7, 1987.

---

**Blacks in the Military: The Victory and the Challenge,** *Alvin J. Schexnider, Ph.D.*

## FOOTNOTES

[1]Quoted in Richard O. Hope, *Racial Strife in the U.S. Military* (New York: Praeger Publishers, 1979),

p. 30.

[2]Charles C. Moskos, Jr., *The American Enlisted Man* (New York: Russell Sage, 1970), p. 111.

[3]Charles C. Moskos and John S. Butler, "Blacks in the Military Since World War II," published manuscript prepared for the Study on the Status of Black Americans (National Research Council, 1987), p. 4.

[4]Martin Binkin, Mark J. Eitelberg with Alvin J. Schexnider and Marvin M. Smith, *Blacks and the Military* (Washington, D.C.: The Brookings Institution, 1982), pp. 31–32.

[5]*The New York Times Magazine*, March 24, 1968, p. 37.

[6]Daniel P. Moynihan, "Who Gets in the Army," *New Republic*, November 5, 1965, p. 22.

[7]Ibid.

[8]Whitney Moore Young, Jr., "When the Negroes in Vietnam Come Home," *Harper's*, June 1967, p. 66.

[9]See Morris Janowitz and Charles C. Moskos, Jr., "Racial Composition in the All-Volunteer Force," *Armed Forces and Society*, Vol. 1 (Nov. 1974): 109–23 and Alvin J. Schexnider and John S. Butler, "Race and the All-Volunteer System: A Reply to Janowitz and Moskos, *Armed Forces and Society* Vol. 2. (Spring 1976): 421–432.

[10]Kenneth J. Coffey, *Strategic Implications of the All-Volunteer Force* (Chapel Hill: University of North Carolina Press, 1979), p. 66.

[11]Charles C. Moskos, Jr., "The Enlisted Ranks in the All-Volunteer Army" in John Keely (ed..) *The Military in American Society* (Charlottesville: University of Virginia Press, 1978).

[12]Charles C. Moskos, "Success Story: Blacks in the Army," *The Atlantic*, May 1986, p. 67.

[13]Ibid.

[14]*The New York Times*, October 11, 1987, p. 42.

[15]Solomon Arbeiter, "Guns, Butter, or Sheepskins? The Military, Business and College Competition for High School Graduates in the 1980's," *The College Board Review*, Fall 1985, p. 31.

[16]See, for example, Mexender Astir, *Minorities in American Higher Education* (San Francisco: Jossey Bass, 1982), especially pp. 26–32; and the American Council on Education's *Fifth Annual Status Report on Minorities in Higher Education* (Washington, D.C., 1986), pp. 14–15.

[17]Binkin, et al., op. cit., p. 66.

[18]Ibid., p. 67.

[19]Alvin J. Schexnider, "Black Youth at the Crossroads, The Armed Forces and Higher Education," *Black Issues*, February 15, 1987.

[20]Moskos and Butler, op. cit., p. 8.

[21]Ibid., p. 8.

[22]Ibid., p. 18.

[23]Ibid., p. 18.

[24]Quoted in *Black Issues in Higher Education*, November 1, 1987, p. 2.

[25]American Council on Education's *Fifth Annual Status Report*, op. cit., p. 14.

[26]Quoted in the American Council on Education's *Fifth Annual Status Report*, p. 15.

[27]Moskos, op. cit., p. 64.

[28]Reference is made here to strained relations between then Mayor of Cleveland Carl B. Stokes and

General B.O. Davis, Jr., and more recently between Mayor of Philadelphia Wilson Goode and General Leo Brooks.

[29]"The Armed Forces Only Black Four-Star General," *Ebony,* November, 1987, p. 160.

---

**Economic Status of Blacks 1987,** *David H. Swinton, Ph.D.*

### REFERENCES

Swinton, David H. 1986. "The Economic Status of the Black Population," in *The State of Black America 1986.* New York: National Urban League.

_____. 1987. "Economic Status of Blacks 1986," in Janet Dewart (ed.), *The State of Black America 1987.* New York: National Urban League.

U.S. Department of Commerce. 1987. Bureau of the Census. Current Population Report, Series p-60, No. 157, *Money Income and Poverty Status of Families and Persons in the United States: 1986* (Advance Data from the March 1987 Current Population Survey). Washington, D.C.: Government Printing Office.

_____. 1986. Bureau of the Census. Current Population Report, Series p-60, No. 151, *Money Income of Families and Persons in the United States: 1984.* Washington, D.C.: Government Printing Office.

U.S. Department of Labor. 1986. Bureau of Labor Statistics. *Employment and Earnings: January 1987* and *September 1987.* Washington, D.C.: Government Printing Office.

_____. 1986. Bureau of Labor Statistics. *Geographic Profile of Employment and Unemployment, 1986 and 1985.* Washington, D.C.: Government Printing Office.

---

**Black Wealth: Facts *and* Fiction,** *Billy J. Tidwell, Ph.D.*

### FOOTNOTES

[1]In fact, persons who reside in poverty areas may often face above average consumer prices, which means they are able to consume less out of a given dollar of income. Blacks encounter this circumstance to a disproportionate extent. Relevant discussions are provided in Sturdivant (1969).

[2]The analysis is based on data on household wealth collected for the first time by the U.S. Census Bureau, as a part of its ongoing Survey of Income and Program Participation. Covering the year 1984, this database is an unusually comprehensive source of wealth data by race.

[3]All averages in this report represent median values. Other analysts (e.g., O'Hare, 1983) have used the mean, which produces higher averages due to the inflating effect of such extreme values. The median minimizes the effect of extreme values by dividing the distribution into two equal groups at its midpoint. Because the distribution of net worth is heavily skewed toward the low end, the median is the more appropriate measure to use. Doing so results in lower net-worth averages than is the case with the mean and larger differences between blacks and whites.

[4]Several major assets were not covered in the Census Bureau survey. These include equities in pension plans, the cash-value of life insurance policies, and the value of home furnishings and jewelry. The survey approach is not a very efficient means of estimating the value of these assets. Technical information concerning measurement reliability for the covered assets is contained in Appendix C of U.S. Bureau of the Census (1986).

## REFERENCES

Bane, M.J. and Ellwood, D.T. 1983. *The Dynamics of Dependence: The Routes to Self-Sufficiency.* Cambridge, Mass.: John F. Kennedy School of Government, Harvard University.

Bennett, L., Jr. 1969. *Black Power U.S.A.* New York: Pelican Books.

Bluestone, B. and Harrison, B. 1986. *The Great American Job Machine: The Proliferation of Low-Wage Employment in the U.S. Economy.* Washington, D.C.: The Joint Economic Committee.

Browne, R.S. 1970. "Barriers to Black Participation in the U.S. Economy." *The Review of Black Political Economy.* Vol. 1, No. 2 (Autumn 1970), pp. 57–67.

_____. 1974. "Wealth Distribution and Its Impact on Minorities." *The Review of Black Political Economy.* Vol. 4, No. 4 (Summer 1974), pp. 27–37.

DuBois, W.E.B. 1968. *Black Reconstruction.* Cleveland, Ohio: Meridian Books.

Friedman, M. 1957. *A Theory of the Consumption Function.* Princeton, N.J.: Princeton University Press.

Glasgow, D.G. 1987. *The Black Underclass in Perspective.* J. Dewart (ed). *The State of Black America 1987.* New York: National Urban League, Inc., pp. 129–144.

_____. 1984. "Full Employment: A Discussion Paper." Washington, D.C.: National Urban League, Washington Operations.

Goodwin, L. 1972. *Do the Poor Want to Work.* Washington, D.C.: The Brookings Institution.

Morley, S.A. 1984. *Macroeconomics.* New York: The Dryden Press, Chap. 11.

Nelson, W.E., Jr. 1978. "Black Political Power and the Decline of Black Land Ownership." *The Review of Black Political Economy.* Vol. 8, No. 3 (Spring 1978), pp. 253–263.

O'Hare, W.P. 1983. *Wealth and Economic Status: A Perspective on Racial Inequality.* Washington, D.C.: Joint Center for Political Studies.

Parcel, T.L. 1982. "Wealth Accumulation of Black and White Men: The Case of Housing Equity." *Social Problems.* Vol. 30, No. 2 (December 1982), pp. 199–211.

Simms, M. 1984. *The Economic Well-Being of Minorities During the Reagan Administration.* Washington, D.C.: The Urban Institute.

Smith, J.P. and Welch, F.R. 1986. *Closing the Gap: Forty Years of Economic Progress for Blacks.* Santa Monica, Calif.: Rand Corporation.

Smith, W.D. (ed.). 1986. *In Pursuit of Full Employment.* Special edition of the *Urban League Review.* Vol. 10, No. 1 (Summer 1986).

Sturdivant, F.D. (ed). 1969. *The Ghetto Marketplace.* New York: The Free Press.

Swinton, D. 1987. "Economic Status of Blacks 1986." J. Dewart (ed.). *The State of Black America 1987.* New York: National Urban League, Inc., pp. 49–73.

Terrell, H.S. 1971. "Wealth Accumulatin of Black and White Families: The Empirical Evidence." *Journal of Finance.* Vol. 26, No. 2 (May 1971), pp. 363–377.

Thurow, L. 1975. *Generating Inequality: Mechanisms of Distribution in the U.S. Economy.* New York: Basic Books, Inc.

Tidwell, B.J. 1984. "1985 Federal Budget: An Examination of Impact on the Poor and Minorities." Washington, D.C.: National Urban League, Washington Operations.

_____. 1987. "Topsy Turvy: Unemployment among Black Administrators and Managers." *The Forum.* Vol. 3, No. 1 (February 1987), pp. 1-3.

U.S. Bureau of the Census. 1985. *1982 Survey of Minority-Owned Business Enterprises (Black).* Washington, D.C.: Government Printing Office.

U.S. Bureau of the Census. 1986. Current Population Reports. *Household Wealth and Asset Ownership: 1984.* Washington, D.C.: Government Printing Office.

U.S. Commission on Civil Rights. 1986. *The Economic Progress of Black Men in America.* Clearinghouse Publication, No. 91.

Vaughn-Cooke, D. 1985. "No Recovery in the Economic Status in Black America." *The Black Scholar.* Vol. 16, No. 5 (September/October, 1985), pp. 5-13.

## Acknowledgements

The National Urban League acknowledges with sincere appreciation the contributions of the authors of the various papers appearing in this publication; Paulette J. Robinson, technical editor; Michele R. Long, proofreading assistant; and the special contributions of NUL staff, including Cynthia Gresham, Ernie Johnston, Jr., Vernice Williams, Faith Williams, Ollie Wadler, and Farida Syed of the Communications Department; External Affairs; Washington Operations; the Research Department; and the Program Departments.

Order Blank

## National Urban League Publications
### 500 East 62nd Street
### New York, N.Y. 10021

| | Per Copy | Number of Copies | Total |
|---|---|---|---|
| State of Black America 1988 | $18.00 | | |
| Other Volumes in series: | | | |
| The State of Black America 1987 | $18.00 | | |
| The State of Black America 1986 | $18.00 | | |
| The State of Black America 1985 | $17.00 | | |
| The State of Black America 1984 | $15.00 | | |
| The State of Black America 1983 | $14.00 | | |
| Volumes 1976-1982 (Available only in a set) | $150.00 | | |
| Postage & handling: Individual volumes — $1.50 each | | | |
| Set of volumes — $10.00 per set | | | |
| | | Amount enclosed | |

------------------------------------------------------------------------------------------

### "The Family" Lithograph

Limited edition, numbered lithograph of "The Family" by James Denmark, signed by the artist. "The Family" inaugurates the *Great Artists* series created for the National Urban League through a donation from the House of Seagram. Proceeds benefit the National Urban League.

Unframed lithograph 28-$^1/_8''$ by 20-$^1/_2''$. Full color. $1,000 each, includes postage and handling.

For information and to order, contact:

National Urban League, Inc.
Fund Department
500 East 62nd Street
New York, New York 10021

*Please make checks or money orders payable to:*
*National Urban League, Inc.*

# Order Blank

## National Urban League Publications
### 500 East 62nd Street
### New York, N.Y. 10021

| | Per Copy | Number of Copies | Total |
|---|---|---|---|
| State of Black America 1988 | $18.00 | | |
| Other Volumes in series: | | | |
| The State of Black America 1987 | $18.00 | | |
| The State of Black America 1986 | $18.00 | | |
| The State of Black America 1985 | $17.00 | | |
| The State of Black America 1984 | $15.00 | | |
| The State of Black America 1983 | $14.00 | | |
| Volumes 1976-1982 (Available only in a set) | $150.00 | | |
| Postage & handling: Individual volumes — $1.50 each Set of volumes — $10.00 per set | | | |
| | Amount enclosed | | |

---

## "The Family" Lithograph

Limited edition, numbered lithograph of "The Family" by James Denmark, signed by the artist. "The Family" inaugurates the *Great Artists* series created for the National Urban League through a donation from the House of Seagram. Proceeds benefit the National Urban League.

Unframed lithograph 28-$^1/_8''$ by 20-$^1/_2''$. Full color. $1,000 each, includes postage and handling.

For information and to order, contact:

National Urban League, Inc.
Fund Department
500 East 62nd Street
New York, New York 10021

*Please make checks or money orders payable to:*
*National Urban League, Inc.*